To my wife, Dianne,

who loves God with all her heart

and her neighbors, family, and friends, as herself

# Advance Praise for *Being a Disciple Community*

Keith Stillwell has turned loose his pastoral imagination and brought us a fun, introspective, and action-oriented work. He challenges us to turn loose our own imagination to study deeper the Scriptures, to love deeper our neighbors, and to grow deeper as disciples. As we do this, we begin to understand clearer, "What is the church?"

—Bo Prosser, EdD, ACC
Catalytic Coach and Consultant

Written during the Covid-19 pandemic, Being a Disciple Community is a book for such a time as this. As congregational leaders guide groups to clarify how to renew their energies by investing in commitments that really matter, these pages will be exceedingly helpful. As you pursue church health and vitality in this post-pandemic world, Keith Stillwell brings his experience, knowledge and commitment of nurturing disciples and building faithful communities to help you. He provides breadth and depth to the reader providing a holistic manual for meaningful conversations offering pathways for discussions to become decisions that result in intentional actions of renewal. Seldom do you find a work that is both extremely practical for congregational leaders and broadly informational for church members. Herein is a mine of treasures inviting you to dig deeper and explore creative approaches as you create new contextual alloys in your autonomous congregational laboratories. Happy disciple-making and community-building.

—Rev. Dennis W. Foust, PhD
Senior Minister, St. John's Baptist Church

Critical to the spiritual formation of the local church is a genuine understanding and implementation of how to grow as disciples of Jesus. Dr. Stillwell provides extraordinary insight and practical ways in which our churches can develop in how we connect with God and one another. I have found no better educational resource for congregations to grasp what really should be the heartbeat of a faith community. Dr. Stillwell's wisdom in this essential area of the Christian mission will energize our churches for years to come.

—Keith R. Felton, PhD
Senior Pastor, First Baptist Church
Frankfort, Kentucky

Realizing that the church is ever-changing and evolving, Keith Stillwell also recognizes that some things about the church will always remain the same. Such things include worship, teaching, prayer, missions, witnessing, care, and leadership. This book provides a solid foundation for how the church can be a loving, faithful disciple community in spite of cultural changes, or shifting social dynamics, or even a pandemic. Keith draws upon storytelling, personal experience as a minister, Scripture, and a wide variety of ministry resources to show that being a disciple community is not only possible, but necessary, for the church remain vital in an unknown future. I recommend this book to congregational ministers and leaders who feel the sands shifting around them.

—Dr. Karen G. Massey,
Associate Dean
Mercer University's School of Theology

What does it mean to really be the church, and if it were being this, what would it be doing? The Spirit is forming and transforming the church as a disciple community into the body of Christ for the sake of the world God loves. Joining in this work of the Spirit is not only an exciting possibility, it also becomes an electrifying reality! The wide scope of reflections on key focus areas of the church's life, the range of experiences cited, along with the breadth of practical implications make this book a most valuable resource for churches today! I have been blessed to be part of conversations with Keith over many years of this book's making. And I am so excited for all who will now have access to this wonderful resource!

—Dale Ziemer (retired)
Center for Parish Development
Chicago, Illinois

In his book *Being a Disciple Community*, Keith has woven his love for God, others, and self into a beautiful description of living out Jesus' two great commandments—Love God, Love your neighbor. Having known Keith as a colleague and friend for over twenty years, this book is not merely a collection of theories on how to make the church better. Rather it is the embodiment of how Keith has lived his life both as a minister and a child of God. Each chapter is not only well thought out and designed, it is also the heart and soul of Keith Stillwell—a friend, colleague, and Christian. In that sense, one can sense Keith's love for the church and his desire to see her become the church God intended her to be.

—Dr. Tommy Valentine
Associate Pastor of Theology and Pastoral Ministries
Campbellsville University

In these crucial days of the corporate church when people don't want to be told "you much do this/believe that" Stillwell calls us back to intentional, deliberate, transformational CE, breaking out of traditional "you still while I instill" approaches that have little effect on behavior change.

This book comes at a crucial time in which churches are redefining practices in light of a three year pandemic forced hiatus on business as usual.

—R. Michael Harton
Dean of Faculty (retired)
Baptist Theological Seminary Richmond

As we continue to learn to live amid a global pandemic that has upended our lives and our routines, it can be difficult to convince ourselves that being a part of a community of faith is worth the time and effort it requires. This readable, story-driven text is a powerful reminder for both clergy and laypeople that the church still matters, even as we wrestle with what it ought to look like. Dr. Stillwell provides a theological examination of what we do and why we do it as well as a helpful framework for thinking about what to prioritize as we regather and reimagine how to be Christ in our neighborhoods, our cities, and our world.

—Rev. Amanda Standiford
Associate Pastor of Children & Spiritual Formation
First Baptist Church, Frankfort, Kentucky

Smyth & Helwys Publishing, Inc.
6316 Peake Road
Macon, Georgia 31210-3960
1-800-747-3016
©2022 by Keith Stillwell
All rights reserved.

Cover art, *Mary & Martha*, by He Qi
www.heqiart.com
Used by permission

*Library of Congress Cataloging-in-Publication Data*

Names: Stillwell, Keith, author.
Title: Being a disciple community : loving God and neighbor / by Keith
  Stillwell.
Description: First. | Macon, GA : Smyth & Helwys Publishing, 2022. |
  Includes bibliographical references.
Identifiers: LCCN 2021060028 | ISBN 9781641733588 (paperback)
Classification: LCC BV600.3 .S745 2022 | DDC 262.001/7--dc23/eng/20220209
LC record available at https://lccn.loc.gov/20210600288

**Disclaimer of Liability:** With respect to statements of opinion or fact available in this work of nonfiction, Smyth & Helwys Publishing Inc. nor any of its employees, makes any warranty, express or implied, or assumes any legal liability or responsibility for the accuracy or completeness of any information disclosed, or represents that its use would not infringe privately-owned rights.

# BEING A DISCIPLE Community

## LOVING GOD AND NEIGHBOR

### KEITH STILLWELL

# Acknowledgments

Thanks to those who contributed to this book.

Dr. James Stillwell, my brother in Christ but not related, wrote most of chapter 7, "Care." James is an experienced and trained counselor, writer, educator, pastor, and staff minister. James and his wife, Vivian, have four adult children and three grandchildren. James received a bachelor of arts from Carson-Newman College, a master of divinity and master of religious education from Southwestern Baptist Theological Seminary, and the doctor of ministry from the Southern Baptist Theological Seminary, with additional study through the Kentuckiana Pastoral Counseling Consortium. He is a licensed pastoral counselor with offices in Lexington, Frankfort, and Louisville, Kentucky. James has led divorce recovery workshops every semester since 1993 and currently in Frankfort-Midway, Kentucky. James also has been a leader in the Healthy Marriages Movement in Central Kentucky. James's counseling practice emphasizes navigating life's transitions and couples' communication. Previously, James served for twenty-nine years in various church staff ministry roles including education, music, youth, single adults, marriage enrichment, and interim pastor. James is well qualified to write this chapter on care. I was fortunate that James was available and willing to join me in this project. Without his contribution, this book would not have been completed.

Richard Summers, associate pastor of music and administration, First Baptist Church, Frankfort, Kentucky, wrote the section "Congregational Singing" in chapter 2, "Worship."

Keith Felton, pastor, First Baptist Church, Frankfort, Kentucky, wrote the section "Caring Role of the Deacon," in chapter 7, "Care."

Brittany Stillwell, minister with students and families, Second Baptist Church, Downtown, Little Rock, Arkansas, wrote the section "Preparing the Space for Worship," in chapter 2, "Worship."

Kelsey Stillwell, associate pastor for youth and missions, First Baptist Church of Christ, Macon, Georgia, wrote the section "Interfaith Dialogue" in chapter 5, "Missions."

I am thrilled to have on the cover of this book He Qi's depiction of Jesus at the home of Martha and Mary. You can see more of his work at www.heqiart.com.

I owe many thanks to Dale Ziemer and the Center for Parish Development in Chicago, Illinois. The center's printed resources and the conferences they have conducted, along with consultations with Dale Ziemer, have greatly influenced my approach to ministry. From the first conference I ever attended with them, I was impressed with their emphasis on churches discerning and participating in God's mission through biblical/theological study, worship and prayer, and group process, engaging the whole body of Christ to facilitate transformation. I have called on Dale often as a consultant. One of my favorite consulting sessions with Dale was held at Wrigley Field during a Cubs and Reds game, even though his Cubs beat my Reds. I have often relied on Dale's wisdom and guidance on the important ministry of leading a church in God's mission.

Thanks to Dr. William B. Rogers and Dr. Israel Galindo, professors of Christian education at Baptist Theological Seminary at Richmond, Virginia, who guided my doctor of ministry studies and pushed me in the direction of this project.

Thanks to Dr. Karen Massey, Dr. Glenn Hinson, Dr. Michael Harton, and Dr. Denis Foust for reading chapters of the book and offering helpful advice and encouragement.

I am grateful for the churches that have given me the opportunity to reflect on church ministry and practice it:

Hillcrest Baptist Church, Hopkinsville, Kentucky, gave me my first full-time ministry opportunity and ordained me to the gospel ministry.

First Baptist Church, Hopkinsville, and especially the Neighborhood Ministry Team, reached out to the church's neighbors across the street from the church campus. We sought to learn from our neighbors how to be a neighbor and then to show that in concrete ways. Some of my happiest days in ministry were shared with church members, sitting on neighbors' front porches, leading children's activities and community worship in an empty lot in the neighborhood, delivering brownies to our business neighbors and hosting them for our monthly business lunches, sharing hundreds of home-baked loaves of bread with residents all around the church, and enjoying an annual neighborhood block party.

Lexington Avenue Baptist Church, Danville, Kentucky, is where I served for most of my ministry, where most of this book was written, and where we sought to love our neighbors in "Jerusalem, Judea, and Samaria and to the ends of the earth"—both in Danville, Kentucky, and with our partner church in Rabat, Morocco. The Lexington Avenue Baptist family affirmed my ministry and gave me the place and the space to study and try new things and practice some of what it means to be a disciple community that loves God and loves neighbors. They trusted me to be involved in all aspects of the church's ministry that this book seeks to address—cultivating community, worship, prayer, teaching, missions, witness, care, and leadership. Early in the process of developing this resource, a group of church members read chapters with me and met with me several times to give me feedback—Amanda England, Shawn England, Evin Farmer, Anna Layton, Patsy Sharp, Karen Thornton, Henry Wilson, and Linda Wright.

First Baptist Church, Frankfort, Kentucky, gave me a job as interim part-time minister of spiritual formation when I needed it and encouraged me to finish this book and use it as a churchwide study in Sunday school there. Without the encouragement of the church staff, especially Keith Felton and Richard Summers, and the time the church gave me, I would not have finished this book by now and maybe never would have.

I have learned much about Christian community, love of God and neighbor, and how the church works from many colleagues with whom I served on church staff: Jim McKenzie, Bill Adcock, Max Sturdivant, and Emory Riley with First Baptist Church, Hopkinsville, Kentucky; Phil Rector, Dave Garrett, Phil Quinn, Tara Luster, Amanda Standiford, Adam Nash, and Adam Standiford with Lexington Avenue Baptist Church, Danville, Kentucky; Keith Felton, Richard Summers, Marcus Pernell, Jenny Luscher, and Steve Hadden with First Baptist Church, Frankfort, Kentucky, along with others I have failed to mention.

My colleague Dave Garrett, youth minister at Lexington Avenue Baptist for a number of years, was an excellent partner in missions. We complemented each other as we engaged in a partnership with Lexington Avenue Baptist Church youth, children, and adults, and with the beautiful community of Nada Kentucky, forming lasting mutual friendships built around work, play, worship, Miguel's Pizza, and Ale8One.

For several years I served on staff with Amanda Standiford, a talented and creative minister who introduced me to the wonders of Godly Play, among other things.

Tommy Valentine was my pastor, friend, mentor, and guide for seventeen years at Lexington Avenue Baptist Church. His office door was always open for me. He listened to me, challenged me, advised me, encouraged me, and gave me the freedom to explore what it means to be a community that loves God and neighbor.

I am grateful for the support of my family:

My mom, Janice Stillwell Hannel, has always shown me what unconditional love is about in a way that helps me understand the kind of love God asks us to show our neighbors. From as early as I can remember, she took my sister and me to the public library every week and taught me a love for reading. My father, John Stillwell, now deceased, taught me about social justice and loving all people without discrimination. I've learned much from my little sister, Stacy Nall, a leader, teacher, and writer with a love for missions and for children. For many years she has used her gifts on the staff of Women's Missionary Union of Kentucky. Sometimes when I had an important college or seminary paper to write, I asked Stacy to proofread it. On multiple occasions (I'm a slow learner), she gave me the best writing advice I have ever received. It went something like this:

Stacy: "I don't understand what you mean here."

Me: "What I am trying to say is . . . ."

Stacy: "So why didn't you say that?"

I tried to remember her advice in writing this book, though I'm sure many times I forgot.

My daughters, Brittany and Kelsey, both faithful, effective, compassionate, and creative ministers, have taught me much and given me helpful feedback on all aspects of ministry. They like to call themselves the "mini-sisters." They are gifted leaders, preachers, teachers, artists, musicians, and students. They are fierce defenders of the marginalized, the forgotten, the oppressed, the Samaritans. They equip the church to grow close to God, to act for justice and mercy, and to cultivate community. I am so proud of them as women, as ministers, as caring human beings. They also read chapters and offered helpful feedback and correction.

Good-hearted Brianna Jones came into our family a few years ago while a college student. She inspires us by the way she has handled the many obstacles she has faced in life with the courage and strength of a lion.

In my wife, Dianne, I have an example of the Good Samaritan, Martha, and Mary all rolled into one. Like the Good Samaritan, she is the kind of person people seek out when they need someone to listen and care and offer a helping hand. Like Martha, she works tirelessly and efficiently to tend to her family, home, church, and career. Like Mary, she has a quiet strength and spiritual depth and takes time for worship, study, and prayer. For many years Dianne has shaped the lives of children as a public schoolteacher, our own daughters, and me. After years of keeping her distance from certain leadership roles in the church because of my position on staff, she was recently ordained as a deacon at First Baptist Church, Frankfort, Kentucky.

# Contents

Preface
xv

Introduction
1

Chapter 1. Community
9

Chapter 2. Worship
29

Chapter 3. Teaching
55

Chapter 4. Prayer
113

Chapter 5. Missions
145

Chapter 6. Witness
173

Chapter 7. Care
209

Chapter 8. Leadership
229

Benediction
261

# Preface

This book is being published at an odd time—during a pandemic. This is a book about what it means to be the church, how a church loves God and neighbors, and what a church does, yet how a church loves God and neighbors has been dramatically altered during these pandemic days. The church has been forced to adapt and find innovative ways to continue being a disciple community. How we do church has changed, and, when the virus is finally under control, it is likely that the church will find a new normal. From exile in Babylon, far from the temple, Isaiah spoke these words of God: "See, I am doing a new thing" (Isa 43:19). Most of us have been away from our usual places of worship. The way we do church will continue to change. We are learning new practices and methods, some of which we will keep using. Whatever church looks like in the future, we will still be engaging in God's mission; loving God with all our hearts, minds, souls, and strength; and we will continue to form community, worship, pray, teach, engage in missions, witness, and care. My hope and prayer are that this book will be a helpful resource for churches on their journey of being a disciple community, loving God and neighbor, whatever the future brings.

For over thirty years I have served in the church as an associate pastor, focused on discipleship (education and missions). For more than half of that time I have been studying, writing, and developing this resource. Whether I have achieved them or not, these were my goals:

*(1) Ask the most important questions.* What does it mean to be the church? What does it mean to be in the process of becoming a disciple community? What does it mean to be a missional church? For answers, I go to what Jesus called the greatest commandments, based on the Shema, the heart of Jewish law: "You shall love the Lord your God with all your heart, and with all your soul, and with all your strength, and with all your mind; and love your neighbor as yourself" (Matt 22:36-40). Look at the life of the church through the lens of love of God and neighbor, and explore two powerful stories that Luke used to illustrate this love.

*(2) Provide a tool to help churches in this process of becoming a disciple community, loving God and neighbor.* Aid churches in the process of transformation, believing that the church is always in need of being "transformed by the renewing of our mind" rather than "conformed to this world" (Rom 12:2), as we see ourselves in a "mirror, dimly" (1 Cor 13:12).

*(3) Highlight concern for those whom Jesus called "the least of these" (see Matt 25:31-46).* Throughout the New Testament, we see examples of Jesus' care for the marginalized and oppressed, minorities and the poor, and all who have been abused and neglected by others. The church should follow Jesus' examples.

*(4) Address all members of the church, not just professional ministers.* There are many exceptional resources and brilliant writings on what it means to be the church. I have attempted to make them accessible for a church to use in a process of study and transformation around the theme of being a disciple community that loves God and neighbor.

Each chapter contains these sections:

*Conversation with Mary and Sam*—Imagined conversations between me (Keith), Mary (Martha's sister in the Bible), and Sam (my nickname for the Good Samaritan in Jesus' parable). These conversations introduce a key theme or function of the church.

*Being a Disciple Community*—Discussion of a key function of the church and Bible passages, generally from Luke-Acts, especially Luke 10:25-42. Unless noted otherwise, Scripture references are to the NRSV.

*Putting It into Practice*—A variety of additional resources, key ideas, and programs related to the topic and how to put it into practice through the church community.

*Resources*—Resources I have found most helpful in understanding and practicing what it means to be a disciple community that loves God and neighbor.

In addition to what's found in this book, I have also created *Small Group and Churchwide Study Helps*, a chapter-by-chapter guide that can be downloaded at no cost from the Smyth & Helwys book page www.helwys.com/sh-books/being-a-disciple-community/. You also may request a copy from the author (keithstillwell@me.com). Also available for download are suggested next steps for a churchwide emphasis as a follow-up to a churchwide study of *Being a Disciple Community: Loving God and Neighbor.*

# Introduction

"Go and do" (see Luke 10). With these words, Jesus concludes an encounter with an expert in Jewish law—an encounter in which he shares the parable of the Good Samaritan. Interestingly, Luke next records the story of Jesus at the home of Martha and Mary—a story in which Jesus says essentially, "Be still and listen."

Luke presents two contrasting stories. First, Jesus' parable is a parable of action. Nearly half of the words in this parable describe the Samaritan's actions.[1] The Good Samaritan is out on the road, getting his hands dirty and bloody, helping and working, going and doing. Jesus says, "Go and do likewise." Then Luke tells us that Mary is sitting quietly at Jesus' feet, listening. Nearby her sister Martha is busy working. Jesus reprimands Martha for valuing her tasks over him and praises Mary, saying, "Mary has chosen the better part."

So which is it—"go and do" or "be still and listen"? Action or reflection? Go and love your neighbor or be still and know God (Ps 46:10)? Is it missions or Bible study? The Christian community—the church—is called to both ministry and worship; to action and contemplation; to missions out in the world and to prayer in the closet. These two stories—the Samaritan helping the hurting and Mary listening to Jesus—can guide the life of the church. The Good Samaritan and Mary, together, provide examples of what is required of a church that seeks to be a balanced and faithful disciple community.

The parable of the Good Samaritan answers the question, "Who is my neighbor and how can I love my neighbor?" The story of Jesus at the home of Martha and Mary demonstrates how we can love God with our whole being. Together these two stories teach us how to obey the command that introduced them: "You shall love the Lord your God with all your heart, and with all your soul, and with all your strength, and with all your mind; and your neighbor as yourself." The major functions of the church can be thought of as expressions of our love for God and neighbor. We could place prayer, teaching, and worship on the loving God side of this commandment. And we could place missions, witness, and care on the loving-neighbors side.

Be aware, though, that dividing these functions of the church into categories is an oversimplification. While we might connect some functions of the church to loving God and others to loving neighbors, in reality love for God and neighbor is not so easily compartmentalized. Luke presents the command to love God and neighbor as one command in one sentence. Whenever we reach out to our neighbors with acts of compassion, we are also expressing love for God because loving our neighbors is one way we show our love for God. Likewise, when we rest in God's presence, worshiping God and learning from God, we do so in the context of a Christian community, sharing God's presence together as members of the body of Christ. When we open ourselves to God's grace, we are freed to love our neighbors more deeply and are called by God to do so. Whatever we do, we do for God.

Love of God and love of neighbor are intricately related. Therefore, we will speak of some functions as helping the church "love God and neighbor," with God listed first. These "loving God and neighbor" functions—*prayer*, *teaching*, and *worship*—are symbolized by the story of Mary learning from Jesus. We will speak of other functions as helping the church "love neighbor and God," with neighbor listed first. These "loving neighbor and God" functions—*missions*, *witness*, and *care*—are symbolized by the parable of the Good Samaritan. Two other functions surround and support all that the church is and does—those are *community* and *leadership*.

Thus, we could visualize the life and work of the church community this way:

**Loving God and Loving Neighbor**

Community

Worship

Teaching

Prayer

Missions

Witness

Care

Leadership

# INTRODUCTION

# Loving God and Neighbor: The Good Samaritan and Mary

As a church, we would do well to live out of these two stories: a story of courageous, compassionate action and a story of deep devotion and communion with God—an image of love for neighbors and an image of love for God. Let these stories guide us.

## *The Samaritan's Journal*

A body, bloody, bruised, broken,
lying on the side of the road.
Dirt, blood, sweat
caked to his brow.
Is he alive?
No.
Yes.
I think I saw him move.
No.
Maybe.
Yes.
He just gasped for air.
Who did this to him?
Robbers certainly.
This road is known for such.
Are they waiting for me?
Will I be next?
I am afraid, standing here staring at my future, if robbers are hiding behind that rock.
Should I help him?
No.
I should run past on the other side of the road, as quickly as possible.
Is this a test?
"Do unto others as you would have them do unto you," it is said.
"Love your neighbor as yourself," it is written.
I must help him.
Who is he?
I can't tell.
He is too bruised, cut, and bloodied.
Is he Jewish?

If I were lying on the side of the road, a Jew would never make himself unclean for me.
Is he Greek?
A Greek wouldn't waste his time on me.
Is he Samaritan?
I'm not even sure a fellow Samaritan would help me were I in this man's condition.
But I will help him.
Straining, lifting, pulling his limp body,
I try,
but fail.
I can't do this.
Lifting the lifeless body of a grown man from the ground is impossible.
Harder I try.
On my knees.
I clasp his arm tightly and pull till he is sitting—slumping.
I roll him over my shoulders, onto my back.
Groaning, I rise to my feet.
His blood and my sweat mingle.
Across my donkey's back
He rides.
Oil and wine cleanse and heal.
Two days' wages will keep him until I return.
Safe in the inn.

## Mary's Journal

It's hard to describe how I feel sitting at Jesus' feet, listening to him speak. They say he "teaches as one with authority."

Listening, I find this to be true, but not like those I know who are in authority. Instead of intimidation, I experience love and feel secure. He knows what he is talking about, but, more than that, he knows me. It is like he is looking through the me I present to others, down to the depths of my being. He sees the part of me I think is ugly, but to Jesus I am beautiful inside.

I expect judgment but experience grace.
Instead of being shamed, I am honored.
In his presence time stands still.
I live fully in this present moment.
Life begins to make sense.

Priorities become clear.

I feel as if I am in the very presence of God.

Suddenly, the rattling of dishes diverts my attention. Martha is angry, and a sense of guilt returns as I realize that I have left my sister alone with the preparations.

However, again I find Shalom with Jesus' gentle affirmation, "Mary has chosen the better part, which will not be taken away from her."

## Ways of Being a Disciple Community

As they are organized here, the functions of the church—witness, teaching, community, prayer, worship, care, and missions—are related to the practices of the early church as recorded in Acts 2:

> This Jesus God raised up, and of that all of us are witnesses [**witness**]. . . . They devoted themselves to the apostles' teaching [**teaching**] and fellowship [**community**], to the breaking of bread [**worship**] and the prayers [**prayer**]. . . . All who believed were together and had all things in common [**community**]; they would sell their possessions and goods and distribute the proceeds to all, as any had need [**missions and care**]. Day by day, as they spent much time together [**community**] in the temple, they broke bread at home and ate their food with glad and generous hearts, praising God [**worship**] and having the goodwill of all the people. And day by day the Lord added to their number those who were being saved. (Acts 2:32, 42-47)

Since its inception, the church has been worshiping, teaching, praying, witnessing, serving, and caring as a community.[2] When we engage in these practices, we are doing what the church has done throughout its history to form disciple communities.

This resource will explore what it means for the church to be a community that loves God and neighbor and lives out the two stories of the Good Samaritan and Mary at Jesus' feet. The emphasis is on *being* as much as it is on *doing*. Sometimes the church is so caught up in a rush of activity and a drive to be productive that we are not attentive to the quality of the church's *being*—values, prayer, relationships, worship, decision-making, and conflict resolution. We will also focus on how we can love God and neighbor as a community rather than as a collection of individuals. Our North American culture conditions us to view the world as individuals, especially when it comes to spirituality and religion, so we must intentionally take on the perspective of the community.

When we speak of the practices of the church, we mean the disciplines that place us in the hands of God. Jeremiah and others have referred to God as the potter and the people of God as the clay: "Just like clay in the potter's hand, so are you in my hand, O house of Israel" (Jer 18:6). Community, worship, prayer, teaching, missions, witness, care, and leadership are functions of the church that place us on God's pottery wheel so that God can form us into the people God desires. Thus, we sometimes refer to these practices as spiritual formation.

Many helpful terms have been used to describe the process of being a disciple community: spiritual disciplines, discipleship, spiritual formation. In many traditions, the discipling process has been called Christian education or, better, experiential Christian education, since we would not want to suggest a vision of a student passively absorbing factual information from a single instructor. Others speak of "cultivating."[3] The Christian community plants, weeds, fertilizes, and waters, but God gives the growth (as Paul writes in 1 Cor 3:5-9). All of these images are ways of thinking about what it means to be a disciple community. When we live, worship, teach, pray, serve in missions, care, witness, and lead in community, we are being a disciple community. We are being cultivated, formed, fashioned, shaped, educated, and molded as a disciple community.

## Resources

Biddle, Mark. *Deuteronomy*. Smyth & Helwys Bible Commentary. Macon: Smyth & Helwys, 2003.

Bridges, Linda McKinnish. *The Church's Portraits of Jesus*. All the Bible. Macon: Smyth & Helwys, 1997.

Culpepper, R. Alan. "Luke." *New Interpreter's Bible*, vol. 9. Nashville: Abingdon, 1995.

Dodd, C. H. *The Parables of the Kingdom*. London: Nisbet & Co. LTD, 1936.

Funk, Robert. *Parables and Presence: Forms of the New Testament Tradition*. Philadelphia: Fortress, 1982.

Jones, Peter Rhea. *Studying the Parables of Jesus*. Macon: Smyth & Helwys, 1999.

Malina, Bruce J., and Richard L. Rohrbaugh. *Social-Science Commentary on the Synoptic Gospels*. Minneapolis: Fortress, 1992.

Marshall, I. Howard. *New International Greek Testament Commentary: Commentary on Luke*. Grand Rapids: Eerdmans, 1978.

Moeller, Mark. "Parables," *Christian Reflection: A Series in Faith and Ethics*. Vol. 21. Waco: Center for Christian Ethics, Baylor University, 2006.

Patte, Daniel, gen. ed. *Global Bible Commentary*. Nashville: Abingdon, 2004.

Parsons, Mikeal C. *Hearing the Parable with the Early Church*, in *Christian Reflection: A Series in Faith and Ethics, Parables*. Waco: Center for Christian Ethics at Baylor University, 2006.

Ringe, Sharon H. *Luke: Westminster Bible Commentary*. Louisville: John Knox, 1995.

Schaberg, Jane. "Luke." *The Women's Bible Commentary*, ed. Carol A. Newsom and Sharon H. Ringe. Louisville: Westminster/John Knox, 1992.

Stillwell, Keith. *Neighborhood Ministry and an Action/Reflection Bible Study on Luke 10:25-37*. DMin Project, Baptist Theological Seminary at Richmond, VA, 2000.

Vinson, Richard B. *Luke*. Smyth & Helwys Bible Commentary. Macon: Smyth & Helwys, 2008.

## Notes

1. Mikeal C. Parsons, *Hearing the Parable with the Early Church*, in *Christian Reflection: A Series in Faith and Ethics, Parables* (Waco: Center for Christian Ethics at Baylor University, 2006), 21.

2. Maria Harris in her book, *Fashion Me a People: Curriculum in the Church* (Louisville: Westminster/John Knox, 1989), calls these basic practices the curriculum of the church and names them (1) Koinonia: community or fellowship; (2) Leiturgia: prayer and worship; (3) Didache: teaching and Bible study; (4) Kergyma: proclamation or witness; and (5) Diakonia: service. Harris shows how these "curricular forms" are the means by which God fashions the Christian community into the church God desires.

3. Thomas Hawkins, *Cultivating Christian Community* (Nashville: Discipleship Resources, 2001); Inagrace T. Dietterich, *Cultivating Missional Communities* (Chicago: Center for Parish Development, 2002).

*Chapter 1*

# Community

## Conversations with Mary and Sam on Community

Sitting in my office, I had been reflecting on the command, "Love your neighbor as yourself." It's a simple enough statement, I suppose, but I wonder if I'm missing something. I try to imagine how the Good Samaritan might explain this verse that made him famous, or what Mary would say since she spent so much time listening to Jesus. I closed my eyes and spun around in my chair, wishing they were here so I could ask them.

When my chair stopped spinning and I opened my eyes, I was embarrassed to see that someone had entered my office. Maybe two or more people had entered—I couldn't tell because the room and everything in it kept tilting. I regained my balance and what composure I could, and I saw that indeed two people had entered the room, a man and a woman, and they were sitting in the two chairs across from my desk. They were wearing the most authentic-looking Bible costumes I had ever seen (not the typical bathrobes).

"Wow! The costumes are great, but Vacation Bible School is not until this summer. Besides, we've decided to go with a beach theme this year," I informed them.

"We aren't here for Vacation Bible School, whatever that is," the man said.

"Why are you here?"

"We are here because you asked for us," the woman answered.

I was confused. "Who are you and where are you from?"

"I don't have a name," the man answered. "I am from Samaria."

"I am from Jerusalem," the woman said. "My name is Mary."

I wondered if my head was still spinning, but Mary and the man from Samaria were sitting still and looking very much real. "I can't believe you're here. I must say how honored I am to meet you. You are two of my favorite people in the Bible. Next to Jesus. No offense."

"None taken," they said together. "Thank you."

"So you tell us why we are here," the Samaritan man said.

"I've been thinking about the command 'Love your—'"

"What's that?" the Samaritan interrupted, pointing to my seminary diploma hanging on the wall.

"It's a diploma. It means I've been to school to study the Bible, theology, ministry, and such."

"You mean like studying under a rabbi at the synagogue?" Mary asked. "Or the disciples who learned from Jesus?"

"Yes, something like that, only there were many teachers, and it was a seminary, not a synagogue."

"Sorry to interrupt," the Samaritan said, "but I was curious because it looks like something you think is important. Go ahead, you were getting ready to tell us why we are here."

"Yes, I guess you're here because I have a question for you. I've been thinking about the command 'Love your neighbor as yourself' and wondering what that means."

"Since you've been to the seminary school with many professors, why don't you tell us what it means?" the Samaritan said.

"But I asked you first," I protested. Then I remembered a certain gospel story. "Oh, I get it, you're being like Jesus and I'm the lawyer. So I have to answer my own question. I didn't learn this in seminary, but when I was a teenager, I remember something my youth minister said that might be helpful."

Mary and the Samaritan looked puzzled.

"What's a teenager and what's a youth minister?" the Samaritan asked.

"We were a group of youth ages twelve through eighteen, and the youth minister was our teacher. He held a large piece of paper with the word JOY printed down the page. He said, 'J stands for *Jesus*. We must put Jesus first. O stands for *others*. We love others second. Y is for *you*. We should put Jesus and others first, but we should love ourselves because if we don't have a healthy self-esteem, then we can't love Jesus or others.'"

Both of my guests stared back at me blankly.

"I have no idea what you're talking about or what self-esteem is," the Samaritan offered.

"That sounds nice," Mary said, "but it is not exactly how we understand that verse."

"And how do you understand that verse?"

"Well, to start with," she began, "loving your neighbor and loving yourself are not two separate commands." The Samaritan leaned back in his seat and nodded in agreement. "Remember the verse says, 'love your neighbor as yourself.' Not 'love your neighbor and love yourself,' as if your neighbor and yourself are two separate things."

"But they are, aren't they? I am a separate individual from my neighbor."

"That's kind of the point. Some want to be totally separate, but God wants us to love our neighbor as ourselves," Mary explained.

"Now I'm confused."

Mary continued, "Let me use an illustration that Paul used. We are one body in Christ. To say that I am an individual totally separate from the body is like the foot saying I have no part in the body."

"OK, I see your point . . . sort of. But is it contrary to this way of thinking to say that I think of myself as an individual who is part of a community?"

"What is more important, *me* or *we*?" the Samaritan asked, moving to the edge of his seat. I thought he had fallen asleep.

"Mr. . . . uh . . . Samaritan man. Hey, can I call you 'Sam'?"

"Sure."

"Okay, Sam, I guess I would say it's both *me* and *we*."

"Sam asked a good question," Mary noted. "Do you start with community or with the individual? It seems that you think from the perspective of the individual first, then think of the community. We would tend to start and end with the community. So loving your neighbor as yourself is about loving within the community of neighbors. Understand?"

"Maybe. You're going to have to give me more time to think about it, since I've been *me* for a long time."

"That's a good idea, and don't forget to pray about it," said Mary.

"Thanks for your help, both of you. Can I call you again if I need you?"

"Of course," answered Mary. "We'll be hanging around if you need us."

"If you need me, I'll be back, but I'll not be hanging around," Sam corrected. "I've got things to do."

## Community

The church is a disciple community, the interconnected body of Christ. We are the beloved community, loved by God and loving God, loved by neighbors and loving neighbors. We are a family, siblings, loving Jesus and serving Jesus, like Mary and Martha. We are Samaritans caring for our neighbor on the side of the road and, in doing so, caring for God. Whatever we do as a church we do together—worship, pray, teach, serve, witness, care, and equip. We are a disciple community.

### *Individualism*

"I can do it myself" was a favorite saying of both of our daughters when they were very young. "I can do it myself" might mean tying shoes, gluing construction paper, or eating an ice cream cone. Sometimes they could do it themselves. Sometimes they needed a little help, like with tying their shoes (except for those wonderful shoes with Velcro) or eating an ice cream cone (lest the ice cream wind up splattered on the kitchen floor). Their insistence on doing everything themselves was a necessary stage in their development—a stage I appreciate now that they are grown.

"I can do it myself" is also the Western and American ideal. America as a nation was formed out of a passion for freedom and independence, so these values are deeply ingrained in our consciousness: independence, autonomy, individual rights and freedom, and the right to privacy. Many of us in America swell with pride when we hear these words.

The concepts of freedom, autonomy, and independence fit well with the Protestant principle of the priesthood of all believers and the right of the individual to interpret Scripture, as well as with Baptists' emphasis on soul competency and autonomy of the local church. Soul competency means that each individual Christian is responsible and accountable to God to listen and think, study the Bible, pray and discern God's will, and act according to freedom of conscience. Soul competency was a reaction to authoritarianism and corruption in the church and state. The idea of soul competency can be helpful when the majority says, for example, "Slavery is an acceptable institution condoned by the Bible and God," or "Women should not be allowed to vote since the Bible says they are to be in submission to men"—both views that at some time in our history have been held by the majority of church members. Soul competency says that Christians are responsible to follow God and not to blindly follow the majority.

Thus, it is understandable that individualism would come to hold a place of honor both in the nation and the church. However, could it be that by putting so much emphasis on the individual, we have come to neglect Christian community? Jesus said, "Love your neighbor as yourself," and "I am the vine and you are the branches." He gathered around himself a community of disciples. Paul refers to the church as one body—the body of Christ (1 Cor 12). Peter uses these lofty terms to refer to the church: "a chosen race, a royal priesthood, holy nation, and God's own people" (1 Pet 2:9). The emphasis in the New Testament is on the community as a whole more than on the individual. Yet when many of us read the New Testament, we tend to hear it speaking to us as individuals rather than speaking to the community of faith. A "me first" approach to life, prevalent in our society, has crept into the church and in some cases has even been affirmed by the church as gospel. From this perspective, the Christian journey is seen almost exclusively as a personal one. We read the Bible alone and form our own interpretations. Even when we gather for worship, we do so as a collection of individual Christians seeking inspiration and food for the soul to help us in our personal walk with Christ. Corporate (or community) confession is, in some places, a foreign concept, since confession is a private matter between me and God and is no one else's business. A page on a Baptist website offers a statement that perhaps many Christians would endorse: "We affirm soul competency, the accountability of each person before God. Your family cannot save you. Neither can your church. It comes down to you and God." From the point of view of individualism, we are completely on our own when it comes to salvation and our relationship with God.

As much as we might like to think of ourselves as independent, we are never completely so, for "There is no *I* apart from *we*."[1] Thomas R. Hawkins, in *Cultivating Christian Community*, writes,

> God has created people for community. Only within community is authentic humanity possible. There is no life that is not lived in community. "It is not good that the man should be alone" (Genesis 2:18). So, God creates us to be partners in a common life. We discover our deepest selves when we live face-to-face and side-by-side with others in the give-and-take of relationship. Before we can speak in the singular, we learn to speak in the plural. We cannot say *I* without first saying *we*.[2]

Our identity is defined for us by our community. The lenses through which we look at the world are given to us by our families, by the larger communities in which we live, and by our culture. God made us to be dependent on others, and dependence is part of God's plan for church community.

A 1997 document titled *Re-envisioning Baptist Identity: A Manifesto for Baptist Communities in North America* makes a strong case for community against what the authors believe has been a harmful form of individualism often practiced in the church. Written by theologians and church historians, and signed by a number of other professors, professional ministers, and laypeople, the manifesto challenges some assumptions held by many Baptists and other Christians. They write that a mistaken path is taken by those "who would sever freedom from our membership in the body of Christ and the community's legitimate authority, confusing the gift of God with the notions of autonomy or libertarian theories."[3] They contend that many of our ideas about individualism, freedom, and autonomy are more cultural (and modern) than biblical and need to be balanced by a more communal approach to studying Scripture, discipleship, the life of the church, the use of baptism, preaching, the Lord's Supper, and the resistance of the church to worldly powers. The Baptist manifesto is a much-needed counterbalance to individualism.

The following story illustrates the folly of placing too much emphasis on individual self-sufficiency and also highlights the value of community: The Smiths (not their real name) were victims of a major flood in our area—a flood so widespread that it ravaged homes that had never before been flooded. Fifteen families of the church where I served experienced major water damage. The tasks that must be performed to save a home after a flood can be overwhelming. Furniture and other household items must be placed outside to dry, mud and water removed, wet drywall and insulation stripped, and carpet removed, just to start. All of this needs to be done as quickly as possible to prevent dangerous mold and mildew from growing. Thankfully the church community responded heroically, working many hours to help their fellow church members and others in the county.

In checking on our flooded church families, I knocked on the Smiths' door. Mr. Smith opened the door only partway. I offered the help of the church community. "Can we help you with flood cleanup?"

"No thanks. We can take care of it ourselves," he answered.

I was stunned by his refusal. Every other family was desperate for any kind of help they could get. The Smiths were an elderly couple who could not possibly take care of the damage themselves. I cringed at the thought of what was going to happen to their furniture, belongings, and home as it remained soaked behind closed doors. I asked again, "Are you sure we can't help? Many of your church friends are ready to help and have been helping other church members already. They'd be more than happy to help."

"No, we'll be okay," the man repeated, and then he quietly closed the door on his church community.

The flood was a tragedy, no doubt, but out of the flood came a deep experience of Christian community for those families who were flooded and the church family that came to their aid. We realized just how much we needed each other. A week of flood relief efforts culminated in a Sunday evening worship service. Prayers were offered, praises were sung to a God who cares when we are hurting, and flood victims and flood workers shared tearfully of how much the experience brought them closer together and closer to God.

Sadly, the Smiths had no part in this experience though they had been active members of the church for years. This extreme example, for me, exposed the idea of total self-sufficiency not as a heroic ideal but as something stubborn, prideful, silly, and destructive. We cannot live the Christian faith in isolation. Too much emphasis on the individual can keep us from fully experiencing community as God intends. Being a part of a community is not just about giving; it's also about receiving. Or we might say that one gift we can give our neighbors is to allow them to help us.

## Family Systems Theory

Thus far we have focused on individualism as a threat to community. We would not, however, advocate a complete removal of boundaries among members of the congregation so that all diversity of personality, thought, and giftedness is lost—and we become a "glob of glue" to use Peter Steinke's term.[4] Or, as Inagrace Dietterich puts it, "Individuals are not 'absorbed' into Christian community, but discover and are affirmed and empowered in their personal particularity."[5]

Family Systems Theory states that all emotional systems (including biological families and churches) have anxiety and patterns for dealing with anxiety to bring stability. For example, unhealthy approaches to dealing with anxiety are to bring a third person or group into the middle of a conflict and place the anxiety on them, to surrender identity and integrity for the sake of harmony, or to completely disconnect from the group. A healthy approach to dealing with anxiety seeks a balance between separate and close, called "self-differentiation." Self-differentiation, according to Steinke, is

- defining yourself and staying in touch with others.
- being responsible for yourself and responsive to others.
- maintaining your integrity and well-being without intruding on that of others.
- allowing the enhancement of the other's integrity and well-being without feeling abandoned, inferior, or less of a self.
- having an "I" and entering a relationship with another "I" without losing your self or diminishing the self of the other.[6]

## Love Your Neighbor as Yourself

What does "love your neighbor as yourself" mean—that you must first love yourself if you are to love others? If you don't have healthy self-esteem, you will not be able to love others appropriately? Contemporary psychology and pastoral counseling have shown both to be true. Thus, loving your neighbor as yourself could be thought of as part of a threefold command to love God, love others, and love yourself. Alan Culpepper agrees in his commentary on Luke:

> The phrase "as yourself" implies that love for oneself is also expected. Three loves, therefore, characterize the life of one who is already experiencing a measure of that life that will characterize the age to come: love of God, neighbor, and self. Only in this sequence of priority, however, does each require the others.[7]

There is nothing about this interpretation that I disagree with—and this has been my understanding of the verse—yet I have a nagging feeling that we are reading an ancient injunction in light of modern disciplines and a "me first" mindset that was foreign to the community that originally recorded it.

I wonder how "love your neighbor as yourself" would have been understood, before pastoral care and contemporary psychology, by the Hebrew desert nomads who shared the rule verbally and then recorded it in Leviticus so many years ago. How would the crowd surrounding Jesus have understood it that day the lawyer repeated the words? It is difficult to hear these words today without thinking about self-esteem, pastoral care, counseling, and the sanctity of the individual human. So we may hear Jesus say, "First love God, and then your neighbor, but you must have a healthy self-image and love yourself or you will not be able to love God or your neighbor."

I believe all of this to be true and helpful, but what if Jesus means something else by "love your neighbor as yourself"? What if we are imposing a contemporary viewpoint that begins with the individual onto a Scripture verse with a viewpoint that begins with the community? Could it be that we love our neighbors because, within the body of Christ, we are one, not separate individuals? Using Paul's illustration of the body of Christ, we might say, "Love your foot as yourself. Love your hand because it is part of one body. Love your neighbor as a part of your body. Love your neighbor because you are one in the same body—the body of Christ." Ideally there is no difference between loving self and loving neighbors since in Christ we are all created as one community. Simultaneously, we love our neighbors and ourselves.

## Putting Community into Practice

How can we be a disciple community rather than just a collection of independent individuals? We will consider some of the ways a church can practice Christian community through baptism, Communion, fellowship meals, hospitality, understanding family systems, the Enneagram, accountability groups, and the whole life of the church. Think of these as community-building activities that help us love our neighbors as ourselves.

In addition to these specific practices, a church would do well to clarify its unconscious assumptions about the individual and community. In subtle and not so subtle ways, our culture teaches us to cherish as virtues independence, individualism, self-sufficiency, autonomy, freedom from others, and privacy. Churches should examine these often unquestioned values to come to a greater awareness of how extreme individualism can be detrimental to Christian community. Otherwise we may approach the following community-building practices with an individualist mindset and a great deal of skepticism and superficiality.

### *Baptism*

Through baptism, the new believer enters into a new life in a new community. "Do you not know that all of us who have been baptized into Christ Jesus were baptized into his death? Therefore we have been buried with him by baptism into death, so that, just as Christ was raised from the dead by the glory of the Father, so we too might walk in newness of life" (Rom 6:3-4). When the new believer is immersed in the baptismal waters, the old life, with its family and cultural ties and earthly citizenship, is buried—or drowned.[8] The believer is then raised from the waters, wet and gasping for new air within a new world, raised with Christ. Thus, baptism reminds us of the death, burial, and resurrection of Christ.

Far from being "just a symbol," as some refer to it, baptism is at least a powerful symbol of the reality that through Jesus' death and resurrection, the reign of God is revealed and the Christian community participates in God's reign. Even more than a symbol, baptism is the act of identifying with the Christian community and thus a way of life that follows Christ's example.

Baptism is a burial and a resurrection. Buried is a life where our first allegiance may be to self, nation, family, race, or culture. Baptism is a transformation into a new community, a new life, a new family, and a new citizenship. Dietterich writes, "Incorporation into the body of Christ involves movement from the alienating independence of individualism based on self-interest and competition, to the affirming interdependence of a community grounded in the obedience and self-giving of Jesus Christ."[9] Paul describes that grounded community this way:

> for in Christ Jesus you are all children of God through faith. As many of you as were baptized into Christ have clothed yourselves with Christ. There is no longer Jew or Greek, there is no longer slave or free, there is no longer male and female; for all of you are one in Christ Jesus. And if you belong to Christ, then you are Abraham's offspring, heirs according to the promise. (Gal 3:26-29)

Old barriers of race, culture, nation, gender, sexual orientation, and socioeconomic status disappear in the new inclusive Christian community. Through baptism, the Christian is born into a new, diverse family. Jesus said, "whoever does the will of my Father in heaven is my brother and sister and mother" (Matt 12:46-50).

Baptism bestows on believers not only a new family name but also a new citizenship in God's kingdom. The Christian's first allegiance is to God, above all others, including family ties, national interests, or cultural identity. Citizenship in God's kingdom leads to a new way of life: the way of loving God and your neighbor as yourself; the way of the Beatitudes and the Sermon on the Mount; the way of loving your enemies, turning the other cheek, and forgiveness; the way of peace, hope, and joy; the way of reconciliation; the way of becoming a disciple community that follows

Jesus. Within the radically new baptized community, the hated Samaritan is the new model for neighbor love.[10]

Since baptism is a not "just a symbol" but is identification with the Christian community and the Christian way of life, we should take care in how we observe baptism.

*Baptism should be given a prominent place in the life of the community.* Jonathan Wilson encourages churches to "make baptism a central event in the life of the church" by conducting baptism in a central space, at the high points of the community's life, and at the center of the church's teachings.[11] This means that baptism would be conducted in the sanctuary or other location of importance to the community at a time when most of the body is gathered together, during Sunday worship for example and perhaps at the high points in the church calendar like Advent, Lent, or Easter. Baptism is not a private, personal act but a public witness within a community.

*Baptism should be enacted in a way that reminds the new believer, and the whole Christian community, of our new life and identity.* This can be done through the words spoken at baptism and the music, Scripture, and prayers that surround the baptismal service in worship. For example, one church offers a baptismal affirmation in the people's response to the new believers: "That we thank God for their faith in Jesus as Savior and Lord; that their sorrows will be our own; that we will do the work of Christ together—prayerfully, compassionately, and courageously."

*Discipleship should precede and follow baptism.* In the Great Commission, Jesus states, "make disciples, baptizing them . . . and teaching them to observe everything that I have commanded you" (Matt 28:19-20). We must not forget the discipleship and teaching part of this command, or baptism can become a superficial act. Baptism, after all, signals becoming part of a disciple community that follows the teachings and example of Jesus.

## Communion

Jesus gathered his disciples for a last meal, broke bread, and lifted the cup, saying, "Do this in remembrance of me." This meaningful remembrance was reenacted each week by the early church and still is observed by Christians all over the world. Referred to as "Communion," "the Lord's Supper," "Eucharist," "Mass," and "Holy Communion," the meal remembering Jesus is an act of celebration, unity, and witness. When the church observes the Lord's Supper, we remember Jesus' life, teaching, death, and resurrection. The supper is a reminder to the Christian community of its call to be the church on mission for God, embodying a way of life. That God-given way of life is one in which all people are welcomed to feast at God's table. Jesus was often criticized for eating with tax collectors and sinners. Jesus shared a drink of water with a Samaritan woman of questionable character. He ate in the home of Zacchaeus, a hated tax collector and swindler.

The Lord's Supper unites the local body of Christ, and churches of all denominations all over the world, in love for Christ and each other and for a common cause. The early church, and many churches today, couldn't think of gathering for worship without breaking bread and sharing a cup together. The Lord's Supper for many is the central act of worship.

For some churches, perhaps, the Lord's Supper has lost some of its significance. The authors of *A Manifesto for Baptist Communities in North America* warn, "The Supper is so infrequently observed that Christians starve for lack of nourishment."[12] The Lord's Supper in many churches is only occasionally observed and then is treated as an addition to worship rather than a central element. Churches that observe Communion regularly as an essential focus of worship may need to guard against approaching it as a routine instead of a holy remembrance of Christ.

The Christian community gathered for Communion seeks to

- Experience Christ's presence.
- Remember what Jesus taught and the example he gave for loving God and neighbors.
- Reflect on how we can be the church called to God's mission.
- Welcome all people to the table in love.
- Witness to the world that we are followers of Christ.
- Model to the world life as God intends.

Closely related to Communion is the fellowship meal.

## Fellowship Meals

Lexington Avenue Baptist Church, Danville, Kentucky, has a partnership with a predominantly African church in Morocco. Members of the church in Kentucky have visited the church in Morocco, and church members from Morocco have visited Lexington Avenue Baptist. We shared a joke with our friends in Morocco. Each time we gathered for a meal someone would say, "One thing in common," and another would answer, "We like to eat." The sharing of a meal together builds community. In Morocco, especially, dinner is an event lasting two or three hours. In Morocco, it's common to eat and talk around the table for hours.

In most cultures, significant community events are accompanied by a meal or feast. When we say, "we like to eat together," we are in good company, and that company includes Jesus. Linda McKinnish Bridges says that in the Gospel of Luke, "Jesus is constantly either going to a meal, at a meal, or coming from a meal. Place Jesus at a dining room table filled with all kinds of folk whom the religious tradition had rejected, and you will see Luke's portrait of Jesus clear and undiluted."[13] So Jesus followed in the tradition of sharing fellowship meals, while at the same time he broke fellowship meal traditions by eating with the "wrong" kinds of people. Jesus ate with women who were out of place at the men's table, tax collectors who had betrayed their fellow Jews for financial gain, fishermen, "unclean" Samaritans, sinners, and respected Pharisees and lawyers. In doing so, Jesus invited all people to the fellowship table.

The simple act of eating in the same room with other Christians is no guarantee of fellowship. The first deacons were called "to wait on tables" because widows from a certain ethnic group were being neglected (Acts 6:1-6). So, early on, the church's fellowship was broken. We easily forget that the fellowship meal with our church community is not about receiving proper restaurant customer service. It's not about how good the food tastes, how much we get to eat, or making sure we get our favorite dessert. The fellowship meal is not about being served first or sitting with the right people. The fellowship meal is about spiritual and community nourishment through intimacy with God and neighbors. The family night supper (or lunch or breakfast) at church reminds us that we dine with Jesus, who dined with all types of people. Common meals with the Christian community remind us of Jesus' last supper with his disciples, a resurrection breakfast of fish on the seashore with his disciples, and breaking bread after a journey on the road to Emmaus with friends who only at mealtime recognized Jesus.

## *Hospitality*

"Hospitality is the front porch of the church." This image has stuck with me since Rev. James McKenzie preached a sermon by that title at First Baptist Church, Hopkinsville. "When I was growing up, our family had a large front porch with a porch swing," he said. "Whenever a neighbor walked by, Mom or Dad would say, 'Come on up and sit awhile.' Usually they did. Everyone was welcome at our home, and the front porch swing was the place of greeting." He then related this story to the church's emphasis on hospitality and welcoming.

The church, as God intends, is a welcoming place for all people. Welcoming the guest is like welcoming Jesus himself. "I was a stranger and you welcomed me," he said (Matt 25:35). In *Hospitality Evangelism*, Greg Nall and Max Price wonder,

> What would our evangelism look like if we considered a stranger—someone not like us, someone who did not believe like us, someone whose life was very different from ours, someone whose opinions were strange to us, someone whose appearance or language or economic status was foreign to us—as a guest of Christ? What would our evangelism look like if we saw our role as that of hosts?[14]

How can a church offer hospitality?

(1) Greet people when they gather, in the parking lot, at the door in the classroom, and in the sanctuary. Even a caring church can inadvertently miss greeting a guest, leaving them feeling unwelcome. Assigning greeters to strategic locations can help ensure that a guest does not slip in and out of a church gathering without being noticed.

(2) Greet people in worship or "pass the peace" of Christ. In my experience, one of the best ways to create an atmosphere of welcome, and to minimize the chances that someone walks away from worship without being greeted, is to take time during the worship service to invite the congregation to greet one another. I understand that this kind of greeting in worship can be a source of contention, since greeting is focused on our neighbors and worship is the time we spend focused on God. I agree that we allow far too little time for offering God our undivided attention, and some do not fully understand the purpose of worship. If your church is not able to think of greeting as an element of worship or finds it too distracting, perhaps the greeting could be placed early in the service and thought of in this way: the invitation for the congregation to greet one another is a part of how we gather and prepare for the worship of God. The greeting is a time for welcoming everyone into God's presence. Now that everyone has been welcomed, we turn all of our attention to praising and thanking God in worship.

(3) Follow up with guests. Send cards or letters, or visit with guests, especially those who have attended your church for the first time. Offer a

hospitality gift that is unique to your congregation. For example, when my family visited a church in Hawaii, we were given a lei during the greeting.

(4) Most importantly, love your neighbor as yourself. When we love all neighbors without discrimination, hospitality will come naturally. Pay attention to those around you and truly listen to your neighbors. Create an atmosphere where everyone feels accepted for who they are. Make everyone feel at home because they are all part of the family of God.

## Family Systems

A greater understanding of how family systems work can help a congregation function more like the body Christ. Anxiety exists in every congregation and in every organization. Our patterns for dealing with this anxiety will determine how functional or dysfunctional a church community will be. A church could bring these emotional processes to the surface by studying family systems together and engaging in dialogue in order to see the church community as a system of interrelated parts. Instead of choosing to react to tension in destructive ways, such as evasion, opposition, passive submission, or coercion, a church could learn to focus on more "health-influencing" responses such as these:

• *Self, not others.* Act based on your beliefs and goals rather than as a non-self whose chief concern is the approval and reaction of others.

• *Strength, not weaknesses.* Do not become immobilized by fretting over what is wrong with the system or by empowering weak responses. Rather, use the church's strengths.

• *Process, not content.* Do not allow criticism or surface issues to distract the community from its goals and a constructive process.

• *Challenge, not comfort.* Anxiety can be a signal that change is needed. Comfort might temporarily alleviate discomfort without addressing the real causes.

• *Integrity, not unity.* Seeking unity can bring about a shallow peace while surrendering integrity. Conflict is a normal part of life in community that can be a catalyst for growth.

• *System, not symptom.* A symptom generally points to a larger issue within the system.

• *Direction, not condition.* Focus on God's mission and vision for the church, not on whatever problem or condition may be most visible at present.[15]

## Enneagram

The Enneagram is a way of understanding personality types. Many churches have found it helpful for cultivating community and strengthening relationships among family members and church members. The Enneagram identifies nine different personality types that influence how we think, feel, and act—and interact. Knowing and acknowledging these differences can help us relate to others with greater appreciation, understanding, and grace. There is much more to each Enneagram type than their descriptive titles, but typically they are listed as: (1) Perfectionist or Reformer, (2) Helper or Giver, (3) Performer or Achiever, (4) Romantic or Individualist, (5) Investigator or Thinker, (6) Loyalist or Skeptic, (7) Enthusiast, (8) Challenger or Protector, and (9) Peacemaker.[16]

## Accountability Groups

In our culture, which places a high value on personal privacy, the idea of public confession and accountability to the community may seem odd or even evil. Yet Jesus included confession in his model prayer for the Christian community: "forgive us our sins, for we forgive everyone indebted to us" (Luke 11:4).

A few years ago, I received a call from a young man who had been in the youth group at a church I had served. He had graduated from college and was then living in a nearby town. He asked me if I could mentor him. "How about we mentor each other?" I said, and we agreed to meet once a week. He mentored me more than I mentored him. He had been involved in a number of Bible study groups and mentoring relationships through his campus ministry and as a leader in summer youth camps. He had learned the value of accountability in his spiritual journey. I was impressed with his complete honesty and transparency about his prayer life, his thoughts, attitudes, and actions, and even his temptations and challenges. He wanted to be more like Christ and knew that other Christians could guide him and hold him accountable. I learned from him, even if I wasn't as open as he was. When I am in a mentoring relationship like this or participate in a discipleship group, I find that I am more aware each day of my habits, sins, and attention to the spiritual life, since I know that I will be talking about these things with other Christians. As a community of disciples, we follow Jesus together, helping each other along the way, encouraging one another, and lifting each other up when we fall. Self-help groups, like Alcoholics Anonymous, rely heavily on this kind of accountability in a community.

Community is strengthened when we share our lives openly in a Christian community and are held accountable in a nonjudgmental environment of love and trust. This kind of community requires transparency in sharing and grace in receiving. Where do we find such groups? A Sunday school class may offer a certain degree of this kind of openness, but sporadic attendance and the relatively short time frame may make it difficult. Bible study and discipleship groups that focus on reflective reading of Scripture and on group-building dynamics can offer a place to practice accountability. Any two friends who are able to be open, gracious, and good listeners to each other can offer relationships of mutual accountability.

## The Whole Life of the Church

Community is not just another church program. We can be the church with a strong sense that everything we do, we do together as a community centered on Christ. So whether we are gathering for worship, studying the Bible in small groups, going on a mission trip, or playing on the church softball team, we can build community (or tear it down). Community envelops everything we do and everything we are as a congregation.

## Community Resources

Bass, Dorothy C. *Practicing Our Faith: A Way of Life for a Searching People*. San Francisco: Jossey-Bass, 1997.

Bellah, Robert N., et al. *Habits of the Heart: Individualism and Commitment in American Life*. Berkeley: University of California Press, 2008.

Bonhoeffer, Dietrich, *Life Together: Dietrich Bonhoeffer Works—Reader's Edition*. Minneapolis: Fortress, 2015.

Bridges, Linda McKinnish. *The Church's Portraits of Jesus*. All the Bible. Macon: Smyth & Helwys, 1997.

Broadway, Mikael, et al. *Re-envisioning Baptist Identity: A Manifesto for Baptist Communities in North America*. 1997. https://www.nobts.edu/baptist-center-theology/confessions/Re-envisioning_Baptist_Identity.pdf.

Camp, Lee. *Mere Discipleship: Radical Christianity in a Rebellious World*. Grand Rapids: Brazos, 2006.

Cron, Ian Morgan. *The Road Back to You: An Enneagram Journey to Self-Discovery*. Downers Grove: InterVarsity, 2016.

Culpepper, R. Alan. "The Gospel of Luke." Vol. 9 of *New Interpreter's Bible: A Commentary in Twelve Volumes.* Nashville: Abingdon, 1995.

Dietterich, Inagrace T. *Cultivating Missional Communities.* Chicago: Center for Parish Development, 2002.

Hawkins, Thomas R. *Cultivating Christian Community.* Nashville: Discipleship Resources, 2001.

Lohfink, Gerhard. *Jesus and Community: The Social Dimension of Christian Faith.* Trans. John P. Galvin. Philadelphia: Fortress Press, 1984.

Nall, Phill, and Mark Price. *Hospitality Evangelism: Sharing the Bread of Life, Leaders Guide.* Atlanta: Cooperative Baptist Fellowship, 1999.

Richardson, Ronald W. *Creating a Healthier Church: Family Systems Theory, Leadership, and Congregational Life.* Minneapolis: Fortress Press, 1996.

Steinke, Peter. *Healthy Congregations: A Systems Approach.* The Alban Institute, 1996.

———. *How Your Church Family Works: Understanding Congregations as Emotional Systems.* The Alban Institute, 1993.

Wilson, Jonathan. *Why Church Matters: Worship, Ministry, and Mission in Practice.* Grand Rapids: Brazos, 2006.

Yoder, John Howard. *Body Politics: Five Practices of the Christian Community Before the Watching World.* Scottsdale, PA: Herald Press, 2001.

## Notes

1. Hawkins, *Cultivating Christian Community*, 7.

2. Hawkins, *Cultivating Christian Community*, 7–8.

3. Mikael Broadway et al., *Re-envisioning Baptist Identity: A Manifesto for Baptist Communities in North America*, 1997, https://www.nobts.edu/baptist-center-theology/confessions/Re-envisioning_Baptist_Identity.pdf.

4. Peter Steinke, *How Your Church Family Works: Understanding Congregations as Emotional Systems* (Alban Institute, 1993), ch. 6.

5. Dietterich, *Cultivating Missional Communities*, 41.

6. Steinke, *How Your Church Family Works*, 11.

7. R. Alan Culpepper, "The Gospel of Luke," vol. 9 of *New Interpreter's Bible: A Commentary in Twelve Volumes* (Nashville: Abingdon, 1995), 228.

8. Dietterich, *Cultivating Missional Communities*, 24–25.

9. Dietterich, *Cultivating Missional Communities*, 24.

10. Lee Camp, *Mere Discipleship: Radical Christianity in a Rebellious World* (Grand Rapids: Brazos, 2006), 143.

11. Jonathan Wilson, *Why Church Matters: Worship, Ministry, and Mission in Practice* (Grand Rapids: Brazos, 2006), 107–109.

12. Broadway et al. *Re-envisioning Baptist Identity*.

13. Linda McKinnish Bridges, *The Church's Portraits of Jesus*. All the Bible. (Macon: Smyth & Helwys, 1997), 68.

14. Phill Nall and Mark Price, *Hospitality Evangelism: Sharing the Bread of Life*, Leaders Guide (Atlanta: Cooperative Baptist Fellowship, 1999), 4.

15. See Steinke, *How Your Church Family Works*, 109–16.

16. There are numerous Enneagram resources. See, for example, Ian Morgan Cron, *The Road Back to You: An Enneagram Journey to Self-Discovery* (Downers Grove: InterVarsity, 2016).

*Chapter 2*

# Worship

## Conversations with Mary and Sam on Worship

"We've been sitting in my office. Let me show you the rest of our church."

"Yes, let's get moving," Sam said as he hopped to his feet.

I led Mary and Sam across the hall and down into the sanctuary. "This is our sanctuary, where we worship on Sundays."

"Nice," Sam complimented.

"Yes," Mary agreed. "Beautiful."

"Thank you. How does it compare to the worship centers of your day?"

"Well. If you mean the temple in Jerusalem," Mary explained, "to be honest, nothing can compare to its size and beauty. But since the Christians who worshiped on Sunday didn't own buildings, I must say I am impressed with your sanctuary."

"Since we are in the sanctuary, let's talk about worship." I motioned for Mary and Sam to take a seat in the front pew, and I sat on the steps leading to the pulpit area.

"Nice and soft," Sam observed as he rocked on the padded pew.

Mary asked, "Besides comfortable, what is worship like today?"

"Every church is different. There are so many different styles. We use words like liturgical, traditional, contemporary, high, charismatic, and emergent to describe some of the styles of worship. I am sorry to say that sometimes these differences are heated. The differences over worship styles have sometimes been called worship wars. I wish we could get back to your day when the church was more united and worship was faithful to the gospel."

Mary grinned and shook her head. "You're kidding, right?"

Not sure how to answer, I kept my mouth shut and shrugged. Mary continued, "It is sad that there is still conflict about worship, but you don't think the church was without disagreement, do you? Why do you think Paul wrote all of those letters to the churches?"

Sam added, "And I don't know that much about Christian worship, but I know we Samaritans and the Jews had our own version of worship wars. Our ancestors worshiped God on Mount Gerizim. We believed this was the place God commanded us to worship. The Jews worshiped at the temple in Jerusalem. Of all the issues that divided Samaritan and Jew, this may have been number one."

"Yes," Mary agreed, "but Jesus had an interesting answer when a Samaritan woman asked his opinion on the proper place to worship. He said, 'The hour is coming when you will worship the Father neither on this mountain nor in Jerusalem . . . but the hour is coming, and is now here, when the true worshipers will worship the Father in spirit and in truth.'"

"In spirit and in truth," I repeated. "Those are two good words for worship."

"Meditate on those words for a while and see how they apply to the worship wars," Mary suggested.

"Good idea. I will."

I continue, "Okay, so disagreements about worship are not new. Since the debate has been going on for over 2,000 years, maybe the three of us will not be able to settle it here in just a few minutes. Mary, could I ask you something else?"

"Sure."

"I'm interested in that day you met with Jesus in your sister Martha's home. From what I understand about your culture, only men sat at a rabbi's feet to learn. Is it true that when you sat at Jesus' feet as a disciple, you were breaking custom?"

"Yes, that is true."

"From what I understand, it would have been kind of shocking and offensive to most, right?" I asked hesitantly.

Mary was not fazed by the question. "Yes. Women just didn't do that."

"I hope you don't mind me asking this." I was afraid of offending her but was curious as to how she felt and what she was thinking at the time. "Why did you do it? I mean, were you worried what others might think? Were you nervous about how others might react? Were you trying to be a rebel and change the world?"

"You know, to be honest, I didn't think about it. I know that's hard to believe, but I was just caught up in the moment. I guess I knew that Jesus often challenged social customs and was more open to outsiders like women—and Samaritans," she said, placing a hand on Sam's shoulder. "But I didn't consciously decide to sit at Jesus' feet as a disciple. Jesus was always so welcoming, and I was simply in such awe of what he was saying that I was naturally drawn to him. I wanted to hear everything he had to say. I was lost in that moment, and I realized I was in the presence of God. God the creator. God the father of Abraham, Moses, and my sisters Ruth, Esther, and Rahab. God who brought my people out of slavery in Egypt into freedom. The God of love, grace, and joy. God was in Jesus, sitting right in front me, even closer than you and I right now. How much closer can you get to God?" Mary paused, wiping tears from her eyes. "So you can see how I might forget about my sister Martha making dinner and forget about customs and the role of women."

I was speechless for a moment. She recounted the experience with such passion that I felt like I was sitting there at Jesus' feet with her. A tear ran down my cheek. "All I can say is 'wow!'"

"Yes, 'wow' is exactly why I sat at Jesus' feet," Mary affirmed. "That is worship."

## Worship

"Wow!" the children said in unison, unprompted. My wife Dianne was leading a children's sermon on worship. She had just shown them a picture of a colorful caterpillar, then pictures of the caterpillar transforming into a chrysalis. Then she displayed pictures of a monarch butterfly emerging from the chrysalis. "Wow!" they said again, eyes wide in amazement. God's creation is awesome and wonderful, and our response is "Wow!" Worship is the community's "wow" response to the wonder of God: God's creation, God's forgiveness, God's unconditional love, God's calling.

Mary was wowed by Jesus. At the home of her sister Martha, she sat at Jesus' feet listening to his teaching. She was so fully focused on Jesus that she paid no attention to Martha's meal preparations or to the cultural rules of the day, which forbade her to sit at a rabbi's feet to receive instruction. Jesus said that Mary had chosen the better part. What is the better part? Worship? Devotion? Prayer? Spiritual growth? Perhaps all of these. Mary's attention to Jesus, her listening ear and her willingness to learn from Jesus, her desire to be near Jesus, and her love for Jesus provide an example for the disciple community. When we gather for worship, we come as a community to set aside other distractions and sit at Jesus' feet filled with love and ready to hear God. When we do, perhaps Jesus would say that we have chosen the better part.

Many would say that worship is the central function of the church. In most churches worship is given priority in terms of time and space. Worship is generally the most well-attended activity of the church and is perhaps the one and only time when the congregation as a whole comes together. Yet I have the sense that worship is largely misunderstood by the community, and often worship planning is not as thoughtful and purposeful as it could be. If worship is God centered, then why are the first questions we often ask about worship related to our personal preferences: Did I enjoy the music? Was the sermon interesting? Was I spiritually fed? Was I inspired? These questions may have some relevance, but they are not the most important questions if worship is our purpose. These kinds of questions may say something about how we view ourselves and worship: I am a passive consumer of religious goods and services, and the purpose of worship is primarily to meet my needs or to entertain me. Debates about worship are prevalent—contemporary, traditional, liturgical, blended, or emergent? Instead of debating which is the best style, the right style, or the only style, let us as a disciple community engage in humble and constructive dialogue around the question, "What is worship?"

## What Is Worship?
### Ascribing Honor

"Ascribe to the LORD, O families of the peoples, ascribe to the LORD glory and strength. Ascribe to the LORD the glory due his name; bring an offering, and come into his courts" sings the psalmist, and "O come, let us worship and bow down, let us kneel before the LORD, our Maker!" (Pss 96:7-8 and 95:6).

Worship means ascribing worth and honor to a worthy person. In the Old Testament, a variety of terms refer to worship. Two of the most common mean "to bow down" and "service." For the Christian, God is of ultimate worth and worthy of our supreme honor and devotion in worship. So to worship is to bow before God and offer the service of ritual, song, praise, a listening ear, a willing heart, and then ultimately a life of service in response to God's call. The essence of worship is captured in this heavenly scene depicted in the book of Revelation:

> And the twenty-four elders and the four living creatures fell down and worshiped God who is seated on the throne, saying, "Amen. Hallelujah!"

And from the throne came a voice saying, "Praise to our God, all you his servants, and all who fear him, small and great." Then I heard what seemed to be the voice of a great multitude, like the sound of many waters and like the sound of mighty thunderpeals, crying out, "Hallelujah! For the Lord our God the Almighty reigns. Let us rejoice and exult and give him the glory . . . ." (Rev 19:4-7)

## Loving God with Heart, Mind, Soul, Strength

Worship is an expression of our love for God. When Jesus was asked, "What must I do to inherit eternal life?" in Luke, or "What is the greatest commandment in the law of God?" in Matthew and Mark, the answer was, "You shall love the Lord your God with all your heart, and with all your soul, and with all your strength, and with all your mind." Loving God is of utmost importance, and corporate worship is a way of demonstrating that love.

Heart, soul, strength, and mind have different meanings to us today than they did to the Hebrew people and the early Christian church. In Hebrew thought the meanings may vary, but generally the "heart" can refer to our emotions and also to our thought and will and our innermost self; the "soul" is one's whole life and breath; "strength" is, as we would expect, our might, power, strength, and ability; the "mind" is the place of thinking and planning. Despite the differences in connotation, the words taken together have similar meaning to us today. We are to love God with our whole being, with all that we are, holding no part of ourselves back.

Saint Augustine beautifully described worship as an offering of his whole self to God:

> My whole heart I lay upon the altar of thy praise, an whole burnt-offering of praise I offer to thee. . . . Let the flame of thy love . . . set on fire my whole heart, let nought in me be left to myself, nought wherein I may look to myself, but may I wholly burn toward thee, wholly be on fire toward thee, wholly love thee as though set on fire by thee.[1]

William Willimon also describes worship as an act of love:

> We love because we have been loved (1 John 4:19). Our alleged excessiveness in worship is the excess produced by love. The church's worship on Sunday is a way of being in love . . . if you have been loved, you already know something of how lovers need to return love. You already

understand irrational, nonutilitarian, gratuitous, delightfully useless behavior like Christian worship.[2]

We worship God because we love God. We love because God first loved us.

## Responding

Worship is our response to the goodness and love of God. When we remember that "while we were yet sinners Christ died for us," we naturally respond with confession and thanksgiving. When we consider God's creation, we respond with awe and praise, as the psalmist sings, "When I look at your heavens, the work of your fingers, the moon and the stars that you have established; what are human beings that you are mindful of them . . . O Lord, our Sovereign, How majestic is your name in all the earth!" (from the worship hymnal of Israel, Psalm 8:3-4, 9.) "When I survey the wondrous cross," as the words of the Isaac Watts hymn say, "Love so amazing, so divine, Demands my soul, my life, my all." We come together as a community for worship, grateful for a God who has walked with us through the week. As a community, we worship God for what God has done and for who God is.

## Revelation and Response

Worship could be narrowly defined as only those acts of honor ascribed to God. In the strictest sense, then, worship includes only those components that are directed to God: expressions of love, praise, and thanksgiving that are solely for the purpose of honoring God. Sometimes worship is more broadly understood as revelation as well as our response, or a dialogue, as Price and Furr suggest in *The Dialogue of Worship*.[3] Thus, worship includes both the revelation of God and our response to the revelation. Revelation might include Scripture reading, music, sermons, and drama, for example. After encountering God, we then respond in a variety of ways, such as confession of sin, songs or prayers of praise and thanksgiving, offerings, and commitment to God's call and mission.

## Transformation

We can speak of worship even more broadly. In response to our encounter with God in worship, we may be transformed to live lives more consistent with God's will. Part of our response to worship is to act justly, to show mercy, to engage in missions and ministry, and to proclaim the good news.

Worship of God that does not lead to this kind of transformation may not be true worship at all. Through the prophet Hosea, God corrected the people with these words: "For I desire steadfast love and not sacrifice, the knowledge of God rather than burnt offerings" (Hos 6:6). The prophet Jeremiah reminded the people that God's presence in the temple was not assured: "Hear the word of the LORD, all you people of Judah, you that enter these gates to worship the LORD. . . . Amend your ways and your doings, and let me dwell with you in this place" (Jer 7:2-3). Worshiping came with the expectation that the people would live life God's way. "If you truly act justly with one another and do not oppress the alien, the orphan, and the widow, or shed innocent blood in this place, and if you do not go after other gods to your own hurt, then I will dwell with you in this place" (Jer 7:5-7).

Thus, all of life can be our worship response. On Sunday we are the gathered community at worship; during the week we are the scattered church, living life as a people transformed by our encounter with God in worship. Our response to worship is to praise God and live for God by loving our neighbors as ourselves. Everything we do can be an act of love for God. As Brother Lawrence has said, "I turn my little omelet in the pan for the love of God."[4]

**Reverence and Celebration**

Do we have to choose between worshiping with an attitude of reverence or celebration? I hope not.

Psalm 96 seems to suggest both are appropriate. Words like "revered," "holy splendor," "tremble," "honor," and "majesty" might suggest a tone of quiet reverence, humility, and awe as we come before God. Phrases like "sing to the Lord a new song," "let earth rejoice," "let the sea roar," and "let the field exult" and "the forest sing for joy" sound like an energetic and loud celebration.

God is holy and therefore due our reverence, which may lead us to kneel, bow our heads, remain quiet, and demonstrate respect in our dress, posture, language, and solemn demeanor. God's goodness is also cause for celebration, which may prompt us to praise God and smile, laugh, sing, dance, lift our hands, shout, or clap.

**A Pledge of Allegiance**

Worship is a pledge of exclusive allegiance to God. Thus, worship is a radical act. When we say our first allegiance is to God, we are saying our first allegiance is not to something else . . . Rome, America, self, work, recreation and entertainment, even family and friends. To worship God is to submit to the reign of God above all else. It is to declare obedience to the way of Christ that includes loving neighbors and enemies, turning the other cheek, and suffering service. For the early church, worship was an act of disobedience. To worship any god other than the emperor was an act of treason. Worshiping the God of Israel or the God revealed in Christ could cost them their property and even their lives. Christians in the United States may not be in physical danger for worshiping God, but the pressure to submit to other gods of culture and nation is real. The gods of nationalism, individualism, consumerism, and competition influence the way we worship and practice our faith. Lee Camp, in a book subtitled *Radical Christianity in a Rebellious World*, challenges us,

> This is the great irony of American Christianity: exalting the nation that affords us "freedom of religion," we set aside the way of Christ in order to preserve the religion we supposedly are free to practice. We kill our alleged enemies in order to "worship" the God who teaches us to love our enemies. The most important question about our pledge of allegiance is not whether we pledge allegiance to a flag under "one God," but to what god we are pledging our allegiance. Perhaps it is, after all, not the God revealed in Jesus Christ we are worshipping, but the god of the nation-state, the god of power and might and wealth.[5]

When we blindly follow any ruler, government, philosophy, or influential person down a path that is contrary to the way of Christ, no matter how esteemed they may be, we have denied our worship of the God who demands our total allegiance. Let us then remember the words of the Shema, "The LORD is our God, the LORD alone. You shall love the LORD your God with all your heart, and with all your soul, and with all your might" (Deut 6:4-5). To worship other gods is idolatry.

## Elements of Worship

Another way of describing worship is through the elements of a worship service. A number of elements are mentioned here, though others could be added and the ones I have named could be grouped differently. These elements will serve as a sampling and also suggest an order of worship, though this is not intended to be the one and only order of worship.

## Gathering

Gathering is what we do to come together as a community, prepare for worship, and turn our attention toward God. Gathering is not so much worship as it is getting ready for worship. The focus is on the community and our relationships with each other. When we gather for worship, we do so as a community, not as a collection of individuals. In worship the community is united in purpose—honoring our God who is worthy of our devotion. Gathering for worship reminds us that we are not alone—that when we come into God's presence, we find a fellowship of Christians around God.

Gathering for worship attends to our needs as a fellowship. We greet one another and make our guests feel welcome in our community. The greeting may happen informally among worshipers, through words of welcome spoken from the pulpit, or by "passing the peace"—inviting the congregation to share words with each other, such as "The peace of Christ be with you." The gathering could be a place to share relevant information in the way of announcements and prayer concerns. Then we begin to center ourselves and shift our focus to the worship of God. A musical prelude may be considered a part of gathering for worship, as well as lighting candles, opening the Bible, or other such traditions.

## Call to Worship

The call to worship is simply that: a call, invitation, or summons to worship. It is a reminder that something extraordinary is about to happen. During the week we may have gone our separate ways, but at this moment we are together as a community in God's presence. God has truly been with us all week, and right now we are more fully aware that we are with our loving and powerful God. The call to worship may take many forms: a hymn, instrumental arrangement, or other music; responsive reading or Scripture; or a spoken word, for example.

## Invocation

The invocation is a prayer that calls upon God to be with us, or, since God is always with us, we may think of it as an acknowledgment of God's presence.

## Confession and Assurance of Pardon

Confession is a prayer acknowledging our sinfulness before God. When we stand before a Holy God, we recognize that we fall short of God's glory. In the light of God, our sin, individual and corporate, becomes more visible. Our response is to confess our sin before God.

Perhaps confession is the least popular aspect of worship, and in some traditions it receives little attention or none at all. Maybe, for some, confession is viewed as a personal and private matter between the individual and God. Yet Scripture and tradition suggest that confession has a place in corporate worship.

The model prayer offered by Jesus leads us to pray to God, "forgive us our sins, for we ourselves forgive everyone indebted to us" (Luke 11:4). Notice the prayer does not say, "forgive *me my* sins" but "forgive *us our* sins." The Lord's prayer is a communal prayer.

Isaiah's call experience recorded in Isaiah 6 is often cited as a model outline for worship. When Isaiah encountered God in all God's glory and holiness, he was moved to confess, "Woe is me! I am lost, for I am a man of unclean lips, and I live among a people of unclean lips; yet my eyes have seen the King, the LORD of hosts!" Then a seraph touched Isaiah's mouth with a live coal and said, "Now that this has touched your lips, your guilt has departed and your sin is blotted out" (see Isa 6:5-6). Isaiah confessed not only for himself but also on behalf of his community.

Psalms, the worship hymnal of Israel, offers numerous Psalms of Confession, or Penitential Psalms (see Psalms 6, 32, 38, 51, 102, 130, and 143). Psalm 51, attributed to David after he committed the sins of adultery, begins, "Have mercy on me, O God, according to your steadfast love; according to your abundant mercy blot out my transgressions. Wash me thoroughly from my iniquity, and cleanse me from my sin. For I know my transgressions, and my sin is ever before me. Against you, you alone, have I sinned" (vv. 1-4).

The *Didache*, one of the oldest documents available from the early church (first or early second century), offers these words of instruction for Sunday worship:

> Assemble on the Lord's Day, and break bread and offer the Eucharist; but first make confession of your faults, so that your sacrifice may be a pure one. Anyone who has a difference with his fellow is not to take part with you until they have been reconciled, so as to avoid any profanation of your sacrifice. For this is the offering of which the Lord has said, "Everywhere and always bring me a sacrifice that is undefiled, for I am a great king, says the Lord, and my name is the wonder of nations."[6]

Immediately after confession comes the assurance of God's forgiveness: "If we confess our sins, he who is faithful and just will forgive us our sins and cleanse us from all unrighteousness" (1 John 1:9). We worship a God of unconditional love and grace, whose response to our confession is mercy and forgiveness.

## Praise and Thanksgiving

Praise and thanksgiving are our response to God's goodness. We praise God for who God is and thank God for what God has done. This aspect of worship might be thought of as a celebration. Indeed we have much to celebrate. God has forgiven us. God is the creator of our beautiful world. God walks with us each day. God answers our prayers. God, though bigger than our universe, sent Jesus, God's own son, to live among us. In the words of the Doxology:

> Praise God, from Whom all blessings flow;
> Praise God, all creatures here below;
> Praise God above, ye Heavenly Host;
> Praise Father, Son, and Holy Ghost. Amen.

Lexington Avenue Baptist Church has enjoyed a friendship with a Christian church in Morocco, and I have had the privilege of worshiping with them on several occasions. I appreciate how the worship service is both reverent and celebrative. The church is a Protestant church made up of members from a variety of Christian traditions, and the worship style reflects that diversity. Most of the members are African university students. The service begins with a rousing welcome, with music and greetings among members and guests, and then takes a more reverent and quiet tone fitting for a time of corporate confession. After the assurance of pardon, the mood of worship lifts and worship becomes an energetic celebration of God. How appropriate. The praise music is full of life and the people sway, clap, and dance to the rhythm, hearts full of joy. For many of them, life has been difficult, even tragic, yet they have found true joy in God's presence. What other response could there be in that setting but to dance and sing praises to God?

## Offering

Part of our response to God in worship is to offer ourselves: our money, time, and talents. The offertory is usually the time when financial tithes and offerings are received. The offering should include our monetary gifts, but the offering in worship is symbolic of much more than money. The offering is, or should be, a commitment of ourselves to God. The prophet Micah said it well:

> "With what shall I come before the LORD, and bow myself before God on high? Shall I come before him with burnt offerings, with calves a year old? Will the LORD be pleased with thousands of rams, with tens of thousands of rivers of oil? Shall I give my firstborn for my transgression, the fruit of my body for the sin of my soul?" He has told you, O mortal, what is good; and what does the LORD require of you but to do justice, and to love kindness, and to walk humbly with your God? (Mic 6:6-8)

The best offering we can make in worship is a life committed to God.

Where do we place the offering in the order of worship? When it's placed early in the service of worship, we might think of the offering as a gift we give God as we come into God's presence. As we begin to worship, we offer ourselves and our gifts. When it's placed late in the service, we might think of the offering as our commitment to God in response to worship: "I have met you, God. Now I give you myself and all that I have."

## Scripture Reading

The Bible is an important part of God's revelation to the church. When we read the Bible in worship, we may be convicted of sin, called to serve, or taught how to live life as God intends. The words of Scripture may help us articulate our prayer of praise, confession, or commitment, especially when we read the words of others who have offered the same kinds of prayers. We encounter God in the Bible, as it is the story of God's relationship with humanity. Thus, after the reading of Scripture, the reader might say, "This is the word of the Lord," and the people respond, "Thanks be to God."

## Proclamation

Proclamation in worship is sharing the word of God or the good news about Jesus. Proclamation attempts to reveal God and lead worshipers to hear a word from God. Most commonly the message is conveyed through a sermon, but music, drama, multimedia, and other arts could be forms of proclamation depending on their content and purpose. Proclamation may not be worship in the strictest sense, as it is directed not to God but to the people, but at its best, proclamation contains God's revelation and will prompt a worship response from the community.

## Invitation and Commitment

In many Christian traditions, especially in evangelical churches, the invitation is the culmination of the service. Having seen and heard God revealed through Scripture and proclamation and having encountered God in worship, we are invited to respond to God. Responses may vary depending on the nature of God's revelation or the unique situation of the congregation: praise and thanks, repentance, commitment, conversion, a transformed life, answering God's call to some ministry or service, or an offering of self, time, spiritual gifts, talents, or money.

## Benediction

The benediction is a blessing from God, usually spoken or sung. There are numerous blessings in Scripture. One of the most popular scriptural blessings is that found in Numbers 6:24-26:

> The LORD bless you and keep you;
> the LORD make his face to shine upon you, and be gracious to you;
> the LORD lift up his countenance upon you, and give you peace.

"God Be with You Till We Meet Again" is a well-known musical benediction:

> God be with you till we meet again;
> By His counsels guide, uphold you,
> With His sheep securely fold you;
> God be with you till we meet again.
> Till we meet, till we meet,
> Till we meet at Jesus' feet;
> Till we meet, till we meet,
> God be with you till we meet again.[7]

One of my favorite benedictions from Scripture is 2 Corinthians 13:14: "The grace of the Lord Jesus Christ, the love of God, and the communion of the Holy Spirit be with all of you."

Celtic Christianity is known for its creative benedictions. The following is attributed to Saint Patrick:

Christ with me,
Christ before me,
Christ behind me,
Christ in me,
Christ beneath me,
Christ above me,
Christ on my right,
Christ on my left,
Christ when I lie down,
Christ when I sit down,
Christ when I arise,
Christ in the heart of every man who thinks of me,
Christ in the mouth of everyone who speaks of me,
Christ in every eye that sees me,
Christ in every ear that hears me.

I often use some form of the following benediction, with some additional words relating to what we have experienced in worship that day:

As you go from this place to be the church in the world,
May God above you,
Christ beside you,
and the Holy Spirit within you
bless you
until we meet again.
Amen.

We scatter as a community at worship with God's blessing in our ears. We go forth to live every day like a people who have experienced God in worship.

Some might criticize this description of the elements of worship as too limited. They would be justified. There are a multitude of worship traditions that are rich, diverse, creative, and faithful to God. I have only given examples.

## Congregational Singing in Worship

*This section is written by Richard Summers, Associate Pastor of Music and Administration, First Baptist Church, Frankfort, Kentucky.*

Congregational singing is one of the major ways the congregation actively participates in the worship service, though many do not participate. The number one reason I am given for individuals not singing is they don't feel like they have a good voice. I can understand that reasoning, though I believe it is flawed. The Creator whom we worship is the one who gave that voice and desires it to be used to praise God.

With the arrival of grandchildren, our home is once again adorned with artwork. Our soon to be four-year-old granddaughters love to draw, color, and paint pictures for us. Though for their age their art is good, you will not find it hanging in a museum. But I would not trade it for any art anywhere, because this art was made especially for me out of love. It is priceless art, and we proudly display it in a prominent place in our family room. It brings me joy every time I look at it.

I believe God views our offerings the same way. No one sings perfectly. But *all* of us can offer our best, knowing God hears it as glorious music offered out of love. If you are worried about what your neighbor thinks of your singing, don't be! I'm reminded of a humorous story I heard many years ago about a young child who was asked to pray at mealtime. The child obliged, but the prayer wasn't audible to those around the table. The parent said, "We can't hear you," to which the child replied, "I wasn't talking to you."

I wish I could say that no one around you will make a face, or even perhaps make a rude comment, but what I can tell you with certainty is that the One who gave you the voice will love to hear your offering of praise.

## *We Are Not the Audience of Worship*

Following on what Richard Summers wrote about congregational singing, there are important things to know about being a participant in worship. First, who is the audience of worship? Søren Kierkegaard has likened worship to a drama, but not in the way we might think. We may tend to think of the worship leaders (pastor, choir, and others who ascend the platform) as the actors and the congregation as the critical audience. After all, we sit facing the platform or stage, some in theater-style seats, and may even offer our critique of the performance on the way out. This view of worship as drama, according to Kierkegaard, is far off base. On the contrary, God is the audience of worship. The worship leaders are the prompters. Members of the congregation are the actors.

Kierkegaard writes, "In the most earnest sense, God is the critical theatergoer, who looks on to see how the lines are spoken and how they are listened to: hence here the customary audience is wanting. The speaker is then the prompter, and the listener stands openly before God. The listener, if I may say so, is the actor, who in all truth acts before God."[8]

Together we offer our worship to God. We do not attend worship as an audience seeking to be entertained by the worship leaders. It is God we seek to please. Therefore, when we gather for worship, let our first thought be not "what can I get out of this" but "what can I give to God."

Television, sports, movies, radio, the internet, and a multitude of new media devices offer us around-the-clock entertainment. I fear that far too often, we approach worship as if it too were for our entertainment. If the sermon, music, and other elements are for the worship of God, then the question is not "Was the sermon interesting?" or "Did I enjoy the music?" Rather the question is, "Did the elements of worship lead me to worship God?" We are not passive spectators but active participants in the worship of God. What is the thinking behind the placement of the elements of worship? Is the purpose to provide variety to hold the interest of people with short attention spans or to lead the congregation through a meaningful flow of revelation and response? If worship is entertainment, then our people may continually be shopping around for the best show in town. My guess is that many are.

Similarly, we may think the goal of worship is for *me* to be spiritually fed. I know of pastors who were dismissed with this reason given: "We are not being fed." Certainly "we are not being fed" may sound less frivolous than "we are not being entertained," but it is still a passive approach to worship, and the focus is on "me" or "we" rather than on God. If God is truly the audience of our worship, then whether or not we are fed is as relevant as whether or not an actor enjoyed her own performance. Indeed, the actor may have gotten something positive out of acting (and the audience may even be interested in hearing about the actor's thoughts on acting), but the focus is on the audience's reaction. Rodney Clapp is blunt in his criticism of "feed me" worship: "Christians were taught that worship was preeminently their opportunity to be 'fed.' But it was rarely recognized that to be fed is to be infantilized. To say I go to church to be fed is the same as saying, 'I go to church to act like a baby.'"[9]

None of this is to say that worship cannot be enjoyable or interesting or that in worship we should not receive something meaningful. Culturally appropriate worship will consider the interests, gifts, forms, and traditions of the surrounding community. However, we must remember that the focus in worship is on God, not our desire to be entertained or fed. Certainly encountering God in worship can be both interesting and enjoyable, but it should also be challenging. And when God's people actively engage in God-centered worship, they will experience spiritual growth.

I have had the privilege of worshiping with the monks at the Abbey of Gethsemani in Kentucky. The experience of being led in worship by a community of monks who have devoted their entire lives to silence, prayer, and worship is awe inspiring. From my seat in the balcony, the lines of sight were not great and I struggled to see the monks. The readings, music, and rituals of worship were not easy for this Baptist to follow and were taken from three different books and from their memories. I was never sure exactly where we were in the service or what was coming next. You could not say that the service was especially user friendly to me, yet I was struck by the realization, "This is not about me. It's about God." It's not that the monks were not welcoming or were trying to make things difficult for me; it was just that their focus was on God. They did make efforts to accommodate worshipers, but their primary purpose was prayer and worship. They were intent on chanting the psalms, confessing, and listening to God's word. They understood that the audience of their worship was God, and God held their undivided attention. And, in that environment, I worshiped God; the Scripture, readings, and prayers were meaningful; and I felt closer to this community I did not know and closer to my God.

## *Worship as a Community*

The second thing to know about participating in worship is that it's a communal experience. When Dave Garrett, the minister of youth, welcomed the congregation to worship, he would often say something like, "Your presence here today matters to others. Maybe even someone across the room will be encouraged in their faith just by seeing you here today." Dave recognized that when we come together for worship, we do so as a community, not just so we as individuals can have a personal, one-on-one encounter with God. The welcome reminds us that we are a gathered people at worship. We sing hymns and choruses together. An individual may offer a prayer, but the prayer is on behalf of the community. Even when the choir sings, ideally the congregation adds their listening assent to an anthem offered to God.

If we worship as a community, then the quality of our worship depends on the quality of our relationships. Jesus says in the Sermon on the Mount, "So when you are offering your gift at the altar, if you remember that your brother or sister has something against you, leave your gift there before the altar and go; first be reconciled to your brother or sister, and then come and offer your gift" (Matt 5:23-24). Jesus says that reconciliation among the members of the community is essential to the worship of God. So when we fight in business meetings, worship is affected. When we engage in parking lot gossip about fellow members, we diminish our capacity for community worship. How can we sing and pray together with one voice if we don't love each other? On the other hand, we might ask, "How can we come to love each other if we don't worship together?" Deborah Moore Clark writes, "The better job a church does at building a community of healthy relationships, the better chance it has for worship. Worship and community function within a cyclical relationship: worship aids community, and community aids worship."[10]

"How are Brittany and Kelsey?" Bernard asked about my daughters at the entrance to the sanctuary one Sunday morning. Bernard was a greeter, and I could tell by the way he listened that he cared about how my daughters were doing. At the end of the announcements, Dave, our youth minister, said, "We are here to worship, so let's do that now." This was not just a routine phrase for Dave; he was earnestly inviting us to worship. The organist played the prelude, and then we sang, "O Worship the King." While we sang, I looked out over the congregation from my seat on the platform and had the strong sense that we were a community worshiping God together. I know that may sound obvious, and I am confessing that my approach to worship is not always what it should be, but in that moment, I was more fully aware of both God's presence and our togetherness. I knew that I loved these people and we were here together for the common purpose of worshiping the God we love. This kind of emotion can make it hard to sing, and I choked on the words: "O worship the King, all glorious above, O gratefully sing His power and His love."

## Putting Worship into Practice

### *Planning Worship*

As worship planners, how do we decide what elements to include in worship, what to leave out, and where to place the ones we include?

#### Begin by asking, "What is worship?"

Some of my colleagues in education like to ask, "What is the theology behind the practice?" in reference to every practice of the church. The theological question is particularly applicable to worship. "What is God's intent for worship?" is a theological question. A clear understanding of worship can help us be more purposeful in our worship planning. If worship is honoring God, God centered, and God's revelation and our response, then we need to determine the best way for our unique faith community to express that worship.

**Allow quality time for God-focused worship.**
Are we spending significant quality time responding to God with praise, thanksgiving, offerings, and commitment? Are we encountering God in worship? Are we hearing God's revelation through Scripture, proclamation, music, and other means? Do the activities that focus on entertaining, educating, evangelizing, and informing dominate the service so much that there is little time for God-focused worship?

My good friend Phil Rector, former minister of music at the church where I served, wondered, "Is it too much to ask that we would devote just one hour a week to ascribing supreme worth to the one who is worthy to be worshiped? And to put aside secularism, entertainment, and other distractions?" Indeed, this is a question worthy of our consideration. Our weeks are filled with secular pursuits, work to provide a living and meaning to life, entertainment, and other ways of looking out for our own needs and desires. When we gather as a disciple community, it is reasonable that we should expect to put aside our own interests and focus on God for a time, where the priority is not what I will get out of this but what we as a community can offer God. When we encounter God in worship, we are likely to "get something out of it," but that is not the primary purpose of worship.

Finding a balance in worship planning is a challenge because the Sunday morning worship hour may be the only time most of the community gathers. Other agendas, besides worshiping God, vie for our attention. These activities are not necessarily evil and may even be important tasks of the church, like announcements of church ministry opportunities, education, or recognizing members for acts of service. What do we do with these activities that are directed to the congregation as the audience rather than to God? First, we can intentionally guard time for worship activities that are God focused and directed toward God. If other activities are deemed necessary to include in our time together as a community, seek to limit them and try to keep them from dominating the service. Second, we can pay attention to the placement of these extraneous items in the flow of the worship service. Ask, "Where is the most appropriate place for this?" For example, what are we saying when, after the call to worship God, we immediately recognize our Sunday school teachers? Finally, we can be clear about what we are doing. If it's not worship, don't call it worship.

**Consider the issue of cultural relevance.**
Worship in a Protestant church in Morocco will look and feel different from worship in a rural town in Kentucky. The music, instruments, language, and symbols of worship will be influenced by the surrounding culture, and, to a certain extent, this is as it should be. Worship that is authentic and provides opportunities for people to hear God and respond to God must take into consideration the cultural dialect of the people. It is simply not possible to completely avoid the influence of culture, since culture provides much of the language, symbols, and meanings through which we communicate. In worship we want to offer God the best of what we find beautiful and meaningful in life, whether that be a particular instrument or style of music, an art form, or a turn of phrase. It is good for our worship to be relevant to the people of our church and to those who live in the neighborhood, town, city, or village where the church is located.

While we want to be relevant to the culture, we do not want to blindly conform. God is holy and bigger than our culture. The church is to be a contrasting light to the world. Worship should not simply seek to mimic the words, manners, and music of our everyday world. No, worship of the God of the universe must rise above the ordinary and everyday. So we should expect that some of the language, symbols, style, and music we use in worship will not be what we are used to encountering every day in the secular world or on the radio or television or at the movies.

Deborah Clark Moore said it well:

> None of life is profane, not even rock and roll music. But worship seeks to draw us away from the blaring sounds and persuasions of the world toward a newness of life the world cannot match. If we allow contemporary culture to dictate our holy times and override all that is sacred, we may later find we have lost our saltiness and any ability to influence society. Sadly, worship may become little more than a mirror image of the world.[11]

**Educate church members about worship.**
Churches would benefit from study and dialogue around worship. Worship is enhanced when more of the congregation understands why we do what

we do in worship. The most perfectly planned worship service may not be effective if the worshipers think of worship as entertainment or approach worship as passive observers.

### Pay attention to the flow of worship.
What happens first, second, and last in worship? Does the worship flow with intentionality? Or are components arranged based more on a concern for variety than for the flow of worship?

### Focus on intentionality, creativity, and humility.
Finally, I would suggest we approach our worship planning with these three words in mind: intentionality, creativity, and humility. We approach worship with intentionality because worship has a purpose. We want to be thoughtful about how we worship, what we include in worship, and the order of worship. We use our best creativity in worship because God is a creative God. God is worthy of our best gifts and efforts. Using the gifts God has given us creatively in worship shows we care and that worship is important to us. On the other hand, a lazy, complacent, "same old" approach to worship preparation may demonstrate that we think God is not worthy of our best. It is understandable that people who care about worship would have strong feelings about what is best for worship. That is as it should be, but in the end we must be humble and remember that we might be wrong. Thomas Merton's prayer is helpful here: "the fact that I think that I am following your will does not mean that I am actually doing so. But I believe that the desire to please you does in fact please you."[12]

## The Church Year as an Aid to Worship
The traditional seasons of the church year can be an aid to worship. Some worship traditions rely heavily on the liturgical calendar, while others are barely familiar. The readings and emphases of the church year can help us become more balanced and can help us relive the biblical story. I offer the season of Advent as an example.

Instead of just giving in to our culture's way of celebrating Christmas, Advent offers another way. Advent is a season of waiting for the coming of Christ during the four Sundays before Christmas. Waiting is not popular in our "I want it now" culture. Christmas begins the day after Thanksgiving or even sooner. The message of commercial Christmas is that of spending, materialism, capitalism, and greed, the opposite of the way of the Christ of Christmas. The season of Advent helps us relive Israel's longing and hope for a promised future Messiah. Advent teaches us that some things are worth waiting for. Advent can prepare us for the times when we have no choice but to wait, whether for test results, for illness, for conflicts to be resolved, for grief. Sometimes we must wait anxiously for a better day. During Advent, we hear the stories of Israel's prophets, John the Baptist, and the birth announcement to Mary and Joseph, all of whom waited for the coming Messiah. We sing songs of anticipation like "O Come, O Come, Emmanuel." As we light a candle on the Advent wreath each Sunday, we are reminded that we wait in hope, peace, joy, and love. Then on Christmas Day, or Christmas Eve, our waiting ends and we celebrate in worship the birth of Christ because "Joy to the world, the Lord has come."

### Preparing the Space for Worship
*This section was written by Brittany Stillwell, Minister with Students and Families, Second Baptist Church, Downtown, Little Rock, Arkansas.*

Space has the ability to speak to our souls—it can put us at ease or cause tension in our bodies; it can inspire or confuse. The physical space in which we worship and the way we adorn it bears witness to our theology and to the God whom we have gathered to worship. Symbols and adornments can aid in our worship or distract from it. Too often the visuals and the architecture of our sanctuaries are afterthoughts or symbols of the culture in which live, not the God we serve.

During my time as a worship pastor, I quickly learned the importance of worship space. It is an often-neglected aspect of worship that has immense power. Some of the most meaningful conversations I have had as a minister happened when a team of congregants came together to discuss the visuals in our space in a theological way. Their creativity and thoughtfulness ushered me and the rest of the congregation into a spirit of worship in a whole new way. These conversations taught us all that visuals for worship, created by the congregation for the congregation, carry so much more meaning than a purchased piece ever could. I also learned that it is important to share these conversations with the rest of the congregation, taking time to point out and explain the meaning of both new, seasonal visuals and the ones that have been in place for so long that their meaning may be forgotten and overlooked. Short paragraphs in the worship guide explaining the choices on the altar table and brief introductions spoken from the pulpit highlighting the colors of the season helped the entire congregation participate in worship with all their senses. I quickly discovered that the seasons of the Christian year and some of the central symbols of our faith were great places to start when helping a congregation begin to see the value of visuals in worship.

The colors of the Christian year can help us tune in to the rhythm of the seasons, providing visual cues that root us in something bigger, while symbols say something about who we worship and where we put our allegiance. Too many colors and symbols can suggest a mixed and cluttered message. Are the symbols and colors in your space pointing worshipers to the God whom they have come to worship? Here are some symbols to consider: Scripture, light, cross, water, bread, and cup. What symbols are already in your space? How can you draw attention to them and help the congregation to see their meaning with fresh eyes?

The architecture and arrangement of the worship space also bears witness to our theology. Does the seating arrangement suggest that everyone is included as participants, or is the congregation seated as an audience merely observing a show? Are instruments and worship leaders placed in a way that puts them center stage, much like a concert, or in a position that suggests they are an expression of our worship? Do our entry and exit points signal that something different happens in this space? Do they prepare us for worship and for taking our worship into the world? Sometimes the architecture of the space is limited and worship planners have to get creative. For example, for spaces where the platform is lifted and the congregants are seated as observers, consider an altar table on the floor, adorned with important symbols and seasonal colors, to bridge the gap between leaders and participants. Consider placing banners or other symbols/colors of the Christian year throughout the worship space to draw participants into the act of worship.

There are so many possibilities when thinking about the worship space. Have fun and let your theological imagination soar. This too is an act of worship.

### *Inclusive Language in Worship*

Language helps shape how we see ourselves and our view of God, and thus we should be intentional in our use of inclusive language and understand its importance, learning especially from those who are excluded by our language. Our use, or nonuse, of inclusive language in the music, readings, and preaching of worship can help frame how we see our possibilities for the future. For example, with the predominance of male-dominated language—"Good Christian Men, Rejoice," "tho' the eye of sinful man" (from "Holy, Holy, Holy"), "Pleased as man with men to dwell" (from "Hark the Herald Angels Sing"), or the use of "he" exclusively when referring to God or pastoral leaders—girls may grow up feeling that leadership roles are not an option for them or, worse, that they are invisible to the church. God is bigger than our language. God may be like a loving father but is so much more. Our worship is enriched, and God is revered, when we use a variety of images to highlight the multiple attributes of God, including feminine images. Deborah Clark Moore[13] provides a helpful list of "feminine images" found in Scripture. See her chapter titled "Inclusive Language, Inclusive Worship"[14] as well as the writings of Naomi King Walker for more on inclusive language in worship.[15] Altered language may feel awkward at first, but inclusive language will become familiar with use. The use of exclusive language, just because we are used to hearing it, is not worth alienating and excluding our sisters, mothers, and daughters, or any other neglected group.

## Worship Resources

Camp, Lee C. *Mere Discipleship: Radical Christianity in a Rebellious World.* Grand Rapids: Brazos, 2003.

Clapp, Rodney. *A Peculiar People: The Church as Culture in a Post-Christian Society.* Downers Grove: InterVarsity Press, 1996.

Clark, Deborah Moore. *O Come, Let Us Bow Down and Worship: A Spiritual Guide for Leadership.* Macon: Smyth & Helwys, 2003.

Dietterich, Inagrace. *Cultivating Missional Communities* (Chicago: Center for Parish Development, 1995).

Edmonson, Robert J. *The Practice of the Presence of God: Brother Lawrence.* Trans. Hal M. Helms. Brewster, MA: Paraclete Press 1985.

Furr, Gary A., and Milburn Price. *The Dialogue of Worship: Creating Space for Revelation and Response.* Macon: Smyth & Helwys, 1998.

Hendrix, John, Susan Meadows, and David Miller. *Celebrate Advent: Worship and Learning Resources.* Macon: Smyth & Helwys, 1999.

Merton, Thomas. *Thoughts in Solitude.* New York: Staus & Giroux, 1958.

Old, Hughes Oliphant. *Leading in Prayer: A Workbook for Worship.* Grand Rapids: Eerdman's, 1995.

Stookey, Laurence Hull. *Calendar: Christ's Time for the Church.* Nashville: Abingdon, 1996.

Underhill, Evelyn. *Worship*. New York: Harper & Row, 1936.

Van Dyk, Leanne, ed. *A More Profound Allelulia: Theology and Worship in Harmony*. Grand Rapids: Eerdman's, 2005.

Walker, Naomi King. "Inclusive Language and the Church: Does "Man" Include Women?" 23 September 2012. *Notations: Journeying with a Woman Minister of Music*. https://womanmusicminister.blogspot.com/2012/09/inclusive-language-church-does-man_5739.html.

Walker, Naomi King. "Inclusive Language and the Church: Fishers of Men?" 17 September 2013. https://womanmusicminister.blogspot.com/2013/09/fishers-of-men.html.

Walker, Naomi King. "Inclusive Language and the Church: Worth the Effort?" 21 June 2012. https://womanmusicminister.blogspot.com/2012/06/inclusive-language-church-worth-effort.html.

Wilson, Jonathan R. *Why Church Matters: Worship, Ministry, and Missions in Practice*. Grand Rapids: Brazos, 2006.

## Notes

1. Quoted in Deborah Moore Clark, *O Come, Let Us Bow Down and Worship: A Spiritual Guide for Leadership* (Macon: Smyth & Helwys, 2003), 53.

2. Quoted in Clark, *O Come, Let Us Bow Down and Worship*, 12.

3. Gary A. Furr and Milburn Price, *The Dialogue of Worship: Creating Space for Revelation and Response* (Macon: Smyth & Helwys, 1998).

4. In Robert J. Edmonson, trans. Hal M. Helms, *The Practice of the Presence of God: Brother Lawrence* (Brewster, MA: Paraclette, 1985), 146.

5. Lee C. Camp, *Mere Discipleship: Radical Christianity in a Rebellious World* (Grand Rapids: Brazos, 2003), 129–30.

6. From Aloys Dirksen, *Elementary Patrology*, quoted online at EWTN, https://www.ewtn.com/catholicism/library/didache-12503.

7. Jeremiah E. Rankin, "God Be with You Till We Meet Again," 1880.

8. Søren Kierkegaard, *Purity of Heart Is to Will the One Thing* (New York: Harper & Row, 1938), 181.

9. Rodney Clapp, *A Peculiar People: The Church as Culture in a Post-Christian Society* (Downers Grove: InterVarsity Press, 1996), 95.

10. Clark, *O Come, Let Us Bow Down and Worship*, 91.

11. Clark, *O Come, Let Us Bow Down and Worship*, 167.

12. Thomas Merton, *Thoughts in Solitude* (New York: Straus & Cudahy, 1958).

13. Clark, *O Come, Let Us Bow Down and Worship*, 141–42.

14. Clark, *O Come, Let Us Bow Down and Worship*, 135–52.

15. For example, see Walker's "Inclusive Language and the Church: Worth the Effort?" 21 June 2012, *Notations: Journeying with a Woman Minister of Music*, https://womanmusicminister.blogspot.com/2012/06/inclusive-language-church-worth-effort.html.

*Chapter 3*

# Teaching

## Conversations with Mary and Sam on Teaching

I was rereading the story of Mary learning at the feet of Jesus in Luke, but having difficulty concentrating, when Mary and Sam stepped into my office.

"Hello, Keith!"

"Hello, Mary!" I replied. "Hello, Sam!"

"You look deep in thought," Sam observed.

"Not so deep, but trying to be."

"So what's on your mind?" Sam asked.

"I've been thinking about the role of teaching in the church. After all, they call me the associate pastor for discipleship, formerly the minister of education."

"Sounds important," Mary offered.

"Well, yes, I guess it is, but so often my work of equipping the church for discipleship kind of gets pushed aside. I get busy with so many other things, important things, I think—planning, administrative details, phone calls, and 'to do' lists—that I get distracted."

"So," Mary replied, "you understand my sister, Martha?"

"Exactly. I get distracted by many tasks."

"Keith," Mary consoled, "we can all get distracted like Martha did that day. How can we help you focus on teaching?"

"I'm not sure where to begin." I stood and walked over to a bookcase full of books related to Christian education. Pointing to the books, I said, "There are so many aspects of Christian education, it can get overwhelming."

Mary suggested, "Well, let's go to a place where learning happens, and maybe that will help you focus."

"Good idea," Sam agreed.

"Okay, let's go."

I led Mary and Sam down the hall to a Sunday school classroom. A dry-erase board hung on one wall. Bible maps on a stand were in the corner. A small desk for the teacher sat in front of the board. We took our seats in the circle of chairs.

After a pause, Sam broke the silence. "This is where you teach? Looks kind of confining to be a place to learn. Where are the things you are learning?"

"What do you mean?"

"If you are trying to learn to fish," Sam explained, "where are the nets, the water, the fish, and the boats?"

"You know Jesus was not being literal when he said, 'I will make you fish for people'?"

"I know. That's not what I mean. Where is the stuff you are trying to learn? Where is the life you are teaching about?" Sam elaborated. "I learned my lessons out on a dangerous road, where a man was beaten up, passed by, and then rescued. I learned about God's love out on the road with real people, doing things."

"Okay I see. But Mary was taught by Jesus in a home. Wasn't that confining?"

Mary said, "Good point. So what lesson was being taught in that story?"

After pondering the question a moment, I took a stab at it. "Let's see. Wasn't it that we should focus on learning from Jesus and be careful not to be distracted by many other things? Are you telling me not to be so distracted by administrative details?"

"Yes, that is part of the message here, but that is not exactly what I'm getting at. If this was an example of Jesus teaching and me listening, what was he teaching *before* Martha interrupted?"

"Oh. I don't know. Luke doesn't say. So you tell me."

Mary explained, "I'm sure it was something about life in the kingdom, because he spoke of that so often, but I can't recall exactly what he was teaching at that specific time. My point is, the teaching was through the whole experience . . . in Martha's rattling bowls, in me missing my sister's subtle hints to get to work, in the exchange between Jesus and Martha, and in how he interpreted both of our actions. The lesson is in the living."

"Yes! That's it," I exclaimed, excited by the insight. "The lesson is in the living. So, then, about this classroom, I would say that they come here to study the Bible and reflect on life in light of the Scriptures in order to live life more faithfully. But you and Sam make a good point. This can become confining. We do often let our life and our teaching get disconnected."

"I'm glad you learned your lesson," Sam said. "Can we go outside now?"

"Okay, but first let me take you to another room I think you'll like."

I led them downstairs into another classroom. In one corner of the room was a small living area, with a kid-sized kitchen, table, and chairs, and many other household playthings. In another corner was a small bookcase with children's books and a beanbag chair. In middle of the room was a table with paint, crayons, paper, and clay. By the window was a nature center with an aquarium, plants, seashells, and other items from the natural world. Another area of the room was filled with wooden blocks, trucks, and cars.

"Welcome to our preschool room. Much teaching happens here while the kids work, play, and relate. This is life. Teachers call attention to God in life."

"Now that's what I'm talking about," Sam said as he checked out the kid-sized living area.

"Maybe your adult rooms should be like this," Mary added.

## Teaching

When you hear the words "teaching" and "education," what image comes to mind? Do you think of a classroom? My Old Testament class at seminary met in an auditorium. There were maybe fifty to seventy-five students sitting behind tables in rows, while the professor lectured to us about the Old Testament. I didn't get to know my professor or see him outside of class to see how he lived out the teachings of the Old Testament. He didn't know me or whether the Old Testament made any difference in my life. I'm not being critical of my professor. He was a good instructor, and the class gave me a better understanding of the Old Testament. This was for me a formative experience in Christian education, but Christian education and teaching goes beyond a classroom lecture.

We will explore teaching as transformative and relational experiences that occur in life, worship, Bible study, missions, ministry, and personal relationships both inside and outside the church building. We will consider Christian education as spiritual formation. To use Jeremiah's image, we are like clay in God's hands (Jeremiah 18). Spiritual formation is allowing God to mold our thoughts, beliefs, and practices. If we are honest, we might admit that we sometimes cling tightly to our beliefs and way of life, afraid of the changes we may be called to make if we examine ourselves in light of God's kingdom. Hopefully, this chapter will provide some insights from the field of Christian education and from the Gospel of Luke that will help us create an environment in which Christian disciples might be formed and transformed. We are interested in education not just as a mental exercise but as an encounter with Jesus as we, his disciples, journey with him, devoting our whole hearts, minds, souls, and strength to him. Several terms will be used to name this task, including teaching, Christian education, spiritual formation, and discipleship.

## *Jesus the Teacher (Luke 10:25)*

The lawyer addressed Jesus as "teacher." We might have expected the lawyer to use the title "rabbi" in this instance, but "rabbi" is not a term Luke uses. Instead, Luke uses the Greek word translated as "teacher." What does it mean to call Jesus "teacher"? There is little evidence of "rabbi" being used as an official title for a teacher/leader until after Jesus' time, so titles like "teacher," "rabbi," or "master" may have been terms of respect similar to "sir."[1] Regardless of what the lawyer may have intended by referring to Jesus as teacher, we know that Jesus was frequently engaged in the task of teaching, directing, guiding, or instructing his disciples and others. In Luke, Jesus begins his ministry opening the Scriptures in the synagogue and teaching (4:21). Stephen Jones reminds us that "The verb teach was frequently used to describe Jesus' activity," as he traveled through towns and villages and in the streets (Luke 13:22), from a boat (5:3), in synagogues (4:15, 31), and daily in the temple in Jerusalem as the time of his death drew near (19:47).[2] Whatever the lawyer meant by "teacher," this was an apt term for Jesus.

Jones suggests that "teacher" is a title that should be reserved for Jesus only:

> I advocate that we refrain from using the title teacher in the church except in referring to Jesus. Jesus advocated this in himself when he said, *But you are not to be called rabbi, for you have one teacher, and you are all students. . . . Nor are you to be called instructors, for you have one instructor, the Messiah.* (Matt 23:8, 10) Those of us engaged in teaching in the church are not the teachers, but rather facilitators of those seeking to encounter the ever-present Rabbi in their lives. Call us enablers or facilitators, and let Jesus be the teacher of the church, then and now![3]

While Jones's recommendation may or may not be advisable or practical, his point is well taken. The person to whom we assign the role of teacher on any given occasion acts to facilitate our learning at the feet of the master teacher, Jesus. Within the Christian community, it is not the human teacher who is at the center of our learning encounters but Jesus, God, God's word, or the Holy Spirit. Jesus is our teacher.

The fact that Jesus had disciples marks Jesus as a teacher. The term "disciple" comes from the Greek word meaning "to learn." So a disciple was a student, adherent, or follower of a teacher. Disciples of a teacher formed a community and traveled with the teacher, not only listening to the teacher's verbal instruction but also learning from the teacher's example in all aspects of life. David R. Bauer notes,

> Perhaps the central feature of the ministry of Jesus was the calling and instructing of his disciples. In both the synoptic and Johannine traditions, the first specific act of Jesus' ministry is the calling of disciples (Mark 1:14-20; John 1:43-51). The disciples are said to be "with" Jesus (Mark 3:14; Luke 9:18; 22:56); they are the special recipients of his teaching (Mark 4:33-34; 10:23-45; 11:12-26; 13:1-37); and they are charged to perform a ministry that is an extension of his (Mark 6:7-13, 30; Matt 9:35–11:1; Luke 9:1-10; 10:1-12).[4]

The church continues the role of disciples of Jesus and disciple makers, obeying Jesus' commissioning in Matthew to "go make disciples and teach them" (Matt 28:19-20). Thinking of Christian education as discipleship and students—all Christians—as disciples is beneficial. Christian education is a not a task confined to a classroom at church. As disciples, we follow Jesus and learn from him at church and on the road, in the car, at work, at home, and at play. Fellow members of the Christian community mentor and guide us as we follow and learn.

## "Recite Them to Your Children" (Deuteronomy 6:4-5)

"What is written in the law? What do you read there?" Jesus, the teacher, asked the lawyer to answer his own question. The first part of his answer comes from the Shema, the most important confession of Judaism: "Hear, O Israel: The LORD is our God, the LORD alone. You shall love the LORD your God with all your heart, and with all your soul, and with all your might" (Deut 6:4-5). This command is so important it comes with its own teaching methodology:

> Keep these words that I am commanding you today in your heart. Recite them to your children and talk about them when you are at home and when you are away, when you lie down and when you rise. Bind them as a sign on your hand, fix them as an emblem on your forehead, and write them on the doorposts of your house and on your gates. (Deut 6:6-9)

Love of God is not to be forgotten, but written on the heart and taught continually, night and day, at home and away. We can imagine a parent telling a child a bedtime story that begins, "You shall love the Lord your God with all your heart, and with all your soul, and with all your might," and waking that child with the same words in the morning. All throughout the day, each time you look down at your hand you see "Love God." Whenever you engage in conversation with friends who share your faith, there it is written on their foreheads. And, when you return home at the end of the day, you see "Love God" written on the front door. We get a clear picture. All the time, everywhere, we teach.

We assume these instructions in Deuteronomy 6 are to be taken figuratively, but they are also practiced literally, as Biddle explains:

> Orthodox Judaism understands literally the command to bind the words of the Shema on one's head and hands, doorposts and gates. Since before the time of Christ . . . small leather boxes containing manuscripts with the words of the Shema plus three related texts (Exod. 13:1-10, 11-16; Deut. 11:13-21), each in one of four separate sections. . . . Orthodox young men from the age of 13 onward (Shebu. 111:8, 11) begin morning and evening prayers by binding these leather boxes first on their left hands and then their foreheads by means of long leather straps.[5]

Additionally, many Jewish families will follow the centuries-old tradition of affixing to the front doorframe of their homes a small decorative tube-shaped container, called the Mezuzah, with the words of the Shema inside.

When Jesus affirms love of God and neighbor as the answer to life, we are reminded of the context of this command in Deuteronomy, which tells us how we can teach it to our children, everywhere, all the time.

## Jesus Taught in Parables (Luke 10:25-37)

Expanding on his explanation of what it means to love your neighbor, Jesus uses one of his favorite teaching methods, a parable. Mark says Jesus only spoke to the people in parables (Mark 4:34). Peter Rhea Jones notes Jesus' frequent use of parables:

The prominent place of parable in the proclamation of Jesus can be grasped immediately with the notation that a full third of his recorded teaching is comprised of his parabolic sayings, comparisons, and full-blown parables. Indeed, it seems fair to declare that parabolic discourse was the characteristic medium of Jesus. He took slices of everyday life in Palestine and with narrative metaphor addressed his hearers.[6]

Why the frequent use of parables? Jesus said he spoke in parables so that "looking they may not perceive, and listening they may not understand" (Luke 8:10). This may seem odd if we think that the primary goal of the teacher is to explain things clearly so that the learner can understand. But perhaps that is not always the goal in teaching, or even the most important goal. When it comes to the inexhaustible mysteries of the kingdom of God, overly simplistic and clear explanations will not do. Jesus' use of parables gives us insight into teaching and learning, especially when it comes to ultimate meaning and the big questions about God and God's vision for our world. God's kingdom cannot be contained in our concise definitions and simple categories. It is the kingdom of God that parables are meant to enlighten. Ultimately the aim of the parable is not just insight about the kingdom but for the disciple to live in the kingdom. The parable elicits transformation and action. C. H. Dodd provided the classic definition of parable: "a metaphor or simile drawn from nature or common life, arresting the hearer by its vividness or strangeness, and leaving the mind in sufficient doubt about its precise application to tease it into active thought."[7]

We can see why Jesus so often used parables. A parable makes comparisons with familiar situations from everyday life to give us a glimpse into a God who is otherwise completely beyond the comprehension of our finite human minds. Though familiar, parables usually have an odd twist that leaves the hearer thinking, baffled and confused so that they are forced to reflect on its meaning well beyond the encounter. It may be hours, days, or years before insights and understanding come. We might like shortcuts and easy answers, but there are some things Jesus wants to teach us about God, and life as God intends, that are not easily grasped because of the vastness of their meaning and due to our limitations and blind spots.

A parable is a story that gives a picture of the kingdom of God into which the hearer can choose to live. The parable brings the hearer into a new and often surprising world—the world of the kingdom of God. The kingdom of God connects with some aspects of reality, so comparisons, references, parallels, and metaphors are possible. But those references can never completely capture the nature of God's kingdom, so meaning is drawn both from dissimilarities and similarities.

Robert Funk shows how Jesus used the parable of the Good Samaritan and how his audience would have heard it. Point of view makes all the difference in how this parable is understood. As the narrative begins, a man is walking down from Jerusalem to Jericho. The listeners in Jesus' teaching audience would identify with the anonymous man, having traveled that road many times before. They were not surprised when the robbers appeared, knowing this to be a dangerous road. So the listeners sympathized with the now half-dead man and viewed the story from the ditch.

Then, a priest walks by on the other side. Those of the priesthood might have briefly identified with the priest, but only briefly, for as soon as the priest appears, he moves to the other side of the road and passes by the wounded man. Those with feelings of animosity toward the religious establishment would have found some satisfaction at the expense of the clergy at this point in Jesus' parable. A similar reaction would have occurred when Jesus mentioned the Levite passing by. The religious leaders in the audience would have been angry.

But the ordinary Israelites—the religious lower class—listening to the story as if half-dead, would have waited gleefully for the hero to come down the road. Perhaps they expected an ordinary Jew to come, enabling them to leave the ditch and identify with the hero. Neither group expected a compassionate Samaritan to come down the road next. No Jew identified with the despised Samaritan. So the hearers had only two choices: reject the parable altogether as totally unrealistic or identify with the man in the ditch. A proud Jew would not accept help from an unclean Samaritan if they could avoid it. But in this story, they could not avoid it. The man in the ditch was half-dead, without options, and even if he wanted to, he was unable to resist the Samaritan's care.[8]

The audience of a parable is important. A parable is not a speech that can be dropped into any setting with the same meaning. A parable is an event that occurs in a particular time and place within a specific community. The parable does not come with a neat conclusion. That is left to the hearer. The teller does not give all the answers.

Returning to C. H. Dodd's definition, we can see how this parable of the Good Samaritan is drawn from common life on a road Jesus' listeners knew well and may have been standing on at the time of its telling. Jesus arrests the hearer with vividness and a strange twist, causing the hearer doubts about deeply ingrained prejudices and teasing the mind into active thought.

The hymn (poem) "Christ Parables," set to the tune BEACH SPRING, shares these themes in song with verses like, "For Christ's parables that spur us / to reflect in fitting ways / on your faithful love and judgment, / God, receive our prayerful praise" and "Give us ears to hear their stories, / minds to know what they convey; / with these glimpses of your Kingdom / teach and nourish us today."[9]

Stephen Jones summarized four characteristics of parables that might also be our goals for the task of teaching:

(1) Parables are eschatological; that is, they deal with ultimate questions of God, the kingdom, heaven, and end times.

(2) Parables are existential. They focus on human existence and how to live life every day as God intends. Parables are sometimes referred to as "earthly stories with a heavenly meaning" or, as some would say, "heavenly stories with an earthly meaning."

(3) Parables are ethical. They focus on "forgiveness, compassion, and grace" and call us to action.

(4) Parables are evangelistic. Parables "require a response," "invite repentance," "seek faith," "demand obedience," and "warrant change."[10]

In our Christian teaching encounters, let us not settle for simply passing on information about God, Jesus, or the Bible. Instead, let us follow the example Jesus set in his use of parables and allow God and God's word to engage, challenge, provoke, confuse, disturb, and surprise us with kingdom issues of great importance for life every day and eternally.

## *Mary at the Teacher's Feet (Luke 10:38-42)*

Having shared Jesus' story about action and service, Luke turns to a story about sitting and listening, which on the surface may seem contradictory. Luke presents a scene that places women in roles that go against societal norms. The fact that Martha, a woman, invited a male into "her" home would have been unusual. When Mary sat at Jesus' feet listening to what he was saying, she was sitting in the place of a male disciple, under the teaching of a rabbi. Luke's audience and people of Jesus' time would have found Martha's reaction to be appropriate. This part of the home was not Mary's domain.[11]

The teaching encounter begins with hospitality. There could be no sitting as a disciple at the feet of the teacher, Jesus, without first receiving him. Martha acts like the good host that Jesus described earlier in this chapter when the seventy were sent out (vv. 4-7). Martha and Mary provide hospitality to Jesus, welcoming him into their home and providing him with a meal (eventually, we presume, whenever Jesus finishes teaching and finally lets Martha finish her cooking and Mary helps). We might say that Christian education begins with hospitality. We invite Jesus the teacher into our presence, with receptive hearts and minds, openness to having long-held assumptions challenged (like the roles of women), and willingness to be transformed by our encounter with Christ.

Many have noted that the phrase "sitting at another's feet" indicated that one was acting as a student—a disciple—of a teacher. Remember that Paul had been a student of the noted Rabbi Gamaliel, "brought up in the city at the feet of Gamaliel, educated strictly according to our ancestral law" (Acts 22:3). R. Alan Culpepper cites rabbinic literature to describe the roles of teacher and student that play out here: "The scene resonates positively and negatively with rabbinic lore: 'Let thy house be a meeting house for the Sages and sit amid the dust of their feet and drink in their words with thirst. . . . [but] talk not much with womankind.'"[12] So, according to this passage of the Mishnah, Jesus was in the proper place as teacher. But his student should not have been a woman.

When Martha protests, Jesus commends Mary: "Mary has chosen the better part, which will not be taken from her." And so the encounter ends. Attention to Jesus' teaching takes priority over all other concerns. Mary's undivided attention to the words Jesus shared was exactly what Jesus wanted in that moment. There is a time for action, but busyness must not crowd out the important moments spent sitting at Jesus' feet.

Martha's voice is a familiar one. Whenever we pause to study and learn, we may hear Martha's words of guilt from within or from well-meaning action-oriented members of the community, saying, "Get to work. We need to stop sitting around. We need to do something, even if it's wrong." We also hear this voice from our culture, which values hard work and productivity. One of the hindrances to effective Christian education is the feeling that, somehow, we are wasting time when we pause to study and reflect, and we should get busy with the important work of God. Jesus' mild reprimand of Martha and affirmation of Mary counter our need to always be busy doing tasks that produce obvious visible results: "Martha, Martha, you are worried and distracted by many things; there is need of only one thing. Mary has chosen the better part, which will not be taken away from her" (Luke 10:41-42).

This episode with Mary and Martha is not contradictory to the Parable of the Good Samaritan but complementary. Sitting at Jesus' feet equips the Christian community for its mission so that when the church does act, it is more likely do so in a way that is consistent with God's vision for the church. Reflection follows action and leads to action.

### *Jesus on the Road to Emmaus (Luke 24:13-35)*

Luke's account of Jesus' appearance, after his death and resurrection, on the road to Emmaus in Luke 24:13-35 is interesting from the teaching/learning perspective. Jesus is seen examining the Scriptures and teaching with a couple of disciples who are seeking understanding. In the end, Jesus' identity is revealed to them, and they run to tell others what they have learned.

Before reading the following section, take time to read this passage prayerfully and reflectively. I suggest three separate readings, listening for all the different ways teaching and learning occur here. On the first reading, take in the setting. Imagine the seven-mile walk (two hours, more or less) and the sights and sounds along the road. Place yourself in the story in the place of the two friends. When reading through the second time, make notes of all the ways you see teaching and learning taking place. What teaching methods does Jesus use? When and how do learning and insight happen? When the disciples recognize Jesus, what happens next? Read a third time to simply enjoy the story and reflect on what God is saying to you personally through the details. If you are part of a small group, skip the following section and wait to share this experience with your group, answering this question together: "What can the Emmaus Road teach us about teaching?" List everything you observe in this conversation.

### **What the Emmaus Road Can Teach Us about Teaching**

Consider these observations:

- The learning experience is a journey that takes time. In this story, the three walked seven miles (v. 13), which would take about two hours at a somewhat brisk pace of seventeen minutes per mile. At the end of the journey, they spent more time together at a home. Sometimes learning, especially transformational learning, requires time for reflection.

- The two disciples engaged in dialogue: "they were talking and discussing" (v. 15).
- Whether the disciples were aware of it or not, their learning experience took place in the presence of the risen Christ. When we study the Bible and dialogue about faith issues as a community, it is helpful to be aware that we do so in the presence of Jesus, the "way and the truth," and to be held accountable by Christ's presence.
- Jesus acted as a mentor to the two disciples. A mentor is one who guides in the issues of everyday life through personal conversation and example. A mentor walks with another person through life.
- Teaching occurred on the road and in a home. Christian education is not confined to a church classroom. It happens in the church hallways and parking lot, in the fellowship hall and sanctuary, at home around the kitchen table, in the workplace, and at our places of recreation.
- Jesus asked questions. He asked questions that did not require a "yes" or "no" answer but helped the disciples share their experience and what it meant to them: "What are you discussing?" "What things [took place]?" (vv. 17-19). He listened to the disciples' answers and asked follow-up questions. He allowed the two disciples to think and discover answers on their own. Sharing our stories and attempting to work out their meaning with words can help us process the experience. Part of the effective teacher's role is to listen.
- Jesus did ask one question expecting an affirmative answer. He wanted to make an important point. "Was it not necessary that the Messiah should suffer these things and then enter into his glory?" (v. 26)
- At one point during the journey and in the midst of the teaching experience, Luke tells us, "They stood still" (v. 17). Sometimes, amid our walking, talking, and questioning, it is helpful to pause, reflect, analyze, meditate, ponder, and process what we've been hearing and thinking about. Sometimes, when teaching, we need to stop and stand still for a moment or two. As the psalmist intoned, "Be still, and know that I am God!" (Ps 46:10). It is often after a period of intentional silence that quieter, more reflective learners are ready to share their insights.
- Jesus said that the two disciples were foolish and slow to believe (v. 25). They lacked understanding, and they were slow to comprehend when given the information that could have informed them. This may sound harsh of Jesus to say, but it sometimes takes a jolt to shake us out of our set ways of thinking. We all come to the learning experience lacking understanding. That is why we need teaching. We have our blind spots.

We are resistant to change. We live in bubbles of our own perspectives and need to see the world through the eyes of another and most importantly through the eyes of Christ. I'm hearing a Brandon Heath song in my head right now: "Give me Your eyes for just one second, Give me Your eyes so I can see, Everything that I keep missing, Give me Your love for humanity."[13] Note that later in this passage, Luke tells us "their eyes were opened" (v. 31). Learning is an eye-opening experience.

• Jesus offered correction and clarification. Learning is most effective in an environment where learners feel comfortable sharing differences and where ideas can be questioned and challenged.

• Jesus interpreted the Scriptures (v. 27). From Moses to the prophets would have been a reference to the Hebrew Scriptures or the Christian Old Testament.

• The teaching experience engaged the emotions. The disciples looked sad upon remembering the events surrounding Jesus' death (v. 17). Later, after their eyes were opened, we can imagine their excitement when they recalled how their "hearts burned within [them]" and when they hurried back to Jerusalem to tell the others what they had experienced. Jesus introduced his reply to the two, calling them foolish, with the exclamation, "Oh" (v. 25), a term "which implies strong emotions."[14] Do not be afraid of emotions when teaching. Sometimes the emotional impact associated with what our mind acknowledges to be true is what motivates us to real change in behavior and attitudes.

• As with the story of Mary and Martha, the Emmaus Road story brings out the importance of inviting Jesus in. The two disciples "urged him strongly" to "stay with us" (v. 29). When we urgently seek the presence of Christ and invite him into our educational encounters, our eyes may be opened to learn from him.

• The experience was filled with symbolic images. At the home in Emmaus, Luke tells us, "When he was at the table with them, he took bread, blessed and broke it, and gave it to them" (v. 30). This language is similar to that used at Jesus' Last Supper with the twelve (22:19) and at the feeding of the five thousand (9:10-17). These images were rich in meaning for Jesus and the two disciples, for the early Christian community, and for Christians throughout history until today. Symbolic visual images and rituals can enhance the learning experience in ways words alone cannot.

• Breaking bread at the table symbolizes worship and community for Christians, another reminder of worship and the community as a whole as an important setting for Christian education.

- Learning is not just a private personal endeavor but occurs in community, through the mutually accountable relationships of Christians who study, pray, minister, and worship together seeking to discern God's vision. Not that the majority is always right when it comes to the will of God, but a Christ-centered learning community can help correct our excesses and reveal our blind spots.
- This educational experience engaged all of the senses. The smell of baked bread filled the room. They touched the bread as they broke it and passed it to each other. They used their senses of sight and hearing as they watched and listened to the activity and sounds. They tasted the bread as they ate it. This is the bread that Jesus said represented his body broken for humanity. When we teach, we might think about how to meaningfully engage as many of the senses as possible. Some learn better through hearing (auditory), others visually (visual), and still others through touch (tactile). Engaging our senses can help all of us no matter our preferred learning style.
- This learning experience led to, and included, immediate action. After learning that they had been in the presence of the risen Christ, within the same hour, the two disciples made the seven-mile return journey to Jerusalem (which might have taken them about an hour and a half at a thirteen-minutes-per-mile jog or an hour and forty-five minutes at a fast fifteen-minutes-per-mile walk). In Jerusalem, they shared with the eleven disciples the good news of what they had learned, that Jesus was alive and appeared to them on the road (vv. 33-35). When we teach, we hope that students apply what they learn and live out of their new understandings of God's kingdom. Christian teachers seek to facilitate a transforming encounter with the living Christ that leads to new ways of acting, thinking, and feeling.

You will find more in this story that is relevant to the teaching/learning experience.

Christian educator Thomas Groome aptly summarizes the Emmaus story from an educational perspective:

> I see the risen Christ portrayed here as the educator par excellence. He begins by encountering and entering into dialogue with the two travelers. Rather than telling them what he knows, he first has them tell the story of their recent experience and what their hopes had been. In response he recalls a larger Story of which their story is part, and a broader Vision

beyond what theirs had been. We might expect the typical educator to tell them what "to see," but he continues to wait for them to come to their own knowing. He spends more time in their company. Surely the dialogue on the road carried over into their table conversations. Eventually, in their table fellowship together, they "came to see." Thereupon they set out immediately to bear witness to what they now knew.[15]

Certainly, the Emmaus Road teaching and learning experience is not one of classrooms and lectures to passive students.

## Putting Teaching into Practice
### What Is Christian Education?
What is Christian education, and what is its purpose?

For some, perhaps, the model of Christian education is that of the expert teacher passing on information to the students. Communication is one-way, from teacher to student, usually taking place in a classroom. The goal might be to gain some new interesting or useful information consistent with what we already believe and to come away with good feelings. Education, by this way of thinking, is building up our knowledge base. Daniel Aleshire critiques this kind of "banking" model of Christian education: "The biblical image of 'knowing' has little similarity to modern perceptions of knowing as the possession of information—like some commodity to be banked and bartered." The biblical image of knowing includes loving and experiencing, like that of a marriage relationship. "To be a people of faith is not just to know about God; it is to know God," Aleshire writes. "To know God is to experience the Presence, to express love, and to hold tenderly the mystery of that encounter."[16]

Our scientific age has tended to treat knowing as purely impersonal and objective. That which we study is something to be analyzed and examined as if under a microscope. The modern approach to education values objectivity over subjectivity. Parker Palmer writes, "We are well-educated people who have been schooled in a way of knowing that treats the world as an object to be dissected and manipulated, a way of knowing that gives us power over the world."[17] At times the church has adopted this approach, treating God, Jesus, the Bible, and truth as impersonal objects or subjects to be controlled and analyzed. The title of Palmer's excellent book offers a more helpful understanding of the goal of Christian education: *To Know as We Are Known*. In 1 Corinthians 13:12, Paul writes, "Now I know only in part; then I will know fully, even as I have been fully known." Knowing, especially when it comes to matters of faith, is an intimate personal relationship. The truth we seek is not a thing. Jesus said, "I am the way, the truth, and the life" (John 14:6). Palmer further explains,

> In truthful knowing we neither infuse the world with our subjectivity (as premodern knowing did) nor hold it at arm's length, manipulating it to suit our needs (as in the modern style). In truthful knowing the knower becomes co-participant in a community of faithful relationships with other persons and creatures and things, with whatever our knowledge makes known. We find truth by pledging our troth, and knowing becomes reunion of separated beings whose primary bond is not of logic but of love.[18]

Christian educator John Hendrix described the situation in Christian education for many churches in this way:

> Many Christians are attached to the Bible by an invisible ten-foot pole which joins them and keeps them apart. The pole has been constructed through years of the dry, lifeless recounting of biblical material unrelated and irrelevant to the deep needs of the heart. In this strange and bizarre position the Christian maneuvers—swinging, punching, jabbing—keeping others away but unable to bring the living Word any closer.[19]

Attempting to narrowly define Christian education can be like putting Christian education and God in box, but perhaps the definitions listed below, none of which will be final or exhaustive, can broaden our understanding of the church's educational ministry. These definitions, along with the ones by the authors above, can provide examples for a church seeking to develop its own educational purpose statement or mission statement.

• Karen Tye names four ways of understanding Christian education: (1) Religious Instruction: "The terms *teaching, instruction, transmitting the faith, conserving the faith, indoctrination, catechesis, belief formation*, and *schooling* suggest this understanding." (2) Socialization Process: "Terms like nurture, socialization, habit formation, enculturation, and even conversion, depending on how one understands this process, point to this definition." (3) Personal Development Approach: "The words *growth, faith development, spiritual formation, moral development*, and *character formation* are suggestive of this approach." (4) Process Liberation: "The terms *critical thinking* and *transformation* point to this approach."[20]

- For Lawrence Little, "The supreme purpose of Christian education is to enable persons to become aware of the seeking love of God as revealed in Jesus Christ and to respond in faith to this love in ways that help them grow as children of God, live in accordance with the will of God, and sustain a vital relationship to the Christian Community."[21]
- Palmer's famous definition of teaching is helpful: "To teach is to create space in which obedience to truth is practiced."[22]
- Charles R. Foster, in his book *Educating Congregations: The Future of Christian Education*, lists the goals of education as "Building Community," "Making Meaning," and "Nurturing Hope."[23]
- Donald Miller described the goal of discipleship this way, making clear that education extends beyond the walls of the church and into the world: "Christian education is to provide a context within the congregation in which persons can discuss the problems facing them, commit their lives to Jesus Christ as Savior and Lord and to the church as the people of God, and participate as a body of disciples in the mission of God in the world."[24]
- Paul Dietterich with the Center for Parish Development states the purpose of a disciple community: "To develop a community of disciples who are learning with one another to live as a sign, foretaste, and instrument of the reign of God."[25]
- The Great Commission in Matthew is "Go therefore and make disciples of all nations, baptizing them in the name of the Father and the Son and the Holy Spirit, and teaching them to observe everything that I have commanded you" (Matt 28:19-20).
- H. Richard Niebuhr was concerned that educational goals be stated simply and directly. He wrote that the purpose of the church and its ministry is "the increase of the love of God and neighbor."[26]

Drawing from these Christian educators and others, I would suggest the following goals for Christian education:

- Developing mature faith throughout all the stages of life, from birth through adulthood.
- Experiencing God in a life-changing encounter. For example, pray and not merely study about prayer. Be in a loving community and not just talk about love.
- Being "transformed by the renewing of your minds" (Rom 12:2).
- Discovering our gifts and calling and being equipped to use those gifts in ministry.

- Nurturing community, learning together in mutually accountable relationships.
- Participating in dialogue with people in Christ's presence, like Jesus and the two disciples on the road to Emmaus.
- Sharing the wonderful stories of our faith and living them.
- Liberating people from whatever enslaves them: sin, oppression, injustice, poverty, bitterness, or prejudice.
- Nurturing by caring, loving, parenting, growing, raising, modeling.

Five stories from Scripture could be used as discussion starters or a series of Bible studies to help small groups reflect on the church's educational ministry:

(1) Jeremiah 18:1-6: "like clay in the potter's hand."
(2) Matthew 28:19-20: "make disciples of all nations."
(3) 1 Corinthians 3:1-9: "I planted, Apollos watered, but God gave the growth."
(4) Luke 24:13-35: "Were not our hearts burning within us while he was talking to us on the road, while he was opening the scriptures to us?"
(5) Deuteronomy 6:1-9: "Recite them to your children and talk about them when you are at home and when you are away."

A variety of perspectives on the definition, purpose, and goals of Christian education have been presented. Together, these descriptions can inform our teaching ministry through the church. How do you define Christian education? What would you say is the goal of Christian education? Church educational leaders could benefit by writing a Christian education mission statement after a time of study, prayer, and dialogue.

## What Is the Curriculum or Content of Christian Education?

For many churches, the task of curriculum planning in the past was easy, and maybe it still is. The curriculum is whatever the denominational publishing house produces each quarter for Sunday school classes of all ages. The task was, or is, easy if you ignore the many contexts in which we learn and if you are not interested in planning a curriculum that supports the specific mission and vision of your church at this particular time. There are advantages to using an ongoing curriculum resource from a trusted publisher, and even when the overall curriculum of the church is carefully planned, we may still choose to use a dated curriculum as the primary resource for Bible study groups. Whatever printed resources we may use, the curriculum is more than the published materials. When it comes to the topics we study and the resources we use, it makes sense that we should be proactive.

When we think about teaching in church, a Sunday school class or other small group may come to mind, and while this may be a key component of a church's educational ministry, it is by no means the only place where teaching and learning occurs. Maria Harris calls curriculum "the entire course of the church's life," present in "worship, community, proclamation, and outreach."[27] We should not ignore the many areas where learning happens. Additionally, Harris speaks of three curricular forms: (1) the explicit curriculum, what we present as our curriculum; (2) the implicit curriculum, what is taught through our procedures and organization, maybe unknowingly or unintentionally (What does the church budget say about our priorities? Are there restrictions or preferences for who is selected to serve in various positions of leadership?); and (3) the null curriculum, what we teach by what we ignore (What topics, perspectives, or ministries are left out? What does their omission mean?).[28]

Maybe curriculum planning is more complex than we have thought but also a greater opportunity than we imagined. The teaching task of the church deserves our careful planning. How do we provide balance in the content of Christian education? There is no simple answer to this question.

One advantage to using a quality dated curriculum from a publisher is the balance they can provide. Following the liturgical calendar of the church can also provide balance. If we always choose the topics we will study, there is a chance we could become focused only on what is already familiar and appeals to our narrow interests. It is good, at least occasionally, to have content chosen for us to expose us to new perspectives and challenge us in areas that may need changing. With or without a set of ongoing curriculum resources, church educational leaders can be intentional about content over time.

It can be helpful to consider some traditional content areas to help us evaluate our curriculum plan.[29] Leon McKenzie and R. Michael Harton, in *The Religious Education of Adults*, offer a sample "Three-Year Curriculum 'Map' for Congregational Religious Education,"[30] including "central questions" for each content area and possible courses of study. Following are the four core content areas with each subdivided into subject areas:

- Biblical Knowledge and Understanding
    - Understanding the Bible
    - Old Testament Studies
    - New Testament Studies
- Christian Heritage and Doctrine
    - Historical Development of the Church
    - Our Baptist Heritage [or other faith tradition heritage]
    - Christian Doctrine and Baptist Interpretation [or other faith tradition interpretation]
- Life Together
    - Church Membership
    - Church Polity
    - Functions of the Church
- Applied Spirituality
    - Ethical Decision-making
    - Christian Perspectives on Ethical Issues
    - The Church in the World

Ultimately, to develop a thorough and balanced curriculum plan, a church should engage in a process of discernment.[31] Lexington Avenue Baptist Church teenagers and youth teachers met to develop a six-year curriculum plan. Dave Garrett, the youth minister, introduced the process this way: "How will your faith be different when you graduate from high school? Your first-grade faith was not enough for you in high school. Your seventh-grade faith will not be enough when you leave here. What can we do for the next six years (or less) to help you grow in your faith?" Thus they set about planning a six-year curriculum, month by month, intended to help them mature in faith by the time they graduated from high school. This was a good way to frame the curriculum-planning task.

Following are some considerations for a curriculum planning process:

- Engage in a process of prayer and discernment. What is God's mission for your church, and how can the curriculum of the church in all its forms and contexts support that mission?
- Involve members of the Christian community in the planning process, including people representative of the diversity of your church family.
- What do we say we teach (explicit)? What do we teach through the way we do things (implicit)? What are we teaching by what we ignore (null)?

- Consider the various groups in your church, including age groups, and their developmental needs and life situations.
- What are the felt needs of the congregation? What benefits or rewards (for example, personal growth or noble cause) would motivate members to participate?[32]
- How can we be intentional about Christian education throughout the "entire course of the church's life,"[33] through worship, preaching, fellowship, and service?
- Who will teach? What gifts, experience, and expertise are available within our congregation or the local community? More than any prescribed topics, teachers will have the biggest influence on the actual curriculum.
- What topics, issues, subjects, or biblical texts do we wish to explore and teach over the course of a year, or over several years, in order to be balanced and to grow as disciples? Where is the Spirit of God leading us?
- Is the curriculum diverse and inclusive of a variety of perspectives, especially those of minority voices? Curriculum is often written from a white European, male perspective. Be intentional about including diverse and inclusive viewpoints.
- If your church uses the liturgical calendar, how might the curriculum utilize and complement the liturgical year?
- What printed and other resources can best support our curriculum?

## *Who Are the Learners/Disciples?*

Not all learners are the same, so a cookie-cutter approach to teaching that does not take the learner into account will not be as formative as it could be. Who is the learner? What is their life situation? What are their hopes and dreams? What causes them stress? How is God working in their lives? Where are they in their development—cognitively, socially, and spiritually? Teaching and learning is a relationship.

There are a number of ways to think about the learner. Respected theories of human development can provide valuable insights into the learner. There is no way to adequately present the depth and breadth of these theories here, but I will seek to introduce some key ideas relevant to the task of Christian formation in the church and encourage further study in these areas.

### Jean Piaget and Stages of Cognitive Development

Before Piaget's theory of developmental stages, it was generally thought that children and adults learned the same way. The only difference was that adults have accumulated more knowledge than children. Piaget proposed that learning occurs in four stages from birth through adolescence.[34] His work is still widely used today. The first stage, according to Piaget, is the Sensorimotor Stage, approximately birth to age two. During this stage the infant learns by using all the senses, grasping objects with their hands, placing them in their mouths, and observing movements. The second stage is the Pre-operational Stage, from about age two, as language develops, until around age seven. At this time children are beginning to learn to think using symbols. They can be imaginative though not always logical. The third stage is the Concrete Operational Stage, during which elementary and preadolescent children begin to think more logically but not abstractly. Now they can begin to imagine how someone else feels and that others have different points of view. During the Formal Operational stage of development, the adolescent's mental abilities expand as they learn to think abstractly. Their problem-solving skills improve greatly. They are able to imagine a variety of scenarios in their minds before acting them out concretely. Deeper reflection on theological concepts is now possible.

Teaching should take these stages into account. For example, provide a rich sensory environment for all children, especially the sensorimotor infant, with plenty of manipulatives to explore; words, music, and interesting sounds to listen to; and most importantly the caring touch of adults. Pre-operational children can be allowed to pretend and use their imaginations, acting out and telling stories, expressing themselves artistically, and answering questions like "How do you think Martha felt when Jesus told her that Mary made a better choice" (Luke 10:42)? The logical progression of a Bible story can be understood; however, theological concepts and abstractions are still lost on the Concrete Operational child. Social interaction becomes even more important as children learn to imagine what their friends are thinking and feeling. The Formal Operational child, while still benefiting by using all the senses, engaging in social interaction, and thinking logically, is also ready to start thinking abstractly. They are developing the capacity to think of God as more than a powerful person in heaven above. They are ready to begin exploring deeper theological issues such as faith, Holy Spirit, resurrection, heaven, and grace, though they are just beginning.

## Lev Vygotsky and Social Learning Theory

Whereas Piaget's theory held that children learn after they reach a level of cognitive development, Lev Vygotsky, Russian psychologist and teacher, proposed that learning leads to development. Through collaborative learning, the guidance of teachers and mentors, and the influence of culture, children and adults learn and develop. Vygotsky introduced the idea of the Zone of Proximal Development, which is the difference between what a learner is capable of doing independently and what they are capable of doing with the help of a teacher or a more advanced peer or in collaboration with others. The image of scaffolding is a way of understanding how teaching and learning occur. Through social interaction, prompts and suggestions from teachers, and a wide variety of teaching methods, the student learns to accomplish a new task or comprehend a concept within their ability to learn at that time (the Zone of Proximal Development). The new learning occurs with assistance at first, until mastered independently. With this new base of development in place, the student is ready to build on that base to construct a new level of development, again through social interaction and with the help of teachers.

Cynthia Jones Neal, in a chapter on Christian nurture titled "The Power of Vygotsky," writes that Jesus modeled scaffolding in his encounter with the disciples on the road to Emmaus:

> One can readily notice how Jesus used questions to draw out His companions' current level of understanding. He allowed their mistakes to become apparent. However, He used their misunderstandings as a springboard to give a clearer picture, a fuller interpretation of the prophecies in the Scriptures concerning Himself. Although He used questions and explanations, He also allowed them to struggle in their discovery process. He walked with them along the way—their way. He did not disclose His identity initially. I suspect that might have clouded the issue, which was that they needed to understand the Scriptures. It was not until their eyes were opened, when He broke bread, that full realization came for them. At that point, Jesus left. The structure was in place.[35]

In the church setting, Vygotsky's theories would suggest the importance of collaborative learning, intergenerational encounters, and the role of teachers, mentors, and peers. The idea of the Zone of Proximal Development reminds the Christian educator of the need to understand the learner—to know where the student is now in their development and how much are they able to grow at this point—lest we bore the learner with activities or ideas that are too easy, or overwhelm them with what is well beyond their abilities.

## Erik Erikson and Psychosocial Stages of Development

Erik Erikson in his classic work *Childhood and Society*[36] identified psychosocial stages of development beginning in infancy. The individual emerges from each stage with one of two poles becoming more characteristic of their psychosocial development.

*Stage 1: Trust versus Mistrust (roughly birth to age one).* In Erikson's first stage of development, the infant learns to trust, or mistrust, depending on whether or not their basic needs are met or whether or not they are hurt or protected from harm. So, for example, when a parent or other caregiver responds to the cries of the infant, the infant learns trust. Thus it is essential that church nurseries be safe places where babies' diapers are changed when needed, they are fed when hungry, and their needs are met in a timely manner. "The infant's first achievement, then," according to Erikson, "is his [or her] willingness to let the mother out of sight without undue anxiety or rage . . . ."[37] If the church is a place where caregivers can be trusted, the groundwork is laid for the baby to grow to trust others and eventually God.

*Stage 2: Autonomy versus Shame, Doubt (roughly ages two to three).* This stage, which is sometimes called the "terrible twos," serves an important developmental function. The toddler learns autonomy by using their favorite words, "me do it" and "no." This is a challenging time for parents and caregivers, who must set reasonable limits while allowing the child to learn to act independently. Responding too harshly to inappropriate behavior can lead the child to be filled with a sense of shame. By providing stimulating age-appropriate activities that children can complete on their own, and by lovingly setting limits when needed, caregivers help children develop a healthy sense of autonomy.

*Stage 3: Initiative versus Guilt (roughly ages four to five).* This stage is played out, literally, in social relationships with friends and adults. When children initiate interactions with others, they may overextend their boundaries or act too aggressively. The pushback to this overreach can lead to guilt, which to a degree can be helpful to their development, but too much guilt can be debilitating. In the church setting, we encourage social interaction among children while teaching appropriate ways of relating and offering gracious correction when necessary. For example, "I cannot let you hurt your friend."

*Stage 4: Industry versus Inferiority (roughly ages six to twelve).* In this stage, according to Erikson, the child "learns to win recognition by producing things." Les Steele sums up this stage well: "children have a desire to develop skills and abilities to help them feel useful, competent, and good about themselves. They enjoy mastering tasks and facts; if this occurs, then a corresponding sense of competency yields a grounded sense of self-esteem."[38] Plenty of social interaction at church, cooperative games and learning activities, and age-appropriate activities that challenge children and give them a sense of accomplishment will help them develop confidence that God has given them talents that they can use for the benefit of themselves and others.

*Stage 5: Identity versus Role Confusion (adolescence).* The key question for adolescent development is, "Who am I?" The teenage search for identity is well known. The church can help teens in this stage of their development by providing a safe nonjudgmental space for them to explore that identity. Adolescents need positive role models, empathetic listeners, and a healthy social environment where bullying is forbidden and verbal putdowns are minimized.

The early developmental stages lay a foundation for spiritual development all throughout life. Early childhood formation should be a priority in our church's Christian educational ministry. Faith development for the child will be more or less difficult depending on how they navigate these stages. Will it be easy for children as they become youth and adults to trust and have faith in their parents, in members of their church family, and in God, or will their early childhood experiences make it difficult for them to trust anyone, including God? Will they learn to be confidently autonomous, able to say "no" when necessary, to think for themselves, and to give themselves to Christ, or will they be filled with shame and doubt and be overly dependent on others? Will they be given opportunities to choose and work on their own so that they learn to be self-directed, or will they be afraid to make mistakes and helpless without the direction of others? Will they grow up to see themselves as gifted by God and use those gifts in ministry, or will they be immobilized by feelings of inferiority? These lessons, taught through interaction with family, members of the Christian community, and other children at church, are more important than memorizing Bible verses or learning Bible stories only for the sake of knowing about them, though we hope the verses and stories help convey trust, autonomy, initiative, and industry.

Erikson further identifies three stages of adulthood:

*Stage 6: Intimacy versus Isolation.* As the young adult engages in relationships with significant others, or not, they experience intimacy and/or isolation. Emerging from the teenage years with an appropriate sense of self, they are ready to give themselves to others in love and intimacy. The church, as the body of Christ, should be an ideal place for the practice of community.

*Stage 7: Generativity versus Stagnation.* The middle adult typically deals with questions of productivity. Will they bear children of their own? Will they contribute to society? Will they find meaningful employment? Will they contribute to future generations? Will they experience stagnation? The church community supports adults in their work and family life and offers opportunities for them engage in ministry of ultimate importance.

*Stage 8: Ego Integrity versus Despair.* The older adult will look back on the successes and failures of life with an overall sense of wholeness and satisfaction or may be overwhelmed with feelings of regret. The church can help adults reflect on life from a faith perspective, offering grace for those feelings of regret and celebrating where life is lived with integrity.[39]

## James Fowler and Stages of Faith

James Fowler, in his book *Stages of Faith: The Psychology of Human Development and the Quest for Meaning,* and other writings set forth the idea that faith development occurs in six predictable stages, though few people progress through all six stages.

*Pre-stage: Infancy and Undifferentiated Faith.* Before Stage 1, Fowler names a Pre-stage, Infancy and Undifferentiated Faith, roughly birth to age two. Similar to Erikson's first psychosocial stage of "Trust versus Mistrust," Fowler writes that "the quality of mutuality and the strength of trust, autonomy, hope and courage (or their opposites) developed in this phase underlie (or threaten to undermine) all that comes later in faith development."[40]

*Stage 1: Intuitive-projective Faith.* Most typical of children ages three to seven, Intuitive-projective Faith is learned through stories, images, feeling, and actions caught from significant adults. The child's imagination plays an important role in this stage of their faith development. The child's religious descriptions may not make sense logically, as symbols, images, and stories are fit together in seemingly random patterns. Fowler suggests that "parents and teachers should create an atmosphere in which the child can freely express, verbally and non-verbally, the images she or he is forming."[41] The

Stage 1 child has learned self-awareness without understanding that others may have a different perspective.

*Stage 2: Mythic-literal Faith.* In the Mythic-literal stage, "the person begins to take on for him- or herself the stories, beliefs, and observances that symbolize belonging to his or her community."[42] Faith stories are logical, concrete, and literal. A Stage 2 faith has learned to distinguish real and make-believe. Justice is based on fairness, with rewards and punishments given based on adherence to moral rules. The person in this stage is better able to take on the perspectives of others. God is thought of in anthropomorphic terms, described with human qualities and actions. This stage is mostly found in school-age children, but some adults will remain in this stage.

*Stage 3: Synthetic-conventional Faith.* Synthetic-conventional Faith generally develops during adolescence as personality and self-identity emerge. Interpersonal relationships and being known and accepted by a group are extremely important in this stage, as self-identity is formed as a member of the group. Since the self-identity is still developing, there is little independent perspective beyond that of the group to which the person conforms. Synthetic-conventional Faith relies on external authority. For these reasons, Fowler writes, "In many ways religious institutions 'work best' if they are people with a majority of committed folk best described by Stage 3."[43] So it is easy to see how a church might be satisfied for most of its member to maintain a Stage 3 faith of unquestioned commitment to the beliefs and practices of the church. The beliefs and value system of Stage 3 are tacitly held (that is, unexamined). Like fish in a fish bowl, people in Stage 3 are unable to view the system from the outside or to understand that there are other systems (fish bowls). Transition to Stage 4 can be precipitated by the experience of leaving home—"emotionally or physically, or both"[44]—through marriage, college, entering the workforce, or joining the military, as the Stage 3 person encounters those from other groups and perspectives. Being confronted with contractions in accepted religious beliefs and practices and discovering the imperfections of religious leaders may cause a crisis of faith that nudges a person toward a higher stage of faith. Churches can facilitate faith development through mission trips, engagement with other cultures, and interfaith dialogue that places members in contact with people who have differing worldviews. Critical reflection on our unexamined (tacit) value systems can help us transition to a Stage 4 explicit (examined) system.

*Stage 4: Individuative-reflective Faith.* Individuative-reflective Faith usually begins in young adulthood with exposure to the wider world of diverse cultures and perspectives. This is a time of disequilibrium as unexamined beliefs and values are called into question and compared to alternative value systems. Whereas authority in Stage 3 comes externally from the group, in Stage 4 authority shifts internally to the self. The emphasis is on individuality, independence, and self-fulfillment. The individual makes her or his own judgments about values and beliefs. Previously accepted religious symbols, practices, and Bible stories may be rejected as naïve. People at this stage may altogether reject traditional faith of any kind.

*Stage 5: Conjunctive Faith.* Conjunctive Faith is rare before midlife. With it comes a greater acceptance of diversity, complexity, mystery, and paradox. Conjunctive Faith has been referred to as the "second naïveté."[45] Previously rejected religious symbols and practices are reaffirmed as tools to help one encounter God and the truth, rather than as merely ends in themselves. Stage 5 knowing, according to Fowler, is characterized by a "willingness to let reality speak its word, regardless of the impact of that word on the security or self-esteem of the knower. I speak here of an intimacy in knowing that celebrates, reverences and attends to the 'wisdom' evolved in things as they are, before seeking to modify, control or order them to fit prior categories."[46]

*Stage 6: Universalizing Faith.* Stage 6, Universalizing Faith, is extremely rare. Fowler names people like Gandhi, Martin Luther King Jr., Mother Teresa, Thomas Merton, and Dietrich Bonhoeffer as examples of people who reached a Universalizing Faith.[47] These individuals' perspectives and actions often run counter to the surrounding culture. They see all people as part of a universal family. They selflessly serve others, loving life without being overly attached to life. Many of them are persecuted and martyred in life but later revered in death.

While there is a predictability and readiness due to age and biological and intellectual development, progression through these stages of faith is not automatic.[48] Some move more slowly than others from one stage to the next, while some remain in earlier stages throughout their adult lives. In all of this, the community plays a key role. The ongoing "sponsorship" of the community makes a significant difference for people as they move from one stage to the next and as they grow within a stage of faith. "Sponsorship," according to Fowler, is the way a "community provides affirmation, encouragement, guidance and models for a person's ongoing growth and development."[49]

The writings of Jean Piaget, Lev Vygotsky, Erick Erikson, and James Fowler are worth further study for application to Christian education, along with others such as John Westerhoff's "Styles of Faith" and Lawrence Kohlberg's "Stages of Moral Development."[50]

## Personality Types

Some understanding of personality types among the learners, such as the Myers-Briggs personality types[51] and the Enneagram,[52] can help a teacher adapt methods to the personality types of a group and can help a group understand each other for a more constructive learning environment.

## Guiding the Faith Development of Children

As we guide children in their faith development, we should consider these key words:

*Life.* Like adults, children learn through life experience. With children, especially with preschoolers, we can bring life into the classroom through the use of experiential learning centers. Children visit centers like home living, blocks, and nature and interact with each other, learning to share and deal with conflict, imitating adults and practicing basic skills, guided by loving teachers.

*Choices.* We want children to grow up making wise choices and eventually choosing to follow Jesus. They learn how to choose by being given the opportunity to make choices rather than always being directed by adult teachers. Children can be allowed to choose which activity center to visit, what art materials to use for a project, or what song to sing during group time. Providing a learning environment in which children can make choices builds confidence and can help them learn in the ways best suited to their learning styles.

*Love.* Bible stories about God's love make sense to children when they experience love demonstrated by their teachers, parents, and other adults in their lives. Children learn boundaries, but more importantly forgiveness and grace, when after misbehaving they hear the teacher say firmly, "I cannot let you hurt your friend," but then continue to receive warmth, love, and smiles from the teacher.

*Creativity.* Give children the freedom to use their imaginations and to create—to paint, draw, build, and work with playdough. Choose blank paper over coloring sheets. Allow the children to decide how to act out the Bible scene.

*Play.* Play is not something we do to entertain children until they are old enough to do real church. Adults could learn from children that play is not wasting time. Play is a child's work. Play is how they learn. Play is social, creative, and imaginative. Play is joy. Play is all of this, but it is also valuable without any specific goals or outcomes. Play is graceful. According to the Godly Play approach to children's religious education, "Being graceful is a manifestation of God being with us. The result is effortless movement, life play. We are no longer clumsy, trying too hard and stumbling. It is at this graceful point that I would like to suggest that we find play at its most authentic in Godly Play."[53]

*The Story.* The sacred Story is from the Bible but is much more than that. The story is our story, the child's story, full of life. Rather than a multitude of disconnected stories, the stories are the Story of God's love, which the teacher helps bring together and bring to life. My seminary children's Christian education professor, Kathryn Chapman, said that one of the teacher's greatest tools is to tell the Bible story well. *God, Jesus, church, prayer, worship,* and *the Bible* are some key words children hear in the story.

*Age Appropriate.* Children are not simply miniature adults. They develop in stages physically, mentally, morally, emotionally, and socially. For example, young children are concrete literal thinkers, so the use of metaphors and abstract concepts are lost on them. Not every Bible story or theological concept is suitable for children. We don't need to "hurry" our children, as David Elkind would say.[54]

## Teens

I asked my youth minister daughter, "What is the most important thing to know about teaching teens?" She said that whatever curriculum you start with you have to adapt. The group may include a homeschooled child who is not used to a classroom setting or working in groups, a teen who has been abused, a teen suffering with a mental illness whose reality is different from everyone else's reality, or a straight-A student. Every group is different. Every student is different. "That's good," I said, "but I don't have room here for the potential life situation of every teen." So she summed it up: "Throw out your plans. Know your kids."

Depending on what age we would endeavor to teach, we may not need to throw out all of our plans, but certainly we should know our learners.

## Intergenerational

Segregating church members by age for spiritual formation has some advantages. Teaching methods and content can be geared to the developmental level of the learner. However, churches that rely exclusively on age-graded discipleship so that children, teens, and adults always worship, pray, minister, and learn separately are missing opportunities to learn from those with more experience in the faith. We may miss out on mentoring relationships. Children learn to pray, worship, and work by observing adults and participating with adults. Not only do children and youth learn from adults how to pray, worship, and work; they are also encouraged to value prayer, worship, and work as they catch the passion of adults. The relationships work both ways. When adults, including senior adults, share their faith with others, the process of explaining and modeling helps them reflect on and further develop their own faith. Older adults can benefit from the fresh perspectives of younger adults, teens, and children. Regardless of the educational advantages of intergenerational learning, all ages learning and growing together seems more consistent with the vision of the church as many members in the one body of Christ.

### *How Do We Teach?*

As already noted, the picture many have of teaching is that of a teacher lecturing to a class, with some interaction through question-and-answer discussion.

Learning Modalities, the Theory of Multiple Intelligences, the Shared Praxis Approach, the Experiential Learning Model, and the Story-linking Process would suggest that lecture and discussion alone are not the best methods for all students and certainly not the only way to teach.

## Learning Modalities

The Learning Modalities, or learning styles, are visual, auditory, and tactile/kinesthetic. Early research, primarily on elementary school students, showed that students "vary with respect to their modality strengths."[55] The researchers found that about 30 percent were primarily visual learners, 30 percent were mixed, 25 percent were auditory learners, and 15 percent were kinesthetic learners. So if all of our teaching is verbal, we put a majority of our members at a disadvantage. We should ask ourselves if we are satisfied with reaching only about a fourth of the community in the ways they learn best. Returning to the Shema of Deuteronomy 6:4-6, we see how the Israelites were instructed to teach the Shema using all three of the learning modalities: "recite" and "talk" (auditory); "sign," "emblem," and "write them" (visual); "lie down," "rise," "bind," and "fix" (kinesthetic).

If in our study of the Bible we truly want to connect with all of the learners, not just auditory learners, then we need to use a variety of teaching methods: pictures, videos, demonstrations, and symbolic objects for visual learners; drama, physical objects that can be held or manipulated, and other activities involving movement for kinesthetic learners; and dialogue, lecture, and music for auditory learners. Worship, in most cases, already utilizes the three learning modalities, though, in my experience, most elements of worship are more geared toward those who are auditory learners. Worship may involve the kinesthetic learner through, for example, sitting, standing, kneeling, singing, holding and eating the bread and drinking from the cup, laying on of hands, baptism, dance, or drama. Visual learners might find a multitude of visual images and symbols like the cross, banners, the Lord's Supper table, stained-glass windows, choir robes, architecture, interpretive movement, a processional, the pastor's facial expressions and gestures, an object in the children's story, flowers, organ pipes, videos, a bulletin, or printed words in the Bible. Auditory learners will hear Scripture readings, sermons, prayers, songs and instruments, and perhaps greetings, laughter, crying, "Amen," or silence. Worship planners should be intentional about including elements of worship that appeal to all of the senses. Take a look at Sunday's worship bulletin. Beside each element of worship write "auditory," "visual," or "kinesthetic." List additional unwritten elements of the worship service or worship space and label those as well. Does your worship service rely heavily on the use of one or two of the learning modalities to the neglect of others?

## Multiple Intelligences

Dr. Howard Gardner, Harvard professor of education, presented the theory of multiple intelligences (MI) in the book *Frames of Mind: The Theory of Multiple Intelligences*.[56] The theory of multiple intelligences has not received as much attention in church educational ministries as it might, at least not directly, but it is a concept that is well worth our attention. Gardner proposed that there are multiple intelligences, not just the one single intelligence traditionally measured by IQ and other similar standardized tests, that can indicate how smart a person is in a wide range of fields. Gardner contends that these tests measure linguistic and logical mathematical intelligence, but there are other intelligences. Using extensive research and a strict criteria, he identified eight (and possibly nine) relatively independent intelligences: (1) Verbal-linguistic (Word Smart), (2) Musical (Music Smart), (3) Logical-mathematical (Logic Smart), (4) Spatial (Picture Smart), (5) Bodily-kinesthetic (Body Smart), (6) Interpersonal (People Smart), (7) Intrapersonal (Self Smart), (8) Naturalist (Nature Smart), and (9) Existential (Life Smart).[57] Gardner conducted research with stroke patients, which showed how a patient could lose one capacity, such as speech, but maintain other abilities, such as singing. Thus, one of his criteria was that the intelligence be associated with specific faculties of the brain that could be isolated by brain damage. He studied cognitive development in ordinary and gifted children, and he observed how prodigies, like Albert Einstein and Pablo Picasso, could be highly proficient in one area and mediocre in others. Out of this kind of research and more, he developed his eight criteria for inclusion as one of the intelligences.[58]

Using the various intelligences, not just logic and language, can help students of all ages learn most effectively. A learner who is weak in linguistic intelligence may be able to more easily process the content if presented in song, through movement or pictures, or when given time for silent reflection. Using methods geared toward a variety of multiple intelligences—all of them over time—will maximize learning for everyone.

The eight intelligences, as described in *Teaching and Learning through Multiple Intelligences*,[59] are presented below with comment:

> **Linguistic Intelligence** consists of the ability to think in words and to use language to express and appreciate complex meanings. Authors, poets, journalists, speakers, and newscasters exhibit high degrees of linguistic intelligence.[60]

Christian education in the church is typically focused on the Bible—the written word—much of which began as the spoken word in oral tradition. So methods using words, written and spoken, will have a prominent place. Teaching can be enhanced by a variety of linguistic methods such as dramatic readings, multiple translations of the Bible, dialogue, storytelling, brainstorming, journaling, poetry, biographies, mini-lectures, interviews, quotes, creative and descriptive writing, and listening.[61] For example, in a Bible study on Jesus at the home of Mary and Martha, participants might be asked to write a journal entry reflecting on the event from the perspective of Mary or Martha.

**Logical-mathematical Intelligence** makes it possible to calculate, quantify, consider propositions and hypotheses, and carry out complex mathematical operations. Scientists, accountants, engineers, and computer programmers all demonstrate this intelligence.[62]

The use of math may at first seem to have few applications in Christian education, but this intelligence involves problem-solving, reasoning, and making connections. We want our theology to be logically consistent. Teaching methods geared to the logical-mathematical intelligence might include inductive and deductive logic, analogies, theology, sequencing Bible stories, graphs and charts, and quality questions.[63] For example, with the Emmaus Road story (Luke 24), participants could estimate how long it might take them to walk seven miles at a conversational pace and again at a hurried pace. The story of Jesus at the home of Martha and Mary could be examined with questions: "If Martha followed Mary's example, who would make dinner? Does Jesus' teaching in this story contradict Jesus' teaching in the previous parable, which ends with the command to 'go and do'?"

**Bodily-kinesthetic Intelligence** enables one to manipulate objects and fine-tune physical skills. It is evident in athletes, dancers, surgeons, and craftspeople. In Western societies, physical skills are not as highly valued as cognitive ones, and yet elsewhere the ability to use one's body is a necessity for survival and an important feature of many prestigious roles.[64]

One of the recurring issues of Christian education in the church is how to deal with children who just can't sit still and listen. I was one of those children. Multiple Intelligence education would suggest that we not try to make them sit still, at least not for extended periods of time. Movement might be the way they learn best and can be used to help them and all learners of any age. Teaching methods for the bodily-kinesthetic mind might include areas designated for physical activities, drama, puppets, role play, simulations, dance, manipulatives like blocks, cooperative games and activities, prayer walks, mission trips and field trips, hands-on missions and ministry projects, and exercise breaks during other learning activities.[65] For example, the Emmaus Road story could be told and discussed while taking a walk together at a leisurely pace to a destination and then returning at brisk pace while participants discuss how the story applies to their lives and their church.

**Spatial Intelligence** instills the capacity to think in three-dimensional ways like sailors, pilots, sculptors, painters, and architects. It enables one to perceive external and internal imagery; to recreate, transform, or modify images; to navigate oneself and objects through space; and to produce or decode graphic information.[66]

The saying, "a picture is worth a thousand words," is especially true for the spatially minded person. Christian tradition and our churches are full of symbolism, stories, and messages conveyed through pictures, art, architecture, and representational objects like crosses, fish, praying hands, the Communion bread and cup, stained-glass windows, the Lord's Supper table, steeples, and the arrangement of church sanctuaries. To appeal to spatial intelligence, teaching methods might use, for example, pictures, videos, flow charts and visual outlines, cartoons, board games, architecture, and art in many forms such as paper, clay, pencils, markers, paint, crayons, collage, and cameras.[67] So, in the case of the story of Jesus at the home of Martha and Mary, a variety of artists' representations could be presented and the artists' intent and meaning discussed.[68]

**Musical Intelligence** is evident in individuals who possess a sensitivity to pitch, melody, rhythm, and tone. Those demonstrating this intelligence include composers, conductors, musicians, critics, and instrument makers, as well as sensitive listeners.[69]

Music has long played an integral role in Judeo-Christian expressions of faith. The letter to the Ephesians encourages the church to "sing psalms and hymns and spiritual songs among yourselves, singing and making melody to the Lord in your hearts" (Eph 5:19). Churches are familiar with music as a tool for worshiping God, sharing the tenants and stories of the faith, and motivating Christians to live the faith. The forms are diverse, including psalms, hymns, chants, spirituals, choruses, orchestras, bands, rap, and contemporary music, just to name a few. Music can be used to create an environment for learning, relaxation, focusing, invigorating, and transitions. The words of songs can convey Bible stories, Christian themes, theological concepts, and calls to service. Music encourages participation with the use of voices and various instruments. Music helps us remember and internalize the message.[70] For example, the hymn "Open My Eyes That I May See" (words and music by Clara H. Scott, 1895) could reinforce the message of Jesus on the Road to Emmaus. With this story, participants might be asked to choose background music for each part of the story that could be used if it were made into a movie.

> **Interpersonal Intelligence** is the capacity to understand and interact effectively with others. It is evident in successful teachers, social workers, actors, or politicians. Just as Western culture has recently begun to recognize the connection between mind and body, so too has it come to value the importance of proficiency in interpersonal behavior.[71]

Interpersonal is what the church is—a community, a fellowship. Interpersonal relationships are how the church extends hospitality and interacts in business, committee, and leadership team meetings. When Jesus said "Do this in remembrance of me," he was instituting an interpersonal community observance. Loving your neighbor as yourself is both interpersonal (neighbor) and intrapersonal (yourself). We appeal to the interpersonal intelligence by creating an environment that is like a family, modeling helpfulness and fairness, a win/win situation, clear rules, high expectations, and a warm, positive, and nurturing atmosphere.[72] Teaching methods include collaborative and cooperative games and learning activities, intergenerational experiences, conflict management, appreciating differences, understanding diverse perspectives, multicultural experiences, board games, simulations, role play, problem-solving, and just about anything that requires working together or dialogue. Interpersonal learning occurs especially in small groups, during leadership meetings, and through missions and service.[73] For example, a small group studying the Emmaus Road encounter might conclude by breaking bread together and sharing stories of times when participants have experienced the presence of Jesus in surprising ways.

> **Intrapersonal Intelligence** refers to the ability to construct an accurate perception of oneself and to use such knowledge in planning and directing one's life. Some individuals with strong intrapersonal intelligence specialize as theologians, psychologists, and philosophers.[74]

The Genesis creation account declares that humans are created in God's image (Gen 1:27). Disciples are being formed intrapersonally (as a self) and interpersonally (as a community) into the likeness of Christ. Loving your neighbor as yourself assumes that the disciple has a well-developed sense of the intrapersonal "self." We can help nurture intrapersonal intelligence with teaching methods that encourage healthy self-esteem, setting and achieving goals, thinking skills, identifying and expressing feelings, journaling, personal feedback, self-directed learning and choices, and time for reflection.[75] For example, when asking a question, request that participants pause for a minute of reflection before answering. You might ask, "How would you have felt if you were Martha (or Mary)?"

> **Naturalist Intelligence** consists of observing patterns in nature, identifying and classifying objects, and understanding natural and human-made systems. Skilled naturalists include farmers, botanists, hunters, ecologists, and landscapers.[76]

The naturalist's mind can appreciate the wonder and beauty of God's creation. Saint Bernard of Clairvaux has written, "You will discover things in the woods that you never found in books. Stones and trees will teach you things that you never heard from your schoolteachers." Learning that occurs inside a church building can be a challenge for the naturalist. Decorating the room with live plants and flowers can help the naturalist in all of us feel more at home. Since some of the strengths of the naturalist intelligence include observation, identification, and classification, these same abilities could be applied to elements of a Bible story. Skills of the naturalist intelligence can be utilized in a variety of ways in teaching: looking at the big picture and the interconnectedness of all things, improving observation, perceiving relationships, and understanding interdependence. Bring children closer to nature with nature walks. A nature center in the preschool and children's rooms can help instill a sense of wonder and awe for the natural world. Church service, ministry, and partnerships that take us outside the walls of the church can bring us closer to nature. One of the advantages of Lexington Avenue Baptist's partnership with a mission church in the mountains of Eastern Kentucky is the opportunity to experience nature. In this community, more of life happens out in the world, surrounded by scenic mountains.

Existential intelligence did not meet all of Gardner's qualifications to be added to his list, but it is worth mentioning due to its relevance to Christian education. The core ability of existential intelligence, according to Gardner, is

> the capacity to locate oneself with respect to the furthest reaches of the cosmos—the infinite and the infinitesimal—and the related capacity

to locate oneself with respect to such existential features of the human condition as the significance of life, the meaning of death, the ultimate fate of the physical and the psychological worlds, and such profound experiences as love of another person or total immersion in a work of art.[77]

Existential intelligence is concerned with the ultimate questions of life. Existential intelligence may be especially prominent among theologians, pastors, psychologists, philosophers, scientists, writers, and artists.

From the Christian education perspective, we are using existential intelligence when we explore questions like "What is the nature of God? What is the Trinity? What is the meaning of life and death? What happens to people after death? Why do evil and suffering exist? What does it mean to love God and neighbor? How is the Bible relevant to my life?" Or, in the words of the psalmist, "What are human beings that you are mindful of them?" (Ps 8:4).

The above discussion of the multiple intelligences has neatly separated teaching methods for each intelligence for the purpose of explanation, but some teaching methods can connect with a number of the multiple intelligences. Imagine, for example, the use of drama with the story of Jesus at the home of Martha and Mary. Participants take on the roles of Jesus, Martha, and Mary. Actors are given time to read the Scripture passage and reflect on the person they will represent: "What exactly are you doing during this story? What are you thinking? What are you feeling?" The person playing the part of Jesus could be asked to think about what Jesus was teaching and how they will portray this part of the story. Perhaps the actor could choose a Scripture passage to read that contains some of Jesus' instruction or be prepared to speak in their own words the kinds of things Jesus might say in this situation. Before acting out the scene, actors and observers could plan how Jesus, Martha, and Mary will be situated in the room. Will any props or visuals help convey the story? When ready, the actors will act out the scene, interacting in ways consistent with the story, improvising missing details and conversation, and moving and speaking in character. When the drama is complete, debrief with a series of reflection questions: "What were each of you feeling as you played your role? What new insights into the characters and the story did you gain? If you were to repeat the dramatization, is there anything you might do differently? What does this story mean for you and your life? What can our church learn from this story?"

Drama like this can touch a variety of the intelligences. Personal reflection, especially getting into character, uses intrapersonal intelligence. Planning, acting, and debriefing together is an interpersonal experience. The discussion before and after, the script, and the dramatic dialogue all utilize the verbal-linguistic intelligence. The actors embody the characters and move throughout the drama appealing to the bodily-kinesthetic intelligence. The scene depicted in 3D space, the placement of the actors—Jesus seated, Mary at his feet, and Martha in the kitchen—and the use of props and other visuals will engage the visual-spacial intelligence.

Following are some general teaching strategies for using multiple intelligences with small group studies in the church:

1. Intentionally include teaching methods aimed at each of the eight intelligences for each session or systematically over a series of sessions.

2. Organize your teaching schedule around the multiple intelligences in eight steps. For example: a. group sharing, b. Bible story presentation, c. drama, d. art, e. personal reflection, f. music, etc.

3. Set up eight learning centers, one for each intelligence. Perhaps begin or end with a group time in which a variety of approaches could be used.

4. Know the learners, and teach to the strengths and build on weaknesses. With strengths, use more advanced methods. With weaknesses, use teaching methods to help learners develop competency and build confidence with a less familiar intelligence.

## Shared Praxis Approach: Bringing Life to Faith and Faith to Life

Thomas Groome has long been a proponent of the Praxis Approach to Christian education, or, more simply stated, "Bringing life to faith and faith to life."[78] Groome is concerned that Christian education in the church is too often disconnected from life and a long way from the teaching approach of Jesus. "Until quite recently," he writes, "the typical mode of religious education was a very didactic process of a teacher telling (usually children) what to believe and how to live. It did little to actively engage participants or to draw upon their own lives—their experiences, or what I call here their praxis."[79]

The praxis approach to Christian education seeks to bring life to faith and faith to life with a process involving five movements:

### LIFE

(1) Naming Present Action: As honestly and perceptively as possible, the participants recall their own ways of thinking, feeling, and acting, especially as it relates to a Scripture text or faith theme being taught. For example, in a Bible study on the Road to Emmaus (Luke 24), we might ask participants to "describe a time when you have had a surprising encounter with Jesus."

(2) Reflecting on the Participants' Stories and Visions: In dialogue with the group, participants reflect on their experiences (present action) to discover the assumptions and beliefs behind their actions. How is the experience related to the participant's larger story and vision? For example, from the Emmaus Road story, we could ask, "What keeps you from seeing Jesus?"

### FAITH

(3) Representing the Christian Story with Meaning and Persuasion: The Christian Story is the faith story, or whatever theme or symbol the group is considering. In the case of a typical Bible study, the Christian story is the biblical text. Groome explains, "Whatever the symbol might be from Christian Scripture and Tradition—a dogma, doctrine, scripture text, sacrament, and so on—the intent is to teach it clearly, highlighting the truth and spiritual wisdom it reflects for our lives and the response it invites."[80] For example, continuing with Emmaus Road story, we might ask, "What does this story teach us about where and how we might encounter Jesus?"

### LIFE

(4) Appropriating the Truths and Wisdom of the Christian Faith into Life: A dialogue occurs between the participants' personal stories and the biblical story. The intent is "that participants come to see for themselves what the teachings and wisdom of Christian faith might mean for their everyday lives."[81] For example, with regard to the Emmaus story, we might ask, "If you take this story to heart, what response does it invite?"

(5) Making Decisions in Light of Christian Faith: Given what has been learned from faith and life, how will the participants now think, feel, and behave as a result? "Movement 5," Groome writes, "gives people an opportunity to choose and decide how they might live in response to the teachings and spiritual wisdom they have encountered in Christian Story and Vision."[82]

## Experiential Learning Model

The Experiential Learning Model and learning styles developed by David Kolb contends that learning occurs generally in a four-stage cycle "grounded in experience" that is repeated, and that each of us will tend to have a preferred learning style or mix of learning styles.[83] The cycle begins with experiences, activities, and relationships (concrete experience); then we examine and reflect on the experience from a variety of perspectives and make observations about the experience (reflective observation); next, we begin to form abstract concepts, theories, and models from our observation of the experience (abstract conceptualization); and finally, based on our conclusions, we make decision and plans, solve problems, and modify our behaviors for new experiences (active experimentation). This is an oversimplification of a more complex learning process. Any particular learning experience will not be as clear-cut and step by step as I've described it here. The learning cycle is more like a continuous spiral (a slinky) than a circle. The cycle is repeated. We live life, reflect on life, form ideas, make plans, and live life again.

Individuals will tend to learn best at certain points in the cycle, although we all utilize all of the learning styles to some degree. Experiential learning reminds us of the role of real-life, real-world, hands-on experiences in the learning process and the importance of examining and reflecting on these experiences in order to adapt and make applications to new experiences.

The four experiential learning styles are

(1) Diverger: Between concrete experience and reflective observation is the diverger. Divergers are good at brainstorming, seeing a variety of options, and using their imaginations. People, relationships, feelings, and emotions are important to them. These are people who lead with their hearts. Among them you will find artists, performers, counselors, and servants of all types.

(2) Assimilator: Between reflective observation and abstract conceptualization is the assimilator. The strength of the assimilator is reasoning. They are most interested in ideas and concepts. They are able to integrate the multiple and broad ideas of the diverger into a coherent theory or model that makes sense of the information. The assimilator enjoys thoroughly studying the Bible to discover the truths found there. They lead with their heads. Among them you will find theoretical scientists, mathematicians, and Bible scholars.

(3) Converger: Between abstract conceptualization and active experimentation is the converger. Convergers are problem solvers, organizers, technicians, and planners. They utilize the assimilators' theories and models and find ways to apply them in practical ways. They may lead with the head, but they have in mind how ideas will be used by the hands and feet. Among them you will find engineers, applied scientists, technicians, skilled workers, and inventors.

(4) Accommodator: Between active experimentation and concrete experience is the accommodator. Accommodators are action oriented. They carry out the convergers' plans and solutions. They like face-to-face interaction. Their preferred problem-solving method is trial and error. They lead with their hands and feet. Among them you will find politicians, salespeople, workers, accountants, and managers.

Let us imagine a small group at church going through the experiential learning cycle. There are four people in this Bible study group: diverger, assimilator, converger, and accommodator. While they are at the church engaged in their Monday morning Bible study, a stranger enters the church asking for assistance. His hair is disheveled, his hands are dirty, and his clothes are worn. He says that he is homeless and hungry. The group is not sure what to do, but the church has food vouchers to a nearby grocery, so they give him one and point the way. When they return to their Bible study, the diverger speaks first: "There has got to be more that we can do. I get angry when we get taken advantage of, but it breaks my heart to see people suffer like that. The song we sang Sunday and the story the pastor told convicted me. Could we open a food pantry or start a jobs program? What if we took up an offering or added a benevolent fund to the budget? Should we start a political advocacy group for the homeless? What other organizations in our community are helping? What if we offered a class on understanding poverty?" The assimilator suggests that group take a week to reflect on and study the issue. The following Monday, the assimilator makes some observations: "A careful study of Scripture clearly shows that the church is called to care for the poor." He reads Matthew 25, interprets the passage, and continues, "Statistics show that at any one time there are an average of 500 homeless people in our town. In interviews with business persons in our church, local officials, and social workers, we find that there are a variety of reasons for homelessness, including mental illness, inflation, physical disabilities, and lack of skills, to name a few. Theologians say . . . Economic indicators suggest . . . etc." Now the converger is ready to take over: "What are we going to do about it? Here's a plan. We start a lawn mowing and cleaning service for our church and hire people based on need. They receive an income for their service and church members will use their gifts and talents to train, guide, and encourage them. They will be trained in all aspects of employment: work skills, resume writing, job interviews, money management, leadership, communications, and conflict management, with the goal of moving them into another job." The accommodator, who has been fidgeting in his seat, interrupts, "Okay, okay. Let's get to work. It's about time we did something. You people can talk anything to death. Let's do it, and if this plan doesn't work, we'll try something else." Then he rolls up his sleeves and gets busy implementing the plan, making phone calls, enlisting leaders, securing equipment, and promoting the plan.

The truth is that no person will be wholly a diverger, assimilator, converger, or accommodator. We are all some combination of learning styles with a tendency toward one or more of them.

## An Experiential Bible Study Model

John Hendrix has developed a Bible study model based in experiential learning. With the living Word, Jesus Christ—revealed in the written word, the Bible—at the center of the circle, this Bible study process moves the learners through the four phases of the experiential learning cycle.[84]

## Experiential Bible Study Model

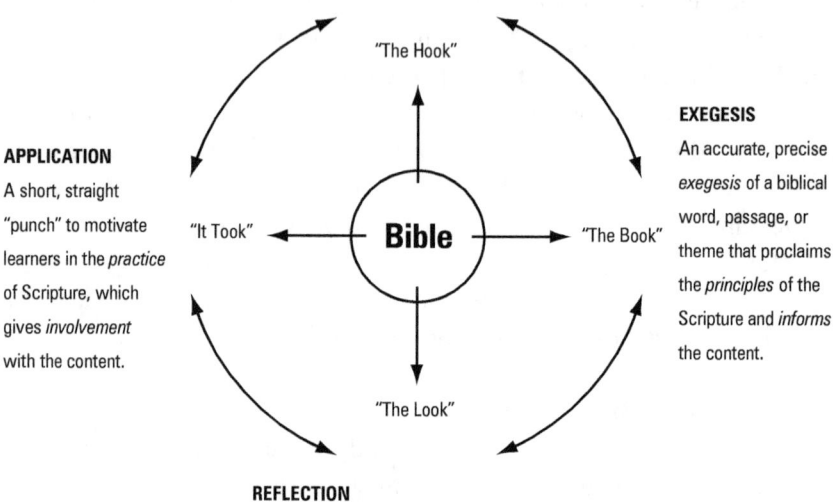

**EXPERIENCE**
A point of *interest*, related to the learner's *experience*, expressed in an unusual way, which gives *immediacy* to the content.

**APPLICATION**
A short, straight "punch" to motivate learners in the *practice* of Scripture, which gives *involvement* with the content.

**EXEGESIS**
An accurate, precise *exegesis* of a biblical word, passage, or theme that proclaims the *principles* of the Scripture and *informs* the content.

**REFLECTION**
The biblical content *reflected* on and held "in solution" with *needs*, *life situations*, and *personal biography*, which provides *intimacy* and *intensity* with the content.

(1) Experience ("Hook"): "A point of *interest*, related to the learner's experience, expressed in an unusual way, which gives *immediacy* to the content."[85] The faith that we bear witness to—the Word—is experiential. The letter of 1 John notes that the good news is based in real-life experience: "We declare to you what was from the beginning, what we have heard, what we have seen with our eyes, what we have looked at and touched with our hands, concerning the word of life—this life was revealed, and we have seen it and testify to it, and declare to you" (1 John 1:1-2). Learning activities that "hook" experience could include questions, stories, and imaginative exercises that call to mind life experiences, but this should also include experiential activities planned as a part of the learning event, such as simulation games, role play, use of art materials, field trips, and interactive group process. When it comes to learning about prayer, worship, or service, we should pray, worship, and serve.

(2) Exegesis ("Book"): "An accurate, precise exegesis of a biblical word, passage, or theme that proclaims the *principles* of the Scripture and *informs*

the content."[86] We all come to the text with our biases and our preconceived ideas about what it says. We read it through the lens of our own assumptions. Careful Bible study is intended to help us, as much as possible, hear the text on its own terms. What did this text mean in its original context, and how does it fit into this particular book of the Bible and in the biblical narrative as a whole? A teacher can encourage good study by creating a safe environment where a variety of perspectives might be heard and understood through group dialogue and from biblical scholarship found in commentaries, dictionaries, and other sources. Hendrix recommends examining the threads of Scripture verse by verse and then reweaving them. Scripture is examined from a number of angles, such as sensory, context, language, style, connections, with empathy, and as if listening to a good friend.

(3) Reflection ("Look"): "The biblical content *reflected* on and held 'in solution' with needs, *life situations*, and *personal biography*, which provides intimacy and *intensity* with the content."[87] Hendrix adds, "The Bible becomes a mirror through which we see ourselves and others."[88] Reflection combines thinking and feeling. Reflection takes time. Requesting a few moments of silence before answering questions can bring out the reflective learner. Encourage reflection with questions like "Who are the people in this text? How are they related to each other? Why are they responding in this way? If I were in this situation, how would I be responding?"[89] Silence, modeling clay, *lectio divina* (a prayer reading of Scripture), and imaginative exercises are some other tools that could be used to facilitate reflection.

(4) Application ("Took"): "A short, straight 'punch' to motivate learners in the *practice* of Scripture, which gives *involvement* with the content."[90] Application asks, "Now what?" or "So what?" In light of what we have learned from experience, careful study of Scripture, and reflection on both, how will we now live? If we have been faithful in our Bible study task to this point, we have been challenged and transformed to new ways of living out the faith. We are ready to apply what we have learned. Learners could be encouraged to set goals, make plans, make a covenant with God or the group, or practice what is learned as individuals or as a group. Hendrix suggests a number of examples of what application behaviors might look like, such as "A move from reliance on a limited number of sources of knowledge and assistance to multiple sources," "A move from fearfully clinging to the known to risking and experimenting with new behavior," and "A move from an acknowledged truth about the self at a rational level to recognition and acceptance of a personal truth."[91]

### Story-linking Process, Anne Wimberly

Anne Wimberly, an African American Christian educator, has written an excellent book, *Soul Stories: African-American Christian Education*.[92] Wimberly uses the story-linking process, an educational approach out of the African American tradition that dates back to the time of slavery. This process is consistent with the experiential reflection approaches we have been considering. Story-linking moves the learner through four phases: "(1) engaging the everyday story, (2) engaging the Christian faith story in the Bible, (3) engaging Christian faith stories from the African American heritage, and (4) engaging in Christian ethical decision-making." This process leads the learner to find liberation and vocation in life.

\* \* \*

What Shared Praxis, Experiential Learning, and Story-linking have in common is an emphasis on connecting faith and life and the importance of experience in the learning process. Life experience is not only the subject of our teaching, but experiential activities and life itself are vital elements of the learning process.

Everything we do as a church—worship, missions, and ministry—is spiritual formation, but not automatically so. Spiritual formation happens in all aspects of the church's life when we reflect on our experiences as a community: What did that missions experience mean? How would we do it differently? Where was God revealed? Why do we worship? What is worship calling me to do, think, or believe? Do members of our community feel cared for? Is anyone excluded from our community? What does the way we make decisions and conduct business say about who we are?

### Multicultural Learning

Our culture colors the way we view the world, God, and others in ways we seldom recognize. The perspective of those from cultures and socioeconomic groups other than our own can bring fresh insights and perhaps correction to our learning. The best way to gain multicultural perspective is, obviously, through face-to-face interaction with those of different cultures and preferably within those different cultural settings. Hearing and reading a variety of cultural perspectives can also help. See, for example, *Global Bible Commentary*[93] or *Return to Babel: Global Perspectives on the Bible*.[94]

## Touching the Head, Heart, Hands, and Feet

If the goal of Christian education is transformation, teaching must touch the *head*, *heart*, and *hands and feet*. Without touching the head with a faithful understanding of God's word, then our actions may be passionate but misguided. Without touching the heart, we may only acknowledge truth in an objective way, unmoved to change our attitudes and behaviors. Touching the hands and feet is where we live life, putting our knowledge and feelings into action in ministry to the world. A variety of methods will be the best way to nurture mature transforming faith.

## Discipleship Development Coaching

Discipleship Development Coaching (DDC) is an approach to spiritual formation in which a Christian disciple relates to a coach who facilitates growth toward life goals by listening, asking key questions, supporting, and leading the disciple through a six-step process. "Disciple Development Coaching," according to the authors, "is a focused collaborative relationship, resulting in the disciple living out his or her calling more fully."[95] The coach's role is not to push, prod, or advocate any particular result. Instead, the initiative and decision-making lie with the disciple, who is called and gifted by God. A lifelong journey of transformation is the goal. The coach facilitates growth using a six-step process:

1. Ask: Action—Beginning the DDC conversation with a simple question, "What would you like to gain from our conversation?"
2. Listen: Action—Listening to the words and meaning of this disciple's message; listening for the desires of the heart
3. Explore: Action—Exploring the alternatives or options before the disciple
4. Design: Action—Identifying the action steps that lead to accomplishing the goal
5. Commit: Action—Discerning readiness for action and making a commitment to take the fitting action
6. Support: Action—Building the fitting level of support so that this disciple will accomplish this goal[96]

Mentoring, spiritual direction, counseling, and accountability relationships are other ways that disciples may receive personal guidance in the discipleship journey.

## Assessment/Evaluation

After all the work that goes into planning and implementing learning events of whatever type, when the activity is complete, we may be ready to move on to the next demand on our time. We may not feel we have the energy to revisit events that are past. However, we will benefit from time taken to evaluate and assess a learning experience, and our spiritual formation process as a whole, with some key questions such as "What did we learn? Where did growth happen? What was the most meaningful part about the experience, and what made it so? What about that experience is worth repeating? What would we do differently? In what ways did the experience help us carry out our God-given mission? Did the activity help cultivate community?"

Israel Galindo and Marty C. Canaday offer a helpful chapter, "Assessing Effectiveness" (ch. 7) on assessing effectiveness in their book, *Planning for Christian Education Formation: A Community of Faith Approach*.[97]

## Teaching Resources

Aleshire, Daniel. *Faithcare: Ministering to All God's People through the Ages of Life*. Philadelphia: Westminster Press, 1988.

Armstrong, Thomas. *Multiple Intelligences in the Classroom*, third ed. Alexandria, VA: ASCD, 2009.

———. *You're Smarter than You Think: A Kid's Guide to Multiple Intelligences*. Minneapolis: Free Spirit Publishing, 2014.

Barbe, Walter B., and Michael N. Milone Jr. "What We Know about Modality Strengths: Research that Shows Students Have Different Modality Strengths Should Be Used to Improve Learning." *Educational Leadership* 38, no. 5 (February 1981).

Bauer, David R. "Disciple, Discipleship." *The New Interpreter's Dictionary of the Bible, D-H: Volume 2*. Nashville: Abingdon, 2007.

Berryman, Jerome W. *How to Lead Godly Play Lessons*. Vol. 1 of The Complete Guide to Godly Play. Denver: Living the Good News, 2002.

———, Cheryl V. Minor, and Rosemary Beale. *Presentations for Fall*. Vol. 2 of The Complete Guide to Godly Play. Denver: Living the Good News, 2010.

Biddle, Mark. *Deuteronomy*. Smyth & Helwys Bible Commentary. Macon: Smyth & Helwys, 2003.

Campbell, Linda, Bruce Campbell, and Dee Dickinson. *Teaching and Learning through Multiple Intelligences*, third ed. Boston: Pearson Education, Inc., 2004.

Culpepper, R. Alan. "Luke," *New Interpreter's Bible*, vol. 9. Nashville: Abingdon, 1995.

Dietterich, Paul. *Center for Parish Development Missional Convocation: A Foretaste! Transforming Leadership Practices*. Chicago, IL, July 25, 2015.

Dodd, C. H. *The Parables of the Kingdom*. London: Nisbet & Co. LTD, 1936.

Elkind, David. *The Hurried Child: Growing Up Too Fast Too Soon*. Reading, MA: Addison-Wesley, 1981.

Erikson, Erik. *Childhood and Society*. New York: W.W. Norton and Company, Inc., 1950.

Ferguson, Nancy. *The Christian Educators' Guide to Evaluating and Developing Curriculum*. Valley Forge: Judson, 2008.

Forman, Brian, Bo Prosser, and David Woody. *Help! I Teach Youth Sunday School*. Macon: Smyth & Helwys, 2004.

Foster, Charles R. *Educating Congregations: The Future of Christian Education*. Nashville: Abingdon, 1994.

Fowler, James W. *Stages of Faith: The Psychology of Human Development and the Quest for Meaning*. San Francisco: Harper & Row, 1981.

Fulbright, Robert G., ed. *Christian Education through the Sunday School: A Guide to Formations*. Macon: Smyth & Helwys, 1994.

———, chair. *Destinations: Mapping Your Congregation's Missional Journey, A Resource for Church Planning*. Cooperative Baptist Fellowship, 2007.

Funk, Robert. *Parables and Presence: Forms of the New Testament Tradition*. Philadelphia: Fortress Press, 1982.

Galindo, Israel. *The Craft of Christian Teaching: Essentials for Becoming a Very Good Teacher*. Valley Forge: Judson, 1998.

———, and Marty C. Canaday. *Planning for Christian Education: A Community of Faith Approach*. St. Louis: Chalice, 2010.

Gardner, Howard. *Frames of Mind: The Theory of Multiple Intelligences: New Horizons*. New York: Basic Books, 1983.

———. *Intelligence Reframed*. New York: Basic Books, 1999.

———. *Multiple Intelligences: New Horizons*, revised and updated. New York: Basic Books, 2006.

Groome, Thomas H. *Christian Religious Education: Sharing Our Story and Vision*. New York: Harper & Row, 1991.

———. *Sharing Faith: A Comprehensive Approach to Religious Education and Pastoral Ministry*. New York: Harper Collins, 1980.

———. *Will There Be Faith? A New Vision for Educating and Growing Disciples*. New York: HarperOne, 2011.

Harris, Maria. *Fashion Me a People: Curriculum in the Church*. Westminster John Knox, 1996.

———, and Gabriel Moran. *Reshaping Religious Education: Conversations on Contemporary Practice*. Louisville: Westminster John Knox, 1989.

Hendrix, John D. *Nothing Never Happens: Experiential Learning and the Church*. Macon: Smyth & Helwys, 2004.

———. *To Thessalonians with Love: An Interpersonal Commentary on 1 Thessalonians*. Nashville: Broadman, 1982.

Jones, Peter Rhea. *Studying the Parables of Jesus*. Macon: Smyth & Helwys, 1999.

Jones, Stephen, D. *Rabbi Jesus: Learning from the Master Teacher*. Macon: Peake Road, 1997.

Kohlberg, Lawrence. *The Philosophy of Moral Development: Moral Stages and the Idea of Justice*. San Francisco: Harper & Row, 1981.

Kolb, David A. *Experiential Learning: Experience as the Source of Learning and Development*. New Jersey: Prentice-Hall, 1984.

Lapin, Hayim. "Rabbi." In *Anchor Bible Dictionary*, vol. 5 New York: Doubleday, 1992. 600–602.

LeFever, Marlene D. *Creative Teaching Methods: Be an Effective Christian Teacher*. Colorado Springs: David C. Cook, 2004.

Levison, John R., and Priscilla Pope-Levison, eds. *Return to Babel: Global Perspectives on the Bible*. Louisville: Westminster John Knox Press, 1999.

Malina, Bruce J., and Richard L. Rohrbaugh. *Social-Science Commentary on the Synoptic Gospels*. Minneapolis: Fortress Press, 1992.

Marshall, I. Howard. *New International Greek Testament Commentary: Commentary on Luke*. Grand Rapids: Eerdmans, 1978.

McGregor, Wynn. *The Way of the Child: Helping Children Experience God, Leader's Guide and Sessions*. Nashville: Upper Room Books, 2006.

McKenzie, Leon, and R. Michael Harton. *The Religious Education of Adults*. Macon: Smyth & Helwys, 2002.

Miller, Donald E. *Story and Context: An Introduction to Christian Education*. Nashville: Abingdon, 1987.

Moeller, Mark. "Parables." *Christian Reflection: A Series in Faith and Ethics*, vol. 21. Waco: Center for Christian Ethics, Baylor University, 2006.

Myers, Isabel Briggs, with Peter B. Myers. *Gifts Differing: Understanding Personality Type*. Mountain View, CA: Davies-Black Publishing, 1995.

Neal, Cynthia Jones. *Nurture That Is Christian: Developmental Perspectives on Christian Education*. Grand Rapids: BridgePoint Books, 1998.

Palmer, Parker J. *To Know as We Are Known: A Spirituality of Education*. San Francisco: Harper & Row, 1966.

Patte, Daniel, gen. ed. *Global Bible Commentary*. Nashville: Abingdon, 2004.

Piaget, Jean. *Origins of Intelligence in the Child*. London: Routledge & Kegan Paul, 1936.

Price, Max B. *Help! I Teach Children's Sunday School: A Guide to Effective Teaching and Faith Development*. Macon: Smyth & Helwys, 2003.

Prosser, Bo, Michael McCuller, and Charles Qualls. *Building Blocks for Sunday School Growth*. Macon: Smyth & Helwys, 2002.

Ringe, Sharon H. *Luke: Westminster Bible Commentary*. Louisville: John Knox Press, 1995.

Riso, Richard Don, and Russ Hudson. *The Wisdom of the Enneagram: The Complete Guide to Psychological and Spiritual Growth for the Nine Personality Types*. New York: Bantam Books, 1999.

Roehlkepartain, Eugene C. *The Teaching Church: Moving Christian Education to Center Stage*. Nashville: Abingdon, 1993.

Rogers, William B. *Being a Christian Educator: Discovery Your Identity, Heritage, and Vision*. Macon: Smyth & Helwys, 1996.

Schaberg, Jane. "Luke." *The Women's Bible Commentary*, ed. Carol A. Newsom and Sharon H. Ringe. Louisville: Westminster/John Knox, 1992.

Steele, Les. "The Power of Erikson." Chapter 5 of *Nurture that Is Christian*, ed. James C. Wilhoit and John M. Dettoni. Grand Rapids: Baker, 1995.

Taylor, Ted G. "Experiential Learning: The Learning Style Inventory." *Adult Leadership* 19/7 (April 1989).

Tidsworth, Mark, and Ircel Harrison. *Disciple Development Coaching: Christian Formation for the 21st Century*. Macon, Nurturing Faith Inc., 2013. Kindle ed.

Tye, Karen B. *Basics of Christian Education*. St. Louis: Chalice, 2000.

Vinson, Richard B. *Luke*. Smyth & Helwys Bible Commentary. Macon: Smyth & Helwys, 2008.

Waldrop, C. Sybil. *Teaching Preschoolers the Bible*. Nashville: Convention Press, 1991.

Westerhoff, John. *Will Our Children Have Faith?* HarperSanFrancisco, 1976.

Wigger, Bradley. "Multiple Intelligences: Understanding the Many Ways We Learn." www.thethoughtfulchristian.com/Products/TC0388/multiple-intelligences.aspx.

Wimberly, Anne E. Streaty. *Soul Stories: African American Christian Education*, rev. ed. Nashville: Abingdon, 2005.

## Notes

1. "Rabbi," Hayim Lapin, *Anchor Bible Dictionary: Volume 5* (New York: Doubleday, 1992), 600-602.

2. Stephen D. Jones, *Rabbi Jesus: Learning from the Master Teacher* (Macon: Peake Road, 1997), 13.

3. Jones, *Rabbi Jesus*, 25.

4. David R. Bauer, "Disciple, Discipleship," *New Interpreters Dictionary of the Bible*, D–H: Vol. 2 (Nashville: Abingdon, 2007), 128.

5. Mark Biddle, *Deuteronomy*, Smyth & Helwys Bible Commentary (Macon: Smyth & Helwys, 2003), 128.

6. Peter Rhea Jones, *Studying the Parables of Jesus* (Macon: Smyth & Helwys, 1999), 20.

7. C. H. Dodd, *The Parables of the Kingdom* (London: Nisbet & Co. LTD, 1936), 16.

8. Robert Funk, *Parables and Presence: Forms of the New Testament Tradition* (Philadelphia: Fortress, 1982), 31–34.

9. Mark Moeller, "Christ Parables," *Christian Reflection: A Series in Faith and Ethics*, vol. 21 (Waco: Center for Christian Ethics, Baylor University, 2006), 51-53.

10. Jones, *Rabbi Jesus*, 38–39.

11. For further discussion of gender roles in public and private see Bruce J. Malina and Richard L. Rohrbaugh, *Social-Science Commentary on the Synoptic Gospels* (Minneapolis: Fortress, 1992), 348–49. Not all agree that Luke has elevated the role of women to that of men. See, for example, Sharon H. Ringe, *Luke*, Westminster Bible Commentary (Louisville: John Knox Press, 1995), 161–62, and Jane Schaberg, "Luke," *The Women's Bible Commentary*, ed. Carol A. Newsom and Sharon H. Ringe (Louisville: Westminster/John Knox Press, 1992), 275.

12. M. Abot 1:4-5. See Herbert Danby, ed. and trans., *The Mishnah* (Oxford: Oxford University Press, 1933), 449, in R. Alan Culpepper, "Luke," *New Interpreter's Bible*, vol. 9 (Nashville: Abingdon, 1995), 231.

13. Brandon Heath, lyrics © Peermusic Publishing, Sony/ATV Music Publishing LLC, ESSENTIAL MUSIC PUBLISHING.

14. See I. Howard Marshall, *New International Greek Testament Commentary: Commentary on Luke* (Grand Rapids: Eerdmans, 1978), 896, on the use of "Oh" in Luke 9:41.

15. Thomas Groome, *Religious Education: Sharing Our Story and Vision* (New York: HarperCollins, 1980), 136.

16. Daniel Aleshie, *Faithcare: Ministering to All God's People through the Ages of Life* (Philadelphia: Westminster Press, 1988), 50.

17. Parker Palmer, *To Know as We Are Known: A Spirituality of Education* (San Francisco: Harper & Row, 1966), 2.

18. Palmer, *To Know as We Are Known*, 32.

19. John Hendrix, *To Thessalonians with Love: An Interpersonal Commentary on 1 Thessalonians* (Nashville: Broadman, 1982), 13.

20. Karen Tye, *Basics of Christian Education* (St. Louis: Chalice, 2000), 10–12.

21. Lawrence Little, *The Objectives of Christian Education* (New York: National Council of Churches, 1958), quoted in Donald E. Miller, *Story and Context: An Introduction to Christian Education* (Nashville: Abingdon, 1987), 77.

22. Palmer, *To Know as We Are Known*, 69.

23. Charles R. Foster, *Educating Congregations: The Future of Christian Education* (Nashville: Abingdon, 1994).

24. Miller, *Story and Context*, 82.

25. Paul Dietterich, Center for Parish Development Missional Convocation: A Foretaste! Transforming Leadership Practices, Chicago, 25 July 2015.

26. H. Richard Niebuhr, *The Purpose of the Church and Its Ministry: Reflections on the Aims of Theological Education* (New York: Harper and Brothers, 1956), quoted in Miller, *Story and Context*, 78.

27. Maria Harris, *Fashion Me a People*, 63.

28. Harris, *Fashion Me a People*, 68–70.

29. For more help with curriculum content areas, see the following:

A Cooperative Baptist resource for church planning by Bob Fulbright (chair), *Destinations: Mapping Your Congregation's Missional Journey, A Resource for Church Planning* (Cooperative Baptist Fellowship, 2007) and Robert G. Fulbright, ed., *A Guide to Formations: Christian Education through the Sunday School* (Macon: Smyth & Helwys, 1994), 11–15, lists nine content areas: the Biblical Story, Worship, Building Community, Church History, Christian Ethics, Missions/Ministries, Outreach/Evangelism, Formation/Discipleship, and Theology/Doctrine.

In a 1993 study of 150 congregations and 11,122 church members, the Search Institute identified content emphases to help youth and adults grow in faith. See Eugene C. Roehlkepartain, *The Teaching Church: Moving Christian Education to Center Stage* (Nashville: Abingdon, 1993), 119–35. For youth, the content emphases were the Bible, Core Theological Concepts, Friendship, Human Sexuality, Substance Abuse, Values and Moral Decision-making, Concern for Others, and Responsibility for Poverty and Hunger. A separate list for adults named Biblical Knowledge and Understanding, Moral Decision-making, Multicultural Awareness, and Global Awareness.

C. Sybil Waldrop, *Teaching Preschoolers the Bible* (Nashville: Convention Press, 1991), 83–96, provides a preschool Bible scope and sequence with these core areas: God, Jesus, Bible, Church, Family, Others, Self, Natural World.

Jerome W. Berryman, Cheryl V. Minor, and Rosemary Beale, *The Complete Guide to Godly Play, Volume 2* (Denver: Living the Good News, 2010), has a story about the circle of the church year, and Israel Galindo provides a "A Model for Church Life as Curriculum" in *The Craft of Christian Teaching: Essentials for Becoming a Very Good Teacher* (Valley Forge: Judson, 1998), 172–73.

30. Leon McKenzie and R. Michael Harton, *The Religious Education of Adults* (Macon: Smyth & Helwys, 2002), 155–56.

31. For more on curriculum planning, see McKenzie and Harton, who recommend a planning process for "Developing a Model for Congregational Religious Education" in *Religious Education of Adults*, 150; Karen Tye, in *Basics of Christian Education* (St. Louis: Chalice, 2000), provides a "Curriculum Resource Selection Process," 59–65; Israel Galindo and Marty C. Canaday's book, *Planning for Christian Education: A Community of Faith Approach* (St. Louis: Chalice, 2010), presents a comprehensive approach to planning for Christian formation through all aspects of the church's life and includes a chapter on planning centered on the church year; Nancy Ferguson, *The Christian Educators' Guide to Evaluating and Developing Curriculum* (Valley Forge: Judson, 2008), presents a process with plans and worksheets to help an educational leadership team make decisions about curriculum, including content scope and sequence.

32. See "Motivation Theory," in McKenzie and Harton, *Religious Education of Adults*, 145–48.

33. Harris, *Fashion Me a People*, 63.

34. Jean Piaget, *Origins of Intelligence in the Child* (London: Routledge & Kegan Paul, 1936).

35. Cynthia Jones Neal, *Nurture that Is Christian: Developmental Perspectives on Christian Education* (Grand Rapids: BridgePoint Books, 1998), 135.

36. Erik H. Erikson, *Childhood and Society* (New York: W.W. Norton and Company, Inc., 1950).

37. Erikson, *Childhood and Society*, 246.

38. Les Steele, "The Power of Erikson," ch. 5 of *Nurture that Is Christian: Developmental Perspectives on Christian Education*, ed. James C. Wilhoit and John M. Dettoni (Grand Rapids: Baker Books, 1995), 277.

39. Steele, "The Power of Erikson," ch. 5 of *Nurture That is Christian*.

40. James W. Fowler, *Stages of Faith: The Psychology of Human Development and the Quest for Meaning* (San Francisco: Harper & Row, 1981), 121.

41. Fowler, *Stages of Faith*, 132–33.

42. Fowler, *Stages of Faith*, 149.

43. Fowler, *Stages of Faith*, 164.

44. Fowler, *Stages of Faith*, 173.

45. Fowler, *Stages of Faith*, 185.

46. Fowler, *Stages of Faith*, 185.

47. Fowler, *Stages of Faith*, 201.

48. Fowler, *Stages of Faith*, 276.

49. Fowler, *Stages of Faith*, 286–87.

50. See John Westerhoff, *Will Our Children Have Faith?* (HarperSanFrancisco, 1976); Lawrence Kohlberg, *The Philosophy of Moral Development: Moral Stages and the Idea of Justice* (San Francisco: Harper & Row, 1981).

51. Isabel Briggs Myers with Peter B. Myers, *Gifts Differing: Understanding Personality Type* (Mountain View, CA: Davies-Black Publishing, 1995). See www.myersbriggs.org.

52. Don Richard Riso and Russ Hudson, *The Wisdom of the Enneagram: The Complete Guide to Psychological and Spiritual Growth for the Nine Personality Types* (New York: Bantam Books, 1999). See www.enneagraminstitute.com.

53. Jerome W. Berryman, *How to Lead Godly Play Lessons*, vol. 1 of The Complete Guide to Godly Play (Denver: Living the Good News, 2002), 49.

54. David Elkind, *The Hurried Child: Growing Up Too Fast Too Soon* (Reading, MA: Addison-Wesley, 1981).

55. Walter B. Barbe and Michael N. Milone Jr., "What We Know about Modality Strengths: Research that Shows Students Have Different Modality Strengths Should Be Used to Improve Learning," *Educational Leadership* 38/5 (February 1981): 378.

56. Howard Gardner, *Frames of Mind: The Theory of Multiple Intelligences* (Gardner, NY: Basic Books, 1983).

57. See Howard Gardner, *Frames of Mind*, and *Multiple Intelligences: New Horizons*, Revised and Updated (New York: Basic Books, 2006); Bradley Wigger, "Multiple Intelligences: Understanding the Many Ways We Learn," www.thethoughtfulchristian.com/Products/TC0388/multiple-intelligences.aspx. The descriptors in parentheses are from the children's book, Thomas Armstrong, *You're Smarter than You Think: A Kid's Guide to Multiple Intelligences, Revised and Updated* (Minneapolis: Free Spirit Publishing, 2014).

58. Howard Gardner, *Intelligence Reframed* (New York: Basic Books, 1999), 46–55.

59. Linda Campbell, Bruce Campbell, and Dee Dickinson, *Teaching and Learning Through Multiple Intelligences*, 3rd ed. (Boston: Pearson Education, Inc., 2004), xx–xxi.

60. Campbell et al., *Teaching and Learning Through Multiple Intelligences*, xx.

61. For more, see Campbell, Campbell, and Dickinson, *Teaching and Learning through Multiple Intelligences*, ch. 1, 1–30; Thomas Armstrong, *Multiple Intelligences in the Classroom*, 3rd ed. (Alexandria, VA: ASCD, 2009), 84–87.

62. Campbell et al., *Teaching and Learning through Multiple Intelligences*, xx.

63. For more, see Campbell, Campbell, and Dickinson, *Teaching and Learning through Multiple Intelligences*, ch. 2, 31–62; Armstrong, *Multiple Intelligences in the Classroom*, 87–90.

64. Campbell et al., *Teaching and Learning through Multiple Intelligences*, xxi.

65. For more, see Campbell, Campbell, and Dickinson, *Teaching and Learning through Multiple Intelligences*, ch. 3, 63–92; Armstrong, *Multiple Intelligences in the Classroom*, 93–96.

66. Campbell et al., *Teaching and Learning through Multiple Intelligences*, xx.

67. For more, see Campbell, Campbell, and Dickinson, *Teaching and Learning through Multiple Intelligences*, ch. 4, 93–126; Armstrong, *Multiple Intelligences in the Classroom*, 90–93.

68. Richard B. Vinson's commentary on Luke includes two such representations by Allori and Velazquez: *Luke*, Smyth & Helwys Bible Commentary (Macon: Smyth & Helwys, 2008), 344–46. The artist He Qi has a painting of this story, and you may find others.

69. Campbell et al., *Teaching and Learning through Multiple Intelligences*, xxi.

70. For more, see Campbell, Campbell, and Dickinson, *Teaching and Learning through Multiple Intelligences*, ch. 5, 127–52; Armstrong, *Multiple Intelligences in the Classroom*, 96–98.

71. Campbell et al., *Teaching and Learning through Multiple Intelligences*, xxi.

72. Campbell et al., *Teaching and Learning through Multiple Intelligences*, 156–57.

73. For more, see Campbell, Campbell, and Dickinson, *Teaching and Learning through Multiple Intelligences*, ch. 6, 153–84; Armstrong, *Multiple Intelligences in the Classroom*, 99–101.

74. Campbell et al., *Teaching and Learning Through Multiple Intelligences*, xxi.

75. For more, see Campbell, Campbell, and Dickinson, *Teaching and Learning through Multiple Intelligences*, ch. 7, 185–218; and Armstrong, *Multiple Intelligences in the Classroom*, 101–104.

76. Campbell et al., *Teaching and Learning through Multiple Intelligences*, xxi.

77. Gardner, *Intelligence Reframed*, 74.

78. Thomas H. Groome, *Will There Be Faith? A New Vision for Educating and Growing Disciples* (New York: HarperOne, 2011), 18.

79. Groome, *Will There Be Faith?* 264.

80. Groome, *Will There Be Faith?* 331.

81. Groome, *Will There Be Faith?* 337.

82. Groome, *Will There Be Faith?* 342.

83. David A. Kolb, *Experiential Learning: Experience as the Source of Learning and Development* (New Jersey: Prentice-Hall, 1984); John D. Hendrix, *Nothing Never Happens: Experiential Learning and the Church* (Macon: Smyth & Helwys, 2004); G. Ted Taylor, "Experiential Learning: The Learning Style Inventory," *Adult Leadership* 19, no. 7 (April 1989).

84. John D. Hendrix, *Nothing Never Happens: Experiential Learning and the Church* (Macon: Smyth & Helwys, 2004), 18 and chs. 3–6; John D. Hendrix, *To Thessalonians with Love: An Interpersonal Commentary on 1 Thessalonians* (Nashville: Broadman, 1982), 16–23, 134.

85. Hendrix, *Nothing Never Happens*, 18.

86. Hendrix, *Nothing Never Happens*, 18.

87. Hendrix, *Nothing Never Happens*, 18.

88. Hendrix, *To Thessalonians with Love*, 20.

89. Hendrix, *Nothing Never Happens*, 107.

90. Hendrix, *Nothing Never Happens*, 18.

91. Hendrix, *Nothing Never Happens*, 113.

92. Anne E. Streaty Wimberly, *Soul Stories: African American Christian Education*, rev. ed. (Nashville: Abingdon, 2005).

93. *Global Bible Commentary* (Nashville: Abingdon, 2004).

94. *Return to Babel: Global Perspectives on the Bible* (Louisville: Westminster John Knox, 1999).

95. Mark Tidsworth and Ircel Harrison, *Disciple Development Coaching: Christian Formation for the 21st Century* (Macon: Nurturing Faith Inc., 2013), Kindle ed., location 575.

96. Tidsworth *Disciple Development Coaching*, location 678–86.

97. Israel Galindo and Marty C. Canaday, *Planning for Christian Education: A Community of Faith* (St. Louis: Chalice, 2010), 98–113.

*Chapter 4*

# Prayer

## Conversations with Mary and Sam on Prayer

I wanted to talk to my new friends about prayer, so I invited them to my favorite place to pray, the Abbey of Gethsemani Monastery in central Kentucky. They agreed, so we made the hour-long drive through the rolling hills of Kentucky to this secluded, silent monastery. First, we each went our separate ways to enjoy some silent prayer, sitting in the garden and walking the woods around the monastery. Then, we went to the church to join the monks chanting the psalms. There is something ancient and holy about hearing these Gregorian chants offered by monks who have dedicated their whole lives to prayer.

After worship, we found three chairs under a shade tree in an area of the monastery designated for conversation.

"So what do you think of Gethsemani?" I asked.

"This is a great place," Sam answered. "I liked the statues of Jesus praying in the Garden of Gethsemane with the disciples sleeping nearby. Jesus had asked them to stay awake and pray, but they couldn't stay awake . . . and at a time when Jesus needed them most."

"And how about you, Mary?" I asked, turning in my seat toward her.

"This is truly a special place for prayer," Mary offered. "I can see why you like it here. I found it to be a peaceful place for silence and prayer."

"Yes, Mary," I agreed. "That's why I like coming here so much. I find it easy to pray here."

"Why is that?" Mary wondered.

"The silence; the architecture; God's beautiful creation; the worship services; the example of monks who live a life of prayer." I leaned back in my chair, at ease, staring up at the trees above.

"But when it comes to the day-to-day routine back home, I have more difficulty praying," I continued, tensing up at the thought of the more hectic pace of normal life. "I have to admit that I can identify with Martha. I know I should pray more, but I have trouble making the time for it. I have so much to do in a day that I don't feel like I have time to pray. Then, when I do make time, I am interrupted by the phone ringing, a visitor, or a Martha-like voice in my head saying, 'quit wasting time, get to work and do something useful.' Even when I am free from distractions, I find myself constantly looking at my watch. I know that's not right, but I'm just being honest."

Leaning forward in my chair, I asked, "So how do you discipline yourself to turn aside for prayer every day when there are so many things to do and so many distractions around you?"

"Who says we can't pray while we go about the day-to-day routine?" Sam asked. "I believe that we can pray while we work."

"You sound like Brother Lawrence," I said, amused.

"Who?"

"Brother Lawrence worked in the kitchen of a monastery. He talked about praying to the God of pots and pans while he washed dishes. He said, 'I turn my little omelet in the pan for the love of God.' He believed in 'practicing the presence of God' in everything he did."

"Yes, exactly," Sam agreed, "Pray as you go. . . . I like Brother Lawrence. Interesting that he worked in the kitchen like Martha. Sounds like he was a kind of praying Martha."

"We should make all of life a prayer," Mary said. "But we still need to retreat from the noisy world regularly for quiet time with God." She paused for a moment, then asked, "Keith, when you're not working or praying, what kinds of things do you like to do for fun?"

I wasn't sure what this had to do with anything, but after thinking about it, I answered, "Go to a ballgame. Watch a movie with my wife."

"What's a ballgame?" Sam asked.

"It's a game people play with a ball. Sometimes they hit it with a bat . . . uh, stick . . . and run around while the other team tries to catch it. Or in another kind of ballgame you try to throw a ball into a basket."

"And a movie?" Sam inquired again.

"Well, its basically pictures that move, that tell a story or make you laugh. A form of theatre perhaps."

"And how long does a ballgame or a movie last?" Mary continued.

"A couple of hours, generally."

"Wow! That long? Okay, when you watch people run around with a ball or look at moving pictures for two hours, do you hear Martha's voice in your head telling you to get to work?"

"No."

"Do you constantly think about the time and wonder, 'When will this be over?'"

"Not usually."

"So, for those things you enjoy, distractions are not a problem?"

"I guess not."

"Keith, prayer is not so much about making time or disciplining yourself," Mary concluded. "Prayer is about loving God so much that you truly enjoy being in God's presence."

I slumped back in my chair and the three of us sat in silence as I pondered Mary's words.

# Prayer

## *What Mary Teaches Us about Prayer*

Mary's experience of sitting in Jesus' presence, listening attentively, has often been held up as an example of prayer, meditation, and devotion. "Mary has chosen the better part," Jesus said, "which will not be taken away from her" (Luke 10:42). It was not wrong for Martha to work at cleaning house and preparing a meal or whatever these "tasks" were. Martha was attending to the important task of offering hospitality to a guest. When Jesus sent out the seventy missionaries (Luke 10:1-12), he offered a special blessing to all who received them: "peace to this house." And, as we have noted, in the parable of the Good Samaritan Jesus commends the Samarian for his action and says, "Go and do likewise." Martha's problem was not that she was active but that she allowed her "many tasks" to distract her from recognizing God's presence in her home. Martha's daily chores, as necessary as they may be, are temporary. Mary's prayerful relationship with Jesus is eternal.

Let us now return to Martha's house and join Mary at Jesus' feet and see what Jesus and Mary can teach us about prayer.

### Prayer Is Listening

Prayer is meditation, contemplation, and reflection. Perhaps many of us have grown up thinking of prayer, primarily, as talking to God—asking God for things or for God to care for people. Certainly, petition (making requests to God) and supplication (bringing concerns to God on behalf of others) are essential forms of prayer, but prayer is also listening to God. Luke wrote that Mary "listened to what [Jesus] was saying." Prayer is a conversation with God, which involves talking and listening. Since God is God, maybe listening is a good place for us to start. When we are silent before God and pay attention, we may hear God speak to our hearts words (or feelings) of direction, instruction, encouragement, correction, or comfort.

We listen to God in prayer, but we also listen to the community so that we might pray for them. When we listen intently to others in the community, we learn their hopes, hurts, joys, and fears and can pray for them with more empathy and compassion. Our neighbors' concerns become our own, and we share these concerns with God. Loving our neighbors in God's presence can be a form of prayer.

**Prayer Is Being with God**
Jesus is in the room. Jesus is always in the room, and, like Mary, we can sit at Jesus' feet in prayer. God is always present. Prayer is being aware of that presence. When we gather for prayer and begin to name people whom we would like the community to pray for, prayer has already begun. God is in the room, hearing our words and our hearts, before we bow our heads and verbalize our prayer list. When we as a community go about the work of the church—worshiping, conducting business and committee meetings, studying the Bible, mopping the floor, or serving meals—we can do so with a heightened awareness that God is actively present, listening and involved. When the church functions with this kind of awareness of God's presence, then the whole life of the church can become prayer, or prayerful.

Thomas Keating communicates the depth of Mary's experience of being with God:

> Mary is not doing anything but listening, yet as she listens her attention moves beyond the words or even physical appearance of Jesus. She penetrates to the divine Person present in the humanity that is visible and palpable. Her faith is expanding. Listening to the words of Jesus is not so much paying attention to what is said, but rather to the experience that is communicated at the deepest level of our being by the divine presence. This is what attracts us. It is not just the words, but the eternal Word of God that we assimilate and by which we are assimilated. This is what makes us Christians—and at the same time, it makes us pray in our very being. This is the ultimate purpose of every form of prayer, devotion, ritual, or sacrament. The word of God in Scripture orientates us towards the transformation of our entire being.[1]

Even when no words are spoken, prayer is communion with God at a deep level. Prayer is loving God and being fully present to God—heart, soul, mind, and body.

## The Lord's Prayer

After recording the story of Mary listening to Jesus in Martha's home, Luke continues the theme of prayer and devotion by giving us his version of the Lord's Prayer.

As busy as Jesus was—healing, casting out demons, teaching, arguing with religious leaders, and feeding the multitude—he found time for prayer. On one of those occasions, Luke tells us that Jesus "was praying in a certain place, and after he had finished, one of his disciples said to him, 'Lord teach us to pray.'" Jesus answered the disciple's request with a more concise version of the familiar Lord's Prayer:

> Father, hallowed be your name.
> Your kingdom come.
> Give us each day our daily bread.
> And forgive us our sins, for we ourselves forgive everyone indebted to us.
> And do not bring us to the time of trial. (Luke 11:1-4)

By the time the Gospels were written, the Lord's Prayer likely had become formalized through use by the worshiping community. Notice that the wording of the prayer is not "give *me* each day *my* daily bread." The prayer is a community prayer—"us," "our," and "we" instead of "me," "my," and "I"—even though we may tend to think of it as the private prayer of an individual. "So this is a communal prayer," Vinson writes, "even when offered by an individual. In Luke's scene, Jesus has just come from solitary prayer and is answering the question of a single disciple. But his instructions, which we should take to agree with his practice, are to pray thinking of oneself as part of a group."[2] And Willimon and Hauerwas conclude, "Thus the usual place to say this prayer is on Sunday, in church, amid the Body of Christ. Joining our voices with others in the repetition of this prayer, we are reminded that being a Christian is too tough to go alone."[3]

Asking Jesus to "Teach us how to pray" seems like such a basic question, almost like asking, "Teach us how to walk," and in some ways it is, yet we sense that there is more to learn. So let us make the same request Jesus' disciples made: "Lord teach us how to pray."

### "Father, hallowed be your name"

The designation "Father" indicates the relationship of God to Jesus and Jesus' disciples. God is like a father to us (or we can just as easily say "like a mother," since God is so far beyond our understanding of gender). God is like a loving parent who listens when God's children speak. We are family. Jesus then says that God's name is to be hallowed (Matthew adds "in heaven" to "Our Father"). To hallow is to give God honor and respect as the holy God. Together, "Our Father" and "hallowed be your name" acknowledge that God is both near and far (or imminent and transcendent, to use the traditional theological terms). God "our Father"/"our Mother" is personal enough to draw intimately near to humanity, and the "hallowed God" is big enough to create an entire universe.

Willimon writes,

> The God whom we have been taught by Jesus to address as "Our Father" is the one who rules the whole cosmos, who speaks in earthquake, wind, and fire. Any less of a god wouldn't do us much good. . . . Because we call God the Father who is "in heaven," we are bold to pray for such absurdly extravagant gifts as bread for the world, peace among the nations, healed marriages, cured cancer, rain.[4]

Thus, God who is both Father and hallowed is a God who is both approachable and able to respond when we approach.

### "Your kingdom come"

We have heard these words so many times while dressed in our Sunday best, sitting in an attractive sanctuary, among friendly church folk, that we may have forgotten that these are fighting words. "Your kingdom come" is a politically rebellious statement. We are praying that God's kingdom will come, not the world's kingdoms. In that sense, the words are un-Roman, un-American, unpatriotic, against any worldly kingdom that would claim ultimate authority over Christians' hearts and minds. We are not talking about armed rebellion here; instead, we are talking about stubborn and steadfast commitment to the way of God, which might mean turning the other cheek, sacrifice, or, as was true for Jesus, death. "Your kingdom come" means obedience and submission to God.

When we say God is king, not Herod, then we can assume that Herod will not like it and things could get deadly. When the wise men came to King Herod, asking for directions to the home of the newborn king of the Jews so that they might worship him, Herod lied and grumbled and murdered all the baby boys in the area. Praying "Your kingdom come" can be dangerous. Willimon and Hauerwas warn of the potential consequences for us today:

> In the face of this culture's pervasive hedonism, our idolatry of the flag, our worship of ourselves, and our assorted deities, give your life to the holy God of Israel whose name is to be hallowed in all that we do and the world will begin calling you "alien" and "exile." Our culture has a way of driving out of the discussion those who do not bow at the culture's altars.[5]

When we pray for God's kingdom to come, we acknowledge that God's kingdom is not completely here yet—that change is needed. As we submit to the reign of God, we experience a measure of God's kingdom now, and we pray for the day when God's reign will be fully realized.

What does this kingdom of God look like? The language of kingdom reminds us of so much of the New Testament. Jesus said that his purpose was to "proclaim the good news of the kingdom of God" (Luke 4:43). Jesus rejected Satan's offer to rule all the kingdoms of the world, saying, "Worship the Lord your God and serve only him." Jesus painted verbal pictures of the kingdom with parables that often began with the formula, "the kingdom of God is like . . . ." The kingdom of God is like a tiny mustard seed that grows into a tree and like yeast that leavens bread (Luke 13:19 and 21). The kingdom is easy for children (18:16-17) and the poor (6:20) to enter but difficult for the rich to enter (18:25). When we pray for the kingdom to come, we are praying to take part in this new kind of life as God intends, in contrast to the ways of the world's kingdoms.

So when we gather and pray, "your kingdom come," let us not forget that these are strong words and that by saying them we are committing to pattern the life of our community after the example and teachings of Jesus, worshiping and serving God alone as our ultimate authority. We are accepting God's vision, God's mission, for the church.

### "Give us each day our daily bread"

The prayer for daily bread assumes that God cares about our physical needs. The word here translated "daily" comes from the Greek word *epiousion*, which, according to Vinson[6] and other commentators, means "what is necessary for existence" or "daily subsistence rations." Using the prayer Jesus gave us, we are asking for the basic necessities of life—no more, no less; neither the distractions and suffering of an aching empty stomach nor overindulgence, gluttony, and greed. In a culture that praises independence, asking for daily bread acknowledges our dependence on God. Daily bread reminds us of the manna God rained down from heaven on the Israelites in the wilderness (Exod 16:1-36). In their hunger they cried out to God, and God provided bread from heaven. Each day God would provide the manna, but they were only to gather enough for one day. They were to trust God for their daily subsistence. When those with less faith in God tried to store up extra for the next day, they found it spoiled and infested with worms.

For an African refugee fleeing war, genocide, and famine; for the materially poor in Appalachia; or for a multitude of other peoples around the world who do not know where the next meal is coming from, the prayer for daily bread is a prayer for survival. For many of us in America, who have enough money to eat even more each day than is healthy and have money left over for houses, cars, televisions, and more, to pray for daily bread is a prayer to do with less. For many of us, the prayer for daily bread is a prayer that we might lead a less self-indulgent lifestyle.

As we have noted, the Lord's Prayer is a communal prayer. We ask for "our" daily bread, not "my" bread. We share our bread together. Those with more share with those who have less. "Our" daily bread is about feasting together at God's banquet table and loving our neighbors. Bread is a gift from God, not to be horded by a few, to the neglect and starvation of others. The first deacons, or servants of the church, were chosen out of concern for widows who were being neglected in the fellowship meals. From the gift of one small boy's lunch, Jesus shared with a multitude. Jesus was criticized for eating with sinners and tax collectors. When Jesus shared the bread and the cup at his last supper with his disciples, he said "This is my body and blood." And when the resurrected Jesus appeared to two men on the road to Emmaus, they did not recognize him until they broke bread together. Daily bread is shared in community with Jesus.

## "Forgive us our sins, for we ourselves forgive everyone indebted to us"

Every line of Luke's version of the Lord's Prayer is shorter than that of Matthew's, except this one. We best not leave out any of this part of the prayer—not the request for God's forgiveness we so desperately need or the part where we offer the same forgiveness to those who have wronged us.

This petition is part of what it means when God's kingdom comes to earth. The prayerful community is a community of people who, though sinners, have received God's grace and offer that same grace to others. A community that prays the Lord's Prayer is a forgiven and forgiving community. Confession, accountability, unconditional love for neighbors, and forgiveness are marks of a prayerful community.

We have missed the mark. We have failed to live up to the ideals of God's kingdom. Our relationship with God and neighbor is broken. When we do not love God with all our heart, mind, soul, and strength or our neighbors as ourselves, then this failure of relationship can lead to sinful acts like stealing, adultery, and even murder and to worshiping other gods. So praying the Lord's Prayer is confession time. Once again, the word "our" stands out. We might like to think of our sin as an individual and private matter between the lone Christian and God. However, Jesus' prayer brings our confession of sin into public worship. We confess and seek forgiveness for individual transgression, but we also confess and seek forgiveness for our corporate sin. As a community, we sometimes model ourselves after a sinful world more so than God's kingdom, and as citizens we participate in unjust political systems. The prayer of Jesus holds us accountable for individual and corporate sin and calls us to live a life more consistent with life as God intends.

### "Do not bring us to the time of trial"

Some find this phrase troublesome, as if God might lead us into temptation to sin or other trials. That interpretation probably reads too much into the phrase. It might simply be understood as a prayer for God to lead us away from trouble and temptation. We know that trials and temptations are unavoidable in life, yet we pray, "God, we prefer that if it is at all possible, you steer us away from any path that would cause us unbearable suffering or temptations so powerful we may not resist." Thus, this final appeal could be thought of as the church's prayer that we be spared the severe persecution that many Christians have experienced or as a prayer for guidance that we would be wise and walk according to the fruit of the spirit rather than the seven deadly sins.

The words of the Lord's Prayer, both here and in Matthew, are concise and easily memorized, making them conducive for use by the worshiping community. The words serve as a sort of outline for prayer, reminding us of some important elements of prayer. Learning to pray as Jesus taught does not simply mean learning to say the words; it also means living the words. We will learn the words quickly. Learning to live the prayer as a community of faith is an ongoing journey.

## *Praying in Community*

What does it mean to be a praying community? Whenever a Christian community gathers, for whatever reason, typically there is prayer. Especially in worship, we offer invocation prayers, prayers of the people, offertory prayers, prayers of confession and forgiveness, and benedictions. In other "prayer meetings" or in small Bible study groups, we may pray for others who are sick, in the hospital, or grieving. These public prayers in community bring us together as God's people and acknowledge that we are in God's presence.

Apart from the obvious public prayers in worship and small groups, does prayer practiced alone in private have any relevance to the community of disciples? After all, Jesus once said, "whenever you pray, go into your room and shut the door and pray to your Father who is in secret" (Matt 6:6), though we should remember that he was speaking to those who would make a show of prayer in order to gain personal praise. Do our silent prayers offered in our closets mean anything to the community? What place do fasting, contemplative prayer, meditation, *lectio divina*, prayer walking, and other forms of personal prayer have in the disciple community as a whole?

Inagrace Dietterich writes, "Within the life of the church we do not engage in isolated, private, and individualistic practices. Ecclesial practices involve people doing things *with* one another, even if these people are not engaged in this activity at the same time and place."[7] So even our so-called personal or private prayer practices can be done with the sense that we are doing them with the community. What exactly does that mean, and how do we pray with the community when we are alone? What does prayer in the closet have to do with the community? I went on a prayer retreat to the Abbey of Gethsemani Monastery with these questions in mind. From the silence and solitude of my Gethsemani closet, let me suggest some answers.

First, and perhaps most obviously, when we pray in private, we often pray for others. Part of our time alone with God may be spent praying for the community. Thus, praying for the community is a communal act that increases our care for and connection with the community. When we pray for the community, we are united in a powerful way, becoming one in heart, mind, and spirit, whether we are praying for a sick member of the community, for a mission effort, for an understanding of God's direction for the church, or praising God for God's blessings on the community.

Second, when we come together in Sunday school classes, small groups, prayer meetings, or for conversation in the fellowship hall, our prayer experiences from the past week become part of the community dialogue. Our fellow church members learn from our prayer experiences, and we can learn from their feedback. In that way, the community shares our private prayer life and helps deepen the prayer life of the community as a whole. As a teaching and learning community, we guide each other in all aspects of the Christian life, including prayer.

Our spiritual development should edify the community. One person of extraordinary spiritual insight and experience may lead the community to a new depth of spirituality, but if that person leaves the rest of us behind on their spiritual quest, then it ceases to be communal prayer and spirituality. The spiritual director or shepherd doesn't leave the flock behind.

Third, when I take care of my own spiritual life, I am also taking care of the community, since I am a member of the body. To use Paul's illustration, Christians are members of the body of Christ: "there are many members, yet one body. The eye cannot say to the hand, 'I have no need of you. . . .'" Self-maintenance is, therefore, community maintenance, because our spiritual health matters to the body: "If one member suffers, all suffer together with it; if one member is honored, all rejoice together with it" (see 1 Corinthians 12). When we are tending to our prayer life and our relationship with God, we are contributing to the health of the body of Christ.

Fourth, when we are alone with God, we are not alone only with God. When we pray, there is a sense in which we are truly praying with the praying community. Within the mystery of God, when we draw near to God, we draw near to others who are near to God, whether or not they are in the same room. If God is the center of our community, then the closer we move to that center, the closer we get to God and to each other.

Finally, let me say that, while we want to avoid the extremes of individualism, God does care about you and me as individuals. God does love you and me, and God desires to spend time with you and me, for our sakes and not just for how it affects God's community.

## Putting Prayer into Practice

What does it mean to be a community of prayer? Obviously, a prayerful community is one that prays together. Typically, a church will pray together in a variety of ways. In worship we pray to invoke God's presence, confess, praise, bless, and cry out for God's assistance through both spoken word and song. We pray God's blessings on our meetings and Bible study groups. We conduct prayer meetings where we may pray for the sick, for those who have lost loved ones and those facing crisis, for our nation and world, for missions and missionaries, for members who reside in nursing homes, and for God's guidance in important decisions. These forms of community prayer should not be neglected.

In addition to these expected prayers, there are other ways we might pray as a community.

## Praying with the Heart, Soul, Strength, and Mind

I have noted earlier that the terms "heart," "soul," "strength," and "mind" do not mean exactly the same thing to us today as they meant to Luke's original audience, but taken together they mean basically the same thing then and today. "Heart," "soul," "strength," and "mind" refer to the whole person. I will use these terms as we use them today—sort of—to speak to how the community can pray with our whole selves. If the prayer practices seem to overlap categories, that is good, since none of these practices can be confined to a single category. They do overlap, just as heart, soul, strength, and mind overlap. These categories are somewhat arbitrary and artificial but will give us a format for exploring a diversity of prayer experiences.

### Praying with the Heart

*Contemplative Prayer.* What I will say about contemplative prayer will be a gross oversimplification. I do not have the knowledge or depth of experience to adequately explain contemplative prayer the way Saint John of the Cross in *Dark Night of the Soul*,[8] the unknown author of *Cloud of Unknowing*,[9] Basil Pennington in *Centering Prayer*,[10] Teresa of Avila, or Thomas Merton can. So I will refer you to their works. What I will do is discuss some elements of contemplative prayer that may help those of us who are novices in our prayer life.

I grew up thinking of prayer, primarily, as talking to God. Daily prayer was a to-do list: confessing sins, saying thank you, praising God, and asking God's help for a number of people including myself. Certainly there is nothing wrong with any of these kinds of prayers, unless we forget to stop and listen to God and take time simply to be with God.

Contemplative prayer, sometimes called centering prayer or apophatic prayer, is the prayer of silence. Contemplative prayer is to "be still and know" that God is God (Ps 46:10). Contemplative prayer follows Jesus as he withdraws "to deserted places to pray" (Luke 5:16). Contemplative prayer is opening our heart's door to Jesus, who is patiently knocking (Rev 3:20). Contemplative prayer is listening to the still, small voice of God that is not heard in the wind, earthquake, or fire (1 Kgs 19:11-12). Contemplative prayer is Mary sitting quietly at Jesus' feet, listening intently (Luke 10:38-42). Contemplative prayer is being with God and loving God with all your heart.

Thomas Merton in his book *Contemplative Prayer* quotes Gregory the Great's classic definition of contemplative prayer,

> The contemplative life is to retain with all one's mind the love of God and neighbor but to rest from exterior motion and cleave only to the desire of the Maker, that the mind may now take no pleasure in doing anything, but having spurned all cares may be aglow to see the face of its Creator: so that it already knows how to bear with sorrow the burden of the corruptible flesh, and with all its desires to seek to join the hymn-singing choirs of angels, to mingle with the heavenly citizens and to rejoice at its everlasting incorruption in the sight of God.[11]

On the practice of contemplative prayer, Merton writes,

> We wish to gain a true evaluation of ourselves and of the world so as to understand the meaning of our life as children of God redeemed from sin and death. We wish to gain a true loving knowledge of God, our Father and Redeemer. We wish to lose ourselves in his love and rest in him. We wish to hear his word and respond to it with our whole being. We wish to know his merciful will and submit to it in its totality.[12]

Notice that contemplative prayer is not about grasping, striving, controlling, or comprehending but is more about letting go and submitting to God. Contemplative prayer is about letting go of our thoughts and our striving and letting God take control.

Contemplative prayer for some may begin with words something like this: "God, I give up. I've been working hard to try to figure it all out. I've been trying to earn my worth. I've been trying to say the right things. I've tried to understand you. But I'm tired. I don't know what to do or say. I can't do it on my own. I'm just going to sit here quietly and rest and let you hold me, and if you want, speak to me. I'm listening." Then, much silence.

God is so far beyond our ability to comprehend that we simply cannot know God by our own effort, creativity, or will. What we can do is be still and trust in the grace of a loving God to take care of us.

I attribute the experience of waiting for the birth of our second child with deepening my understanding of prayer. Because of some risks to our unborn child, my wife Dianne was put on bed rest several months before the birth and was mostly confined to the recliner in our living room. So we spent a number of hours together each evening, she in the recliner, me in the rocking chair next to her. Often we sat there without saying a word as I read and she worked on various projects. But even though we were not always talking to each other, I had this sense that we were together in a significant way, that I loved her and enjoyed simply *being* with her. I thought about how simply being with God, enjoying God's presence, can be prayer.

*Practicing Contemplative Prayer.* The practice of contemplative prayer is simple but can be difficult. Our minds are not easily quieted and tend to race from one thought to the next. Here are some suggestions for a group or individual engaging in contemplative prayer: (1) Find a quiet place, as free from distractions as possible. Sit up straight in a comfortable position, with eyes closed or focused on a point on the floor or table in front of you. (2) Decide how long you will pray, preferably twenty minutes or more. (3) Do not approach contemplative prayer with any agenda other than to be with God. (4) When practicing contemplative prayer, it can be helpful to use a sacred word. Any word that reminds you of God's presence can work—for example, God, Jesus, love, grace, or peace. The word is not to be repeated continuously but is repeated only when the mind is distracted. Whenever your mind begins to wander, to start trying to figure God out, or to initiate the conversation with God, saying the sacred word can bring you back to the center of God's presence. (5) Reflect on the experience. If in a group setting, group members may discuss the experience.

Walking meditation can be another way of practicing contemplative prayer. The walking path can help keep us focused on God. Glenn Hinson describes how he uses his daily morning walk for prayer:

> My own method, if I can call it that, is to walk three miles every morning before breakfast. I can't describe exactly what I do because I do not have a set routine. Some days I just walk. Some days I am overcome with awe as our great fiery sun comes up over the horizon. Some days I meditate on a passage or passages of scriptures. Some days I intercede for someone

or pray about some concern. I can tell you what results from this time of solitude and attentiveness: I am collected. I am present where I am, really present, not just halfway present. As a consequence, I get more done. My writing is deeper. My relationship with those around me is more satisfying for all.[13]

## Praying with the Soul

The word Luke uses for "soul" is the same word used for "breath" or "life." What would it mean to pray with one's soul or for life and breath to become a prayer? "Pray without ceasing" is the challenging exhortation written in the letter to the church in Thessalonica (1 Thess 5:17). Dr. Glenn Hinson suggests that, as Paul's missionary companion, Luke's emphasis on prayer may have been influenced by Paul, as reflected in Luke 18:1: "Then Jesus told them a parable about their need to always pray and not lose heart."[14] To always pray, or to pray without ceasing, could be a way of making every breath and all of life a prayer, but this would seem to be an extremely difficult if not impossible task. How can we pray without ceasing?

*The Jesus Prayer.* The question, "How can we pray without ceasing?" sent the Russian pilgrim in *The Way of Pilgrim* wandering in search of an answer. He found it in the Jesus Prayer, or the Prayer of the Heart: "Jesus Christ, Son of God, have mercy on me" (or some traditions add, "have mercy on me, a sinner"). He was taught to say this simple prayer first, three thousand times a day, then six thousand times a day, then twelve thousand until "my tongue pronounced the words entirely of themselves without any urging from me."[15] One could pray the Jesus Prayer with every beat of the heart and with every breath we take. "Thus," to pray with the heartbeat, Pilgrim teaches, "with the first beat, say or think 'Lord,' with the second, 'Jesus,' with the third, 'Christ,' with the fourth, 'have mercy,' and with the fifth 'on me.'" Or, to pray with the breath, "as you draw your breath in, say, or imagine yourself saying, 'Lord Jesus Christ,' and as you breathe again, 'have mercy on me.'"[16] "After no great lapse of time," Pilgrim explains, "I had the feeling that the prayer had, so to speak, by its own action passed from my lips to my heart. That is to say, it seemed as though my heart in its ordinary beating began to say the words of the prayer within each beat."[17]

The Jesus Prayer, "Jesus Christ, Son of God, have mercy on me, a sinner," is an ancient Christian prayer that derives from the cry for help from the blind beggar, shouted out to Jesus: "Jesus, Son of David, have mercy on me" (Luke 18:35-43, also Mark 10:46-52 and Matt 20:29-34). The words are simple yet profound. Pilgrim calls the prayer a summary of the Gospels: "What the Gospel is, that the prayer of Jesus is also, for the Divine Name of Jesus Christ holds in itself the whole gospel truth."[18] There is nothing magical about repeating the words; the significance is in the meaning of the words, in the experience of crying out to God and in listening to God's response.

*All of Life as Prayer.* Another way to pray without ceasing is to think of all of life as a prayer. Brother Lawrence, a Carmelite monk, cook, and dishwasher, taught us to "practice the presence of God" in the seemingly mundane tasks of life; "I turn my little omelet in the frying pan for the love of God."[19] Rather than seeking God through a "multitude of methods," he says, "is it not much shorter and more direct to do everything for the love of God, to use every one of our duties to show that love to Him, and to maintain His presence in us by the communion of our hearts with Him?"[20] Brother Lawrence speaks of what could be called unceasing prayer,

> I occupy myself solely with keeping myself in God's holy presence. I do this simply by keeping my attention on God and by being generally and lovingly aware of Him. This could be called practicing the presence of God moment by moment, or to put it better, a silent, secret and nearly unbroken conversation of the soul with God.[21]

John Killinger describes a simple way to pray without ceasing during the everyday tasks of life:

> St. Paul speaks of praying "without ceasing."
>   It is not as hard as it sounds, really. You merely learn to become aware of God's presence with you all the time, whatever you are doing.
>   A friend who commutes to work says that he sits and communes with God every time he stops at a traffic light.
>   You can do it every time you open the refrigerator.
>   Or when you brush your teeth.
>   The trick is simply to turn your thoughts toward God at lots of specific times every day.
>   One way is to practice remembering him while you are performing one specific action all week. When you are making up the bed for instance. Or setting the table. Or picking up your mail. Or walking to school.
>   Then, for the next week, pick another action.
>   What you will discover is that you remember God when you are doing last week's action, too. And the week's before that. It is a cumulative effect. Soon you will be thinking about God a great deal of the time.[22]

We sometimes speak of our lives as alternating between a life of activity like Martha and a life of contemplation like Mary, but Thomas Kelly writes that what we seek is "not alternation, but simultaneity, worship undergirding every moment, living prayer, the continuous current and background of life."[23] Kelly describes what a life of unceasing prayer can look like:

> There is a way of ordering our mental life on more than one level at once. On one level we may be thinking, discussing, seeing, calculating, meeting all the demands of external affairs. But deep within, behind the scenes, at a profounder level, we may also be in prayer and adoration, song and worship and a gentle receptiveness to divine breathings.[24]

Similarly, *The Way of the Pilgrim* describes how it is possible to go about even mentally demanding tasks while being continually aware that we are in God's presence,

> Imagine that a severe and exacting monarch ordered you to compose a treatise on some abstruse subject in his presence, at the steps of his throne. Although you might be absolutely occupied by your work, the presence of the king who has power over you and who holds your life in his hands would still not allow you to forget for a single moment that you are thinking, considering, and writing, not in solitude, but in a place which demands of you particular reverence, respect, and decorum. This lively feeling of the nearness of the king very clearly expresses the possibility of being occupied in ceaseless prayer even during intellectual work.[25]

So Christians can cultivate the awareness that we live and work at the foot of God's throne—not an exacting monarch but a merciful God who asks our obedience.

*A Group Prayer Experience using the Jesus Prayer.* Use these steps to help lead a small group through the Jesus Prayer:

(1) The Jesus Prayer: Introduce the experience and explain the Jesus Prayer. Repeat the Jesus Prayer frequently during the experience. *"Jesus Christ, Son of God, have mercy on me."* This is an ancient Christian prayer known as the Jesus Prayer or the Prayer of the Heart. It comes from a Bible story in which Jesus heals a blind beggar. The man cried out to Jesus, "Jesus, Son of David, have mercy on me!"

(2) Read Luke 18:35-43: Jesus heals a blind beggar. *"Jesus Christ, Son of God, have mercy on me."* Listen to the story prayerfully. Put yourself in the man's place, and imagine what you hear, feel, smell. What are you feeling during the story? Note that many at this time thought that blindness and other disabilities were punishment from God for sin. *"Jesus Christ, Son of God, have mercy on me."* Read Luke 18:35-43 slowly and with expression, especially when the man shouts out to Jesus.

(3) What does it feel like to lose your sight? *"Jesus Christ, Son of God, have mercy on me."* Now close your eyes. I will give you some questions to reflect on. Imagine that you have become blind. What does that feel like? How will being blind affect your work? Your family? Your hobbies? How will you adapt? *"Jesus Christ, Son of God, have mercy on me."*

(4) Where do you need mercy and care? (This could be a special concern, fear, hurt, worry, sin.) Speak to God about an area in your life where you would like to receive God's mercy and care. *"Jesus Christ, Son of God, have mercy on me."*

(5) Jesus is coming. You hear that Jesus is coming. You have heard that he has the gift of healing and has made people well. You have heard that Jesus has helped other people in situations like yours. *"Jesus Christ, Son of God, have mercy on me."*

(6) Pray the Jesus Prayer. Repeat the Jesus Prayer a number of times. You may wish to focus on a different word each time you say the payer, emphasizing "Jesus" the first time, "Christ" the second time, and so on.

Or you might say the prayer in time to your heartbeat: "with the first beat, say or think 'Lord,' with the second, 'Jesus,' with the third, 'Christ,' with the fourth, 'have mercy,' and with the fifth 'on me.'"[26]

Or you could pray the prayer with each breath: "as you draw your breath in, say, or imagine yourself saying, 'Lord Jesus Christ,' and as you breathe out, 'have mercy on me.'"[27] (Allow several minutes for group members to pray the Jesus Prayer. Close this time of prayer by saying aloud the Jesus Prayer.) *"Jesus Christ, Son of God, have mercy on me."*

(7) What do you want Jesus to do for you? Jesus asks you, "What do you want me to do for you?" Answer Jesus. Tell Jesus what you want him to do for you. *"Jesus Christ, Son of God, have mercy on me."*

Imagine how Jesus would answer your request. What does Jesus say in answer to your request? *"Jesus Christ, Son of God, have mercy on me."*

(8) Sharing. Invite group members to talk about the experience, sharing as much as they feel comfortable sharing.

## Praying with the Body

What does your body language say? I watched a show once in which a body language expert observed couples on a dinner date and analyzed what their posture was saying. Did they lean in? Did they fold their arms? How close did they sit to each other? How much eye contact did they make? All of these postures supposedly said something about how each felt about the other. Conversations with the couples after the date mostly confirmed what the expert suspected.

We might ask what our body language says about how we feel about God. Bowing our heads, standing, bowing at the waist, or kneeling can be ways of showing God honor, humility, submission, or remorse. The very act of bowing before God in prayer is a prayer that says, as in the Lord's Prayer, "Hallowed be your name." A hug or serving others with our hands and feet can be an expression of love for God: "as you did it for one of the least of these my children, you did it for me." When the congregation holds hands and prays, they are saying, "We are together in this," that at least two of us agree in what we are asking (Matt 18:19-20). When the church lays hands on a person and prays, that person may feel those many hands on the head and shoulders as the empowering touch of God and the support of a faithful community. Walking and praying can remind us that God walks with us and that we are on a spiritual journey. Daniel Wolpert, in *Creating a Life with God*, writes, "As our physical bodies move through space, our minds move too. And as our minds move, God can enter into our beings because movement creates space and new possibilities."[28] And, in a chapter titled "Praying with Our Bodies," Vernard and Bryant write, "When words do not come, our bodies may shape our prayers for us. We stretch upward and weep; we dance in delight; we fall to our knees or lie prostrate on the earth."[29] Thus, our bodies can be used as both an aid to prayer and meditation and an expression of prayer.

*The Way of Prayer: Companions in Christ* offers a prayer experience using the body that I found to be a meaningful expression of prayer. We were asked to "Imagine how various plants or animals assume postures of prayer: trees swaying in the breeze, flowers turning faces to the sun . . . . Feel free to look out the window or to find a place outdoors for inspiration."[30] Normally I'm self-conscious about that kind movement with my body, but no one was watching, so I tried it. The area where I lived had just been hit by a devastating ice storm, so when I looked out the window for "inspiration," the most obvious features I saw were trees bent to the ground and broken from the heavy weight of layers of ice covering them. So I imagined that I was a tree in my backyard. I held out my arms like branches and felt the ice pull me down as I bent, arms dropping, and twisted awkwardly. Holding that uncomfortable posture, I reflected on the things in life that weighed me down and sometimes kept me from experiencing the abundant life Jesus offers. I contemplated the sins, self-indulgences, distractions, and stresses that pulled me down. Then I imagined God's grace thawing the ice. I felt the water dripping off my branches and sheets of ice beginning to break loose. As the burden became lighter and lighter, I slowly stood upright, straight and tall with my arms outstretched to God. In a compelling way, the postures helped me express prayers of confession and praise and feel God's grace and forgiveness lifting me up.

While there are many other ways the body might be used in prayer, let us consider two examples, walking the labyrinth and fasting.

*Walking the Labyrinth.* Walking the labyrinth is an ancient meditation practice that was adapted by Christians as an aid to prayer, initially used as a substitute for the pilgrimage to Jerusalem. The Christian labyrinth is generally circular in shape and laid on out on the ground or floor. Though the labyrinth may look like a maze, there is no getting lost in it, as one single path winds its way to the center. The same path leads out from the center as one's steps are retraced. When walking the labyrinth, you may at one moment find yourself moving closer and closer to the center until you are walking immediately beside the center, and then you may find that the path takes you back to the outer edges.

Walking to the center is a time for letting go of the things in our lives that would keep us from God. Wolpert suggests that the disciple consider questions like these:[31]

- What is it like to be on this journey?
- Is there anything I need to let go of?
- Is there something blocking me from experiencing God's love?
- Am I in need of forgiveness?
- Is there anyone I need to forgive?

At the center, we rest in God's presence for as long as we like. Here we experience God's presence, listen, pray, and worship.

As we walk our way out again, we prepare to go back into the world with God and live out the implications of our time with God, whatever that may mean. Again, Wolpert offers questions for reflection:[32]

- In what new way might Jesus accompany you into the world?
- What are your thoughts and feelings as you contemplate going back out into your life?
- Do you come with any new insights, experiences, or plans?

Often when I pray, I find that my body is restless, ready to finish as soon as possible and move on to the next place or the next item on the to-do list. The labyrinth keeps my body moving on a path for the twenty, thirty, or more minutes it takes to walk it. The slow, twisting path helps keep my mind and body focused on God. And when I exit the labyrinth, often the focus on God continues as I move on to the other activities of my life.

A group may walk the labyrinth together, and even though participants will walk the labyrinth at a varied pace, there is a sense of community knowing we share a common journey. When you walk the labyrinth with other people, you never know for sure where others are in their journey—whether they are coming or going, whether they are close to the entrance or to the center. You only know if others are on the journey, or in the center, or outside the labyrinth. This is a little bit like the spiritual journey of the community. Often, we don't know on the surface where our neighbors are in their spiritual journeys, but there are times when we can see that a person is resting in the center of God's presence. There are other times when it may be clear that someone has abandoned the journey. The labyrinth reminds us of the importance of sharing our spiritual walk with others so that we can encourage and support one another.

Our town, Danville, Kentucky, has a beautiful outdoor stone labyrinth built behind the Presbyterian church on the campus of Centre College. Once, after I began to walk this labyrinth, a couple came and were looking around the area—not unusual in this public place. I didn't know them, but when they unexpectedly entered the labyrinth, I knew we had something in common. I felt a bond with these strangers for a few moments as we shared the experience together. We were on a spiritual journey. We were community. This experience of community is even more deeply felt when we share it with those we know well and love from our own faith community.

*Fasting.* Fasting is not a very popular form of prayer and devotion. In my experience, fasting gets little attention, and on those infrequent occasions when the church encourages a fast, it seems that for many fasting is out of the question. I once a led a group in a study of Richard Foster's book *Celebration of Discipline*.[33] The group diligently read each chapter and practiced the disciplines each week, but when we came to Foster's excellent chapter on fasting, few in the group participated in the suggested twenty-four-hour fast for the week. I remember as a child a time when my church encouraged members to skip a meal and give the cost of a meal to the world hunger offering. My parents gave the cost of a meal to world hunger, but we did not skip a meal. I can't say that I think of fasting as great fun, and I have too many times ended a fast sooner than planned. We have been conditioned to think that skipping a meal is unhealthy, impossible, or crazy. Foster writes, "In a culture where the landscape is dotted with shrines to the Golden Arches and an assortment of Pizza Temples, fasting seems out of step with the times," and "the constant propaganda fed us today convinces us that if we do not have three large meals each day, with several snacks in between, we are on the verge of starvation."[34] As I write this, I have just watched three food commercials offering bigger burgers or larger portions. Overindulgence and the desire for instant gratification is a problem in our society (as is watching too much television). We should not be surprised, then, that fasting is a neglected spiritual discipline among Christians in our culture, yet materialism is the very reason we need to practice fasting (health permitting).

There are numerous examples of fasting in the Bible. For example, Esther asked the Jews to fast for three days on her behalf before she went to the king to prevent the destruction of her people (Esth 4:16). Jewish law required fasting on the Day of Atonement, a day for repentance and atonement for sin (Lev 23:26-27). Moses fasted for forty days on Mount Sinai when God gave him the Ten Commandments (Exod 34:27-28). The great king David practiced fasting in a time of crisis (Ps 35:13-14). It was while the church in Antioch was worshiping and fasting that God, through the Holy Spirit, called Barnabas and Saul (Paul) to be missionaries to the world (Acts 13:1-3). The prophetess Anna, who rejoiced to see baby Jesus in her old age, was said to practice worship, fasting, and prayer in the temple, "day and night" (Luke 2:36-38). In Jesus' Sermon on the Mount he said, "whenever you fast . . . ," assuming his disciples would fast (Matt 6:16-18). When answering a question about why his disciples did not fast, Jesus pointed to the importance of both feasting and fasting: "The wedding guests cannot mourn as long as the bridegroom is with them, can they? The days will come when the bridegroom is taken away from them, and then they will fast" (Matt 9:15). So again, Jesus assumed there would come a day when his followers would fast.

After Jesus' baptism and before his public ministry began, Jesus went out into the wilderness, where he fasted for forty days. Jesus' response to the devil's temptation to turn stones into bread was, "One does not live by bread alone, but by every word that comes from the mouth of God" (Matt 4:4, see also Luke 4:1-4). Here Jesus gives us the primary purpose for fasting. It is to feast on the word of God. Fasting is not as much about doing *without* as it is about doing *with* God. We deny ourselves food in order to avail ourselves more fully to God. Fasting reminds us that, while we need our daily bread, what we need most of all is God's sustaining presence. Fasting reprioritizes our lives. Life is not about food or any material possessions that might possess us. Life, at its fullest, is about our relationship with God.

What is the purpose of fasting, and what do we do when we fast? Foster offers these reasons for fasting:

(1) "Fasting must forever focus on God."[35] Whatever other reasons we might have for fasting, a spiritual fast begins with God. Fasting is first and foremost an opportunity to focus on God in prayer and worship. When our stomach rumbles, we find ourselves obsessing about food, or feeling that we are getting weak, then we are reminded to listen to God and turn to God for strength. Mealtimes especially may provide a little extra time for prayer and devotion.

(2) "Fasting reminds us that we are sustained 'by every word that proceeds from the mouth of God' (Matt 4:4)."[36] Food does not sustain us. God sustains us. We may think it's our own hard work, talent, and ingenuity that sustain us, but it is God who sustains us. We are wholly dependent on God, not money, power, fame, intelligence, or any other thing. When we are instructed not to look miserable when we fast, that does not mean we should act like we are happy; we should truly be happy. Fasting is feasting on the word of God, feasting in God's presence.

When we fast, we may find that what we are feeling is not happiness but anger, depression, frustration, and grumpiness. This brings us to a third reason for fasting.

(3) "Fasting reveals the things that control us."[37] Fasting can show us how our desire to fill ourselves goes beyond our body's need for nourishment. The emptiness in our lives that we so often try to fill with food and other distractions may come to light during a fast. Paul warns about "enemies of the cross of Christ . . . whose god is their belly" (Phil 3:18-19) and people "who do not serve our Lord Christ, but their own appetites"

(Rom 16:18). Fasting helps keep God in control of our lives rather than the god of overindulgence. As we fast, we might pray, "God, reveal to me those things that control me. Show me the things other than you that I think I can't do without."

Food can be symbolic of the many things in life that vie for our devotion. Thus Foster suggests that there are other ways we might fast in addition to fasting from food. Since the "central idea of fasting is the voluntary denial of an otherwise normal function for the sake of intense spiritual activity," the fast can be applied to other things in our lives.[38] For example, in this electronic information age, a fast from media can be beneficial. A multitude of electronic devices has put all types of media and communication tools literally at our finger tips twenty-four hours a day, wherever we go: cable television, satellite television, streaming, internet, email, Facebook, Instagram, cell phones, smart phones and smart watches, texting and tweeting, radios, GPS, tablets, Zoom, and any other thing that has come out and will come out. With all of these distractions, it might be difficult to hear the still, small voice of God. We may come to believe that we cannot live without our electronic gadgets and computers. A fast from media for a designated period of time could make it easier to listen to God. In the stillness of a media fast, we might hear Jesus say, "One does not live by computer alone, or cell phone, television, or movies, but by every word that comes from the mouth of God."

(4) "Fasting helps us keep our balance in life."[39] We can be overcome by the demands of life. Our wants and needs can become confused. Our priorities can become jumbled. Fasting reminds us of what is truly important and can help us see more clearly what we need and what we only want. Food, and other things in our lives, finds its proper place. As a result of fasting, we may find that food tastes better and we appreciate it more for the nourishment it provides.

(5) We can add a fifth purpose for fasting. Fasting can help us identify with the poor and hungry. In a very small way, when we fast, we identify with those who go without eating, not by choice but because they have no food to eat. We get just a sense of what it must feel like to be hungry every day. And hopefully that feeling leads us to act and to give to put an end to poverty and hunger.

For those who have never practiced fasting and would like to try it, consider these recommendations:

*(1) Check with your doctor.* Some people have medical conditions that prevent them from fasting from food. Check with your doctor about whether or not you should fast. If your doctor does not recommend a full fast, perhaps your doctor can suggest a partial fast. Fasting is not recommended for children. Teenagers need to carefully consider what type of fast is healthy and how long they should fast.

*(2) Start slowly and work your way up to longer fasts.* If you have never fasted, begin by skipping one meal. Next, try a twenty-four-hour fast. After supper, don't eat again until supper the next day. Then you might try a thirty-six-hour fast or longer, which means for at least one full day you will not eat any meals. Drink plenty of water when you fast.

*(3) Don't give up.* The first few times you fast, you may only be focused on food and not receive the full spiritual benefit. Keep at it. Keep practicing and fasting will become more meaningful.

*(4) Fast because you want to grow closer to God.* Remember the primary purpose of fasting, and fast because you want to center on God. Pray and worship God while you fast. Make the five reasons above the focus of your prayer and reflection during the fast.

## Praying with the Mind

*Lectio Divina.* This ancient Christian practice is a prayerful reading of Scripture or divine reading of Scripture. Traditionally, *lectio divina* consists of four steps, or readings, of a passage of Scripture: (1) *lectio*: hearing the word, (2) *meditatio*: reflecting on the word, (3) *oratio*: prayers of response to the word, and (4) *contemplatio*: resting in the word.[40] Let's look at each of these.

(1) Read (*lectio*). We begin with a reflective reading of the Scripture passage. The focus is on listening. Reading the Scripture slowly, we listen for a word or phrase that God places on our hearts. It may be difficult to turn off our analytical minds, but we are not holding the text at a distance to objectively observe and critique it. We are not analyzing the text impersonally. We are listening to how the word of God speaks to us. Indeed, the Scripture is God's word to us, so what is God saying? As Daniel Wolpert says, "Listen for those words that tug at you, that invite you to go deeper into the mystery of God."[41] We listen for the word or phrase that God seems to lift off the page for us at this moment in our lives. After the passage is read, we take a moment to reflect.

(2) Reflect (*meditatio*): The passage is read a second time, perhaps from a different translation and, if in a group, by another reader. Again, we take

time to listen for the voice of God and meditate on the word or phrase that God has placed on our hearts. Wolpert suggests these questions for reflection: "So, allow your heart and mind to follow your word. What images come to mind? What thoughts, what feelings? Perhaps a particular memory is stirred, an unresolved situation in your life in need of healing, in need of Christ's touch."[42]

(3) Respond (*oratio*): The passage is read a third time. This time, having listened deeply to God, we are ready to offer our prayer of response. What response is called forth from you in this passage? Now that God has spoken to you, how will you respond? Our response is prompted by God's word to us. The prayer of response may take many forms: a prayer of praise and thanksgiving for God's goodness; a petition on behalf of oneself or another; confessing and asking God's forgiveness or offering forgiveness to another; or an answer of "Here am I send me" to God's call to act in some specific way.

(4) Rest (*contemplatio*): After a final reading of the text, we rest in God's presence. We allow the word to rest deep within our hearts and minds. No words need to be spoken here, but we simply enjoy God's loving presence. A good question for reflection is, "Do you know how much God loves you?" We ponder the whole experience of our encounter with God and soak up whatever insights or feelings God has offered us.

(5) Return (*incarnatio*): Jane Vennard and Stephen Bryant suggest a fifth step, "*incarnatio*" or "return." When we return to life, we return as a new transformed creation. We leave this encounter with God in Scripture to think, feel, or act differently in accordance with the word spoken to us. We have read God's word, meditated on it, responded to it, and rested in it, and now we go to live out God's word to us.

I might suggest another step, a preparatory step, as long as it does not interrupt the flow or the reflective mood (which can easily happen). In keeping with words beginning with the letter "r," I will call this step "research." In order to minimize the chance that we put words in God's mouth by misunderstanding the Bible, it could be helpful to come to some understanding of the text before we begin the personal encounter that is *lectio divina*. What is the context of the passage in the Bible and in its historical setting? What is the purpose of the writing? What questions need to be discussed so that we can hear a word of God more clearly through the text? Cultural influences and personal biases can make it more difficult for us to hear a transforming word from God. A careful study of the text can help us interpret it more faithfully and honestly. The risk with beginning with this step, though, is slipping into a more familiar analytical stance of holding the text at a distances rather than reflecting, responding, contemplating, and living.

*A Process for Lectio Divina.* Thus a process for *lectio divina* for an individual or group could look something like the following:

(1) Research: Study the word. Begin by choosing a passage in the Bible—a psalm, a story from the Gospels, the assigned Bible text for the day, or any other passage. Study the passage using Bible commentaries or other Bible study tools. Come to a basic understanding of the meaning of the text, asking questions such as Who was the original audience? Why was this book of the Bible written? How does this passage fit in the biblical context? What is the cultural and historical context? What additional information can help the reader understand the passage? It is not necessary to be comprehensive and answer all questions. Limit the time for this step. Sometimes you might consider skipping it.

(2) Read (*lectio*): Hear the word.
- Read the Bible passage.
- In silence, listen for the word or phrase in the passage that speaks to you.
- Be alert to your senses. What sights, sounds, textures, tastes, and smells does this passage elicit?
- Resist the urge to analyze or critique the passage.
- After reading the passage (or hearing it read), listen to God in silence.
- In group *lectio divina*, group members may share their words or phrases at this time without comment or discussion.

(3) Reflect (*meditatio*): Reflect on the word.
- Read the passage a second time. You might choose a different translation (and in a group process a different reader) for each step.
- Ask God to speak to you through this passage and the word or phrase God placed on your heart. Meditate on what God is saying to you.
- After reading the passage (or hearing it read) a second time, listen to God in silence.
- In group *lectio divina*, group members may share briefly (in a sentence or two) how they heard God speaking to them.

(3) Respond (*oratio*): Pray in response to the word.
- Read the passage a third time.
- What response is being called forth from you in this passage? What is God calling you to think, feel, do, or be? How will you respond to God?

- After reading the passage (or hearing it read) a third time, respond to God in silent prayer.
- In group *lectio divina*, group members may share briefly (in a sentence or two) how they responded to God.

  (4) Rest (*contemplatio*): Rest in the word.
- Read the text a final time.
- Allow the word to rest deep within you. Enjoy God's loving presence. Reflect on the entire experience.
- Rest in silence
- In group *lectio divina*, group members may freely discuss the experience.

  (5) Return (*incarnatio*): Put the word into action.
- Given this encounter with God, how will you now live? Maybe you want to decide on one small thing to do now as you return to the world, to your life.
- Pray silently.
- Go live the word.

### The Classics of Christian Devotion

I admit that, for me, reading the ancient classics of Christian devotion can be difficult. The language is often archaic, the perspectives born in a different culture at an earlier time, and the illustrations often unfamiliar. Yet the effort can be well worth it, for the classics are filled with devotional insights that have been meaningful to Christians through the years in a variety of contexts. The classics of Christian devotion offer time-tested guidance in the ways of prayer, like these words from Saint Augustine, "You stir man to take pleasure in praising you, because you have made us for yourself, and our heart is restless until it rests in you."[43]

Following are just a few of my favorite classics: *Confessions*, Saint Augustine; *Pensees*, Blaise Pascal; *Interior Castle*, Teresa of Avila, *Letters and Papers from Prison*, Dietrich Bonhoeffer; *The Seven Storey Mountain*, Thomas Merton; *The Practice of the Presence of God*, Brother Lawrence; *A Testament of Devotion*, Thomas R. Kelly; *Pilgrim's Progress*, John Bunyan; *The Imitation of Christ*, Thomas à Kempis; and *The Way of the Pilgrim* and *The Pilgrim Continues His Way*, anonymous Russian Christian.[44]

### Prayer Resources

Augustine. *Confessions*, A New Translation by Henry Chadwick. Oxford University Press, 1991.

Blythe, Teresa A. *50 Ways to Pray: Practices from Many Traditions and Times.* Nashville: Abingdon, 2006.

Bonhoeffer, Dietrich. *Letters and Papers from Prison: The Enlarged Edition,* ed. Eberhard Bethge. New York: Macmillan Publishing Company, 1971.

Brother Lawrence. *The Practice of the Presence of God,* trans. Robert J. Edmonson. Brewster, MA: Paraclete Press, 1985.

Bunyan, John. *Pilgrim's Progress.* 1678.

*The Cloud of Unknowing,* ed. James Walsh, S. J. New Jersey: Paulist Press, 1981.

Dietterich, Inagrace T. *Cultivating Missional Communities.* Chicago: Center for Parish Development, 1995.

———. *Teach Us to Pray: Nurturing Christian Prayer.* Chicago: Center for Parish Development, 1994.

Foster, Richard J. *Celebration of Discipline: The Path to Spiritual Growth,* rev. ed. San Francisco: Harper & Row, 1988.

———. *Fasting—20th Century Style,* message by Richard Foster. place. asburyseminary.edu/atsconferences/2222/.

Hinson, E. Glenn. *Seekers After Mature Faith: Deepening Devotional Life with Help from Christians of Past and Present.* Nashville: Broadman, 1968.

———. *A Serious Call to a Contemplative Lifestyle,* rev. ed. Macon: Smyth & Helwys, 1993.

———. *Spiritual Preparation for Christian Leadership.* Nashville: Upper Room Books, 1999.

Keating, Thomas. *The Better Part: Stages of Contemplative Living.* New York: Continuum International Publishing, 2000.

Kelly, Thomas R. *A Testament of Devotion.* New York: HarperCollins, 1969.

Killinger, John. *Prayer: The Act of Being with God.* Waco: Word, 1981.

Merton, Thomas. *Contemplative Prayer.* New York: Doubleday, 1996.

———. *The Seven Storey Mountain, Fiftieth Anniversary Edition.* New York: Harcourt Brace & Company, 1998.

Pascal, Blaise. *Pensees,* trans. A. J. Krailsheimer. London: Penguin Books, 1995.

Pennington, M. Basil. *Centering Prayer: Renewing an Ancient Christian Prayer Form.* New York: Doubleday, 1980.

Saint John of the Cross. *The Dark Night of the Soul,* trans. and ed. E. Allision Peers. New York: Doubleday, 1990.

Teresa of Avila. *Interior Castle,* trans. and ed. E. Allison Peers. New York: Doubleday, 1989.

Thomas à Kempis. *The Imitation of Christ.*

Vennard, Jane E., and Stephen D. Bryant. *The Way of Prayer: Companions in Christ.* Nashville: Upper Room Books, 2006.

Vinson, Richard B. *Luke.* Smyth & Helwys Bible Commentary. Macon: Smyth & Helwys, 2008.

*The Way of the Pilgrim* and *The Pilgrim Continues His Way,* trans. R. M. French. New York: HarperCollins, 1965.

Willimon, William H. and Stanley Hauerwas. *Lord, Teach Us: The Lord's Prayer and the Christian Life.* Nashville: Abingdon, 1996.

Wolpert, Daniel. *Creating a Life with God: The Call of Ancient Prayer Practices.* Nashville: Upper Room Books, 2003.

## Notes

1. Thomas Keating, *The Better Part: Stages of Contemplative Living* (New York: Continuum International Publishing, 2000), 19.

2. Vinson, *Luke,* 367.

3. William H. Willimon and Stanley Hauerwas, *Lord, Teach Us: The Lord's Prayer and the Christian Life* (Nashville: Abingdon, 1996), 17.

4. Willimon and Hauerwas, *Lord, Teach Us,* 34–35.

5. Willimon and Hauerwas, *Lord, Teach Us,* 47.

6. Vinson, *Luke,* 370–72.

7. Dietterich, *Cultivating Missional Communities,* 16.

8. Saint John of the Cross, *The Dark Night of the Soul,* trans. and ed. E. Allision Peers (New York: Doubleday, 1990).

9. *The Cloud of Unknowing,* ed. James Walsh, S. J. (New Jersey: Paulist Press, 1981).

10. M. Basil Pennington, *Centering Prayer: Renewing an Ancient Christian Prayer Form* (New York: Doubleday, 1980).

11. Thomas Merton, *Contemplative Prayer* (New York: Doubleday, 1996), 51.

12. Merton, *Contemplative Prayer*, 67.

13. E. Glenn Hinson, *Spiritual Preparation for Christian Leadership* (Nashville: Upper Room Books, 1999), 154.

14. E. Glenn Hinson, personal conversation, email, 2010.

15. *The Way of the Pilgrim* and *The Pilgrim Continues His Way*, trans. R. M. French (New York: HarperCollins, 1965), 13–15.

16. *The Way of the Pilgrim*, 90.

17. *The Way of the Pilgrim*, 19–20.

18. *The Way of the Pilgrim*, 27–28.

19. Brother Lawrence, in *The Practice of the Presence of God*, 146.

20. Brother Lawrence, in *The Practice of the Presence of God*, 146.

21. Brother Lawrence, *The Practice of the Presence of God*, 93.

22. John Killinger, *Prayer: The Act of Being with God* (Waco: Word, 1981), 15–16.

23. Thomas R. Kelly, *A Testament of Devotion* (New York: HarperCollins, 1969), 13.

24. Kelly, *A Testament of Devotion*, 9.

25. *The Way of the Pilgrim*, 176.

26. *The Way of the Pilgrim*, 90.

27. *The Way of the Pilgrim*, 90.

28. Daniel Wolpert, *Creating a Life with God: The Call of Ancient Prayer Practices* (Nashville: Upper Room Books, 2003), 125.

29. Jane E. Vennard and Stephen D. Bryant, *The Way of Prayer: Companions in Christ* (Nashville: Upper Room Books, 2006), 71.

30. Vennard, *The Way of Prayer*, 23.

31. Wolpert, *Creating a Life with God*, 186.

32. Wolpert, *Creating a Life with God*, 187.

33. Richard J. Foster, *Celebration of Discipline: The Path to Spiritual Growth*, rev. ed. (San Francisco: Harper & Row, 1988).

34. Foster, *Celebration of Discipline*, 47.

35. Foster, *Celebration of Discipline*, 54–55.

36. Foster, *Celebration of Discipline*, 55.

37. Foster, *Celebration of Discipline*, 55–56.

38. Fasting, 20th Century Style, message by Richard Foster, jeffreygarner.typepad.com/files/richard-foster-fasting-20th-century-style.pdf

39. Foster, *Celebration of Discipline*, 56.

40. For many of the ideas in this section, I have drawn on the thoughts of Vennard and Bryant, *The Way of Prayer*, 82–85, including the "r" words: read, reflect, respond, rest, and return.

41. Wolpert, *Creating a Life with God*, 43.

42. Wolpert, *Creating a Life with God*, 44.

43. Augustine, *Confessions*. A New Translation by Henry Chadwick (New York: Oxford University Press, 1991), 3.

44. For more suggestions, see Glenn Hinson's, "Experiencing Grace through Other Writings," in *Spiritual Preparation for Christian Leadership* (Nashville: Upper Room Books, 1999) or in *Seekers After Mature Faith: Deepening Devotional Life with Help from Christians of Past and Present* (Nashville: Broadman, 1968), an excellent guide to the classics of Christian devotion, if you can find it.

*Chapter 5*

# Missions

## Conversations with Mary and Sam on Missions

"Let's talk about missions and ministry."

"Yes, finally," Sam said enthusiastically, "my favorite subject."

"I'm not surprised. For many Christians today, you are *the* model for ministry. Matthew 28:19-20—the Great Commission, we often call it—may be the theme verse for missions, but you are the ministry hero—the Good Samaritan, we call you."

"Ha. You're funny," Sam responded, a little annoyed.

"I'm serious. Yours is probably the most popular of Jesus' parables and you're the most beloved character."

"That's hard to believe. In my day 'hero,' 'popular,' and 'beloved' would never be used with 'Samaritan.' They certainly would never call me 'Good Samaritan.'"

"How could anyone not like you, Sam?"

"Ask Mary."

"Mary?"

"He's right, I must confess," Mary answered, lowering her head. "I've learned to love Sam as my neighbor, but it wasn't easy because of the way I was raised. I did not like Samaritans at all."

"Why?"

"I'm ashamed to say it, but we believed that Samaritans were an impure race, part Gentile, part Israelite."

Sam responded, "We believe we are true descendants of the Israelites."

Mary continued, "We recognize the Torah—the first five books of the Bible—plus the Psalms, prophets, and other writings given by God as authoritative."

"We accept only the Torah," Sam noted.

"We worship God at the temple in Jerusalem."

"We worship God at the temple on Mount Gerizim."

Mary turned to me, "Would you like us to go on?"

"No, I think I've got the picture. Let's talk about your story. You are the example for helping others."

Sam added, "If you think this story is just an example story for others to follow, you are missing a major point."

"And that is?"

"A neighbor is not just someone who is like you and who needs your help. A neighbor is also someone who is not like you—maybe even someone you don't like. And the very person you were taught not to like could be the person to help you out of the ditch."

Mary added, "So, as Jesus so often did, he reminded us of God's love for the outcast, the hated, the dispossessed."

"I see."

Sam scooted to the edge of his seat restlessly. "Enough of that. As you said, 'Let's talk about missions and ministry.'"

"Okay, let's do that. There are a couple of issues—tensions, you might say—that we often discuss and sometimes even debate when we talk about missions and ministry. First, is missions local or global? When some think of missions, they think of missionaries in faraway places like Africa, India, or Japan, and mission action is primarily financial and prayer support and education. Others say missions begins at home and, in practice, it ends there for some. They have little interest in supporting any mission effort that is not within our church or town."

Sam, still on the edge of his seat, said, "That's easy. Do both. Why choose?"

"Yes," Mary agreed, "but there are still decisions to be made about how churches will allocate their resources of time and money. No one church can do it all. Each Christian community must discover its unique gifts and calling and respond as God leads. Every church should find a balance. Acts 1:8 provides a good guide. Jesus said you will be my witnesses in Jerusalem . . . ."

Looking at me, Mary added, "Jerusalem is for those who want missions at home," and then she continued reading, "in all Judea and Samaria—"

Sam interrupted, "Hey, thanks for including me."

"—and to the ends of the earth," Mary concluded.

Sam leaned back in his chair and smiled. "I believe that includes everybody, the next door neighbor, the surrounding areas, bad people like me, and the whole world. Next question."

"Okay, *Good* Sam. We'll move on for now. The second issue deals with ministry that is focused on immediate needs versus ministry that is focused on systemic issues, seeks long-term solutions, and includes assets-based community development and advocacy."

"Systemic? Community development? Advocacy? What are you talking about?" Sam shook his head.

"I heard a story once that helped me understand. It goes something like this: 'Imagine a stream. The stream has a strong, rapid current, and you notice people in the stream. They are struggling as they are being swept downstream. They are drowning.'"

"People are drowning?" Sam shouted as he jumped to his feet, "Where? Why are we still sitting here when people are drowning?"

"Calm down. It's just a story."

"And so am I," Sam said, offended. "Are you saying that characters in stories don't matter?"

"Sorry, Sam. I didn't mean to offend you."

"Quick, let's go to this stream and try to save them," Sam commanded as he ran to the once imaginary stream that was now real.

Mary and I followed. Sam arrived first and immediately dove in. He scooped up a child in one arm and grabbed a man by the collar and dragged them both to shore. Mary calmed a woman and pulled her onto her back. I saw a teenage girl, about the age of my younger daughter, go completely under. I was able reach deep, take her hand, and pull her gasping to the surface. For several minutes, the three of us worked frantically to pull people from the stream until most were rescued. A few rushed past us and were well downstream. One by one, more people were floating down the stream toward us. We continued to pull them from the rushing waters.

While Sam waded out to pluck another drowning person from the stream, he looked over his shoulder at me and asked, "So are you going to finish your story?"

"Oh yes, the story. Well, sooner or later, seeing all these people drowning in the stream, we might wonder, 'How are all these people getting in the stream? Did they all fall in? Is someone throwing them in?'"

Mary wondered, "Maybe they were simply wading and didn't realize how strong the current was?"

"Perhaps. So why don't we go upstream and see why all these people are ending up drowning in this stream and see if we can stop it? That is advocacy. That is ministry focused on systemic causes. That is a long-term solution. We should go upstream and see what is going on."

"But people are drowning right here, right now," Sam protested.

"And they will continue to drown unless we can get to the root of the problem."

"So who do you want to let drown?" Sam responded angrily. "How about this little boy?" Sam lifted a curly-headed preschooler from the water. "Do you want me to throw him back so we can take a stroll upstream? Or maybe that woman over there, who could be your mother. Do you want to leave her?"

"Okay, I get your point, but what do we do?"

Mary took charge and said, "Sam, you stay here, and we'll go upstream. You minister to these immediate needs. We'll look for long-term, systemic solutions and be advocates for people drowning in streams, if needed."

With that the story ended and the three of us were back in my office. Oddly, Sam and Mary were dry, but I was still soaking wet.

## Missions

Tyler Wash, a teenager on a mission trip, had heard about Anne Margaret's home. He had heard about the terrible living conditions for this grandmother and her grandchildren, but no one could imagine what Anne Margaret's house was like until they saw it. Tyler went with a group to deliver a meal to this woman who had become a friend to many from our church. He saw holes in the walls that could not stop the wind, the bare, cracked floors that could not hold back the dirt, a roof that could not shed water, and the few pieces of tattered furniture in the indescribably tiny house. When Tyler came back to the cabin where the mission team was staying, he was broken. He couldn't believe anyone could have so little, while he had so much. He sat on the porch and wept. As result of his experience, Tyler has become an advocate for missions. Tyler's story is a familiar one. Many Christians hear God's call to love neighbors and, seeing a neighbor in distress, are moved to compassionate action and a love for missions.

Missions, as I will use the term in this chapter, could be thought of as a combination of ministry functions: witness, proclamation, evangelism, service, social ministries, and justice advocacy. But since so many churches and denominations have missions organizations and "missions" is a term that many find inspiring, we will treat missions as a single, though multifaceted, function of the church. Missions as used here is a piece of the missional church—the church in all of its functions on mission with God in the world. Missions is loving your neighbor as yourself.

"Love God . . . and your neighbor as yourself" was the lawyer's answer to his own question, "What must I do to inherit eternal life?" When Jesus affirmed the lawyer's answer, the conversation might have ended, but the lawyer had another question: "Who is my neighbor?" Jesus answered him with a story—the popular parable of the "Good Samaritan."

## *Missions Is Mutual*

The shifts in Jesus' Good Samaritan story are interesting and insightful for an understanding of neighbor love and missions. The lawyer asked, "Who is my neighbor?" Jesus answered with a parable about a man robbed, beaten, and left on the side of the road. When a story begins this way, we expect there to be a hero, and we—and Jesus' Jewish audience—expect to identify with that hero. However, after two religious leaders pass by without offering assistance, Jesus surprises his audience by bringing a despised Samaritan down the road. The listener is left with no choice about who to be, since the Jewish hearer could never identify with a bad Samaritan. Jesus places the audience on the side of the road, changing the question from "Who is my neighbor?" to "Who was a neighbor to the man?" Jesus offers this interesting twist. We expect the answer to the question, "Who is my neighbor?" to be "The victim who needs our help." Instead, we are the one in need, and "my neighbor" is the one who helps us. In Jesus' parable, we are on the side of the road and the Samaritan is the hero. Isn't that a backwards view of missions? Isn't missions about us going to help the needy?

Many churches are learning that missions involves mutual relationships of giving and receiving. Too often in our mission work, we have gone into communities as if we have all the answers and resources to save the poor and helpless. Chris Rice, a member of the interracial inner-city church Voice of Calvary (VOC), calls this the caseworker mentality. Rice shares this experience:

> One church group we hosted at VOC had worked hard all week renovating a house for a low-income family. After dinner, each household member gave a brief testimony, then one of our Black members talked for fifteen minutes on God's concern for racial reconciliation. After he finished, there was a long pause before one volunteer spoke up: "Thanks for the food, but I'm tired, and I came here to serve Christ, not for Black and White. So I'm going to leave." Soon other group members joined

him in making it clear that they had come to do ministry, not learn about racial reconciliation. For another hour, we tried to point out the contradiction in their commitment but made no headway. As they left the house, we felt devastated.

They had come to do something for the poor. But they weren't willing to listen and learn from the very people they considered themselves serving, only to tell and do.[1]

With this well-intentioned but paternalistic and condescending approach, we may come away feeling good about ourselves and yet contribute to a sense of helplessness and dependence within the community we are seeking to help. Our neighbors, like the Samaritan, have gifts to offer us, and they just might be the ones to save our lives.

Through relationships with Nada, a small community in the mountains of Eastern Kentucky, and a church in North Africa, Lexington Avenue Baptist Church is learning the value of mutual relationships of giving and receiving.

Once, the youth of Nada joined Lexington Avenue Baptist Church youth on a mission trip to another part of Eastern Kentucky to clean up an old hotel that was being transformed into a mission center. Traveling to another town on a mission trip was a new experience for the Nada youth, so they were not sure what to expect. The youth from Lexington Avenue Baptist took the lead, but soon both groups were up to their elbows in dirt, cleaning the rooms of this disgusting old hotel. One of the Nada youth commented, "I never thought cleaning a bathroom could be so much fun." On the way back, the Nada youth spontaneously invited our youth to a swimming hole. This time the youth from Lexington Avenue Baptist were the inexperienced ones. The Nada youth dove in headfirst, clothes and all. The youth from Lexington Avenue were hesitant at first, wading in ankle deep and splashing around a bit, but soon they too jumped in—literally. The two youth groups that got on the bus that morning came back as one wet youth group.

Lexington Avenue Baptist Church members are thankful that on this and many other occasions, the beautiful community of Nada has given them the gift of friendship. Members of Lexington Avenue Baptist, like those of many middle- to upper-class churches, live fast-paced lives. Their friends in Nada teach them how to slow down and enjoy the simple pleasures of life like a soda at the country store, a conversation on the front porch, and the beauty of God's mountain creation.

Lexington Avenue Baptist Church's experiences in North Africa have been similar. The church has developed a friendship with a church in North Africa, made up primarily of sub-Saharan African university students. When the first team traveled to the North African church, they were told that they would be impressed by these young church leaders. They didn't realize how much they would be impressed. In a culture that allowed the church to exist but certainly did not favor Christianity, they had learned not just to survive but to thrive. It is against the law for Christians in this area to share their faith verbally with local citizens. The church had made the decision to obey the law. Many of the typical ministry actions our church members were used to doing on trips like these—home repair, clothes and food distribution—are seen as the responsibility of the government. So we may wonder, "What's a Christian to do if you can't work and you can't talk?" This North African church is teaching their Kentucky friends how to *be* the church. Lexington Avenue Church is used to *doing*. This North African church has learned how to be a witness—a light to the world—by loving their neighbors around them, worshiping God as a community, and developing mature Christians to go out of the universities to be leaders all over the world. Their deep faith, love for God, commitment, and joy are evident in every worship service, Bible study, and conversation. They have taught Lexington Avenue Baptist Church much about *being* church and not just *doing* church.

The kind of missions that Jesus taught in the parable of the Good Samaritan means sometimes being the helper with bandages for the wounded and sometimes being the wounded lying on the side of the road. Missions at its best has us acting as both the Samaritan and the wounded at the same time in relationships where everyone is equal, with gifts and needs.

## *Missions Is Loving the Samaritan Neighbor*

When the lawyer asked, "Who is my neighbor?" he was asking, "Whom am I to love as I love myself?" He wanted to know the limits of neighbor love. The implication of his question was "Who is not my neighbor?" and thus "Whom do I not have to love as myself?" Leviticus 19:18 suggests that a neighbor was a fellow Israelite: "You shall not take vengeance or bear a grudge against any of *your people*, but you shall love your neighbor as yourself." Leviticus 19:34 expands this love for neighbor to include the foreigner living among us: "you shall love the alien as yourself, for you were aliens in the land of Egypt." The lawyer, then, likely considered Samaritans to be outsiders of the wrong race, religion, and nationality, and certainly outside the limits of neighborly love. He expected the answer to the question, "Who is my neighbor?" to exclude Samaritans and others who didn't look, think, or act like him.

Jesus confronted the accepted understanding of who is and is not my neighbor. By making a Samaritan the compassionate hero of the story, Jesus removed all limits on neighbor love. The popular Jewish perspective of Jesus' time was that the Samaritans were wrong in nearly every way a person could be wrong—religiously, nationally, and racially. Samaritans were considered an impure racial mix of Gentile and Israelite. They held beliefs that were strange to the Jewish faith. For example, the Samaritans worshiped at a temple on Mount Gerizim instead of in Jerusalem, believed that Moses existed with God from the beginning, and recognized only the first five books of the Hebrew Bible. This is why it was so unusual for Jesus to travel directly through Samaria instead of going the long way around. And this is why it was scandalous for Jesus to have a conversation with a Samaritan woman.

Missions means loving neighbors—all neighbors without discrimination. Loving neighbors especially includes those who are not like us. "Samaritan" can stand for many different kinds of people: those who are poor and oppressed; those of an economic status, race, profession, religion, or culture different from our own; those who are generally disliked; anyone who is not like us; or anyone we do not like. Since loving the Samaritan and learning from the Samaritan may not come naturally to us, we must be intentional in our mission efforts to love Samaritans, whatever that may mean for own disciple community.

### Missions Is Love in Action: Giving and Going

By pooling our financial resources with other Christians and churches, we can have far more impact than any one person, or church, ever could alone. These shared offerings can support global mission strategies, effective organizations, education, and ministry personnel near and far and can provide food, clothing, building materials, and other essential resources to those who need it most. However, if all we do for missions is give money, we miss the opportunity to engage with our neighbors face to face. So, in addition to financial and prayer support, we can seek out ways to become directly involved, building long-term relationships, getting our hands dirty, looking our neighbors in the eye and calling them by name.

Have you ever thought about what it would take to lift a bloody, lifeless body from the ground and onto a donkey by yourself? It cannot be done without getting close and getting bloody, sweaty, and dirty. Notice how the Samaritan loved his neighbor: (1) he shared the resources he had available—bandages, oil, wine, and his donkey; (2) he became directly and physically involved with his hurting neighbor by embracing him and lifting him up onto his donkey; (3) he opened his wallet and provided financial support—equal to two days' wages; and (4) he promised to come back and do more. Not a bad missions model for the church.

Twice, Jesus asked the lawyer to "do": "do this and you will live" (10:28), and "go and do likewise" (10:37). *Love* is an action word. Love involves loving acts of mercy toward neighbors in need.

## Missions Is Loving God by Loving Neighbors

One of the ways we love God with all our heart, soul, strength, and mind is to love our neighbors. Christian educator Thomas Groome noted how radically Jesus interpreted the law:

> First, he insisted that one cannot love God without loving one's neighbor, and second, he removed all limits to who is "my neighbor" . . . Jesus expanded neighbor to mean all people, even one's enemies. Thus he radicalized the law of Kingdom by making it clearer that it is not "love of God and love of neighbor," but "love of God by love of neighbor," with no limits to "neighbor."[2]

So how can we understand neighbor love? Loving neighbors is the way people love God. Love of God is demonstrated in acts of mercy toward neighbors. Neighbors include the powerless, the marginalized, and the despised. A neighbor, though needy, has something to offer.

Part of what Jesus' encounter with the lawyer and the parable of the Good Samaritan teaches is that neighbors are not just the people who are near. In the kingdom of God, love for neighbor is not limited to next door neighbors, but it does include them.

The Gospels, including the story of Jesus' encounter with the lawyer, demonstrate that through Jesus, God cares for Samaritans, women, tax collectors, sinners, prostitutes, and all who have been overlooked by society. This care, or neighbor love, is lived out in relationships and in the giving and receiving of acts of mercy with those in need. Luke expected that Jesus' command to the lawyer, "Go and do likewise," would be heard and lived in his early Christian community. We may also hear the call to love neighbors —those whose voices are ignored, those living in homelessness and never looked in the eye, survivors of abuse, immigrants in need of support, those the church has forgotten and ignored, those we have passed by on the other side of the road.

## The Missional Church

In this chapter I have used the word "missions" to refer primarily to hands-on activities of the church in the service of others, relationships with people outside the church, and sharing the good news about Jesus.

The missional church movement suggests that the church should think of missions as more than just programs and projects; it should be the very identity of the church. We don't have a mission. We *are* a mission—God's mission. The ways we conduct our business, relate to each other, deal with conflict, worship, pray, study, and minister are all a part of God's mission to the world. The church is a contrast society offering a godly alternative to the sometimes unloving ways of the world.

The Missional Church Network defines a missional church in comparison to a church missions program:

> A church with a missions program usually sees missions as one activity alongside many other equally important programs of the church. A missional church, on the other hand, focuses all of its activities around its participation in God's agenda for the world. God's mission must form and inform everything we do. All activities of the church must be catalyzed by and organized around the missio Dei.[3]

The missional church, in this sense, refers to all of the practices of the church. So being a disciple community is being a missional community. Because the word "missions" is such a popular word in many churches and is so familiar, we will continue to use it to refer to the church at work in the world, serving, building relationships, and proclaiming the gospel. However, let us not forget that everything the church does is a part of that mission.

# Putting Missions into Practice

## Acts 1:8 Missions

*"But you will receive power when the Holy Spirit has come upon you; and you will be my witnesses in Jerusalem, in all Judea and Samaria, and to the ends of the earth."* (Acts 1:8)

After Jesus' resurrection in the Luke-Acts account, just before he is taken up into heaven, his last words to his disciples are these in Acts 1:8. Jesus commissions his followers to bear witness to his life, death, and resurrection, to the love of God they have experienced in Jesus, and to the example of life as God intends, demonstrated in Jesus' own life. They are to share the story of Jesus in Jerusalem, Judea, Samaria, and to the ends of the earth.

Each location Jesus names was filled with significance. A little geography will help us understand and apply this passage. Jerusalem was the Holy City, the political, social, and religious center of Israel. Whether or not the disciples were born in or around Jerusalem, it was their spiritual home. Judea was the larger surrounding region. Jerusalem was a city within the region known as Judea—something like the capital city of Frankfort (Jerusalem) within the state of Kentucky (Judea). Samaria was an adjoining region. Samaria and Judea lay side by side, Judea to the south and Samaria to the north. There is more meaning to the mention of Samaria here than geography. As I have already noted, Jews typically thought of Samaritans as different, unclean, racially impure, and heretical in their religious beliefs and practices. From Samaria, Acts 1:8 jumps to the "ends of the earth." The "ends of the earth" refers to everywhere else or, at least in the disciples' minds, to the far reaches of the Roman Empire. The witness of the gospel, therefore, is for all people everywhere, including the Gentiles.

In Acts 1:8, the witness to the good news about Jesus and God's kingdom begins at home in the city of Jerusalem, expands to the entire surrounding region of Judea, moves north to the neighboring region of unclean Samaria and the hated Samaritans, and then expands to everyone, everywhere all around the world—to "the ends of the earth." Jesus gave his disciples an ambitious mission.

## Acts 1:8 Missions in the Local Church

What would it be like for your church to adopt an Acts 1:8 strategy for missions? The world is a big place. How can the local church community take seriously Jesus' mission in Acts 1:8? To begin with, we can work together. No one church can do it all, but when we work together with other churches we can accomplish much more. Resources shared through denominational and other mission organizations are multiplied many times. Together we can do more than we could ever do alone, like sending ministers, developing comprehensive and balanced strategies, creating educational and promotional materials, providing theological education, and more.

In addition to financial support, the church can be directly involved in face-to-face relationships by developing and maintaining friendships in smaller parts of the world. The church can prayerfully seek out partnerships with specific people groups within its own Jerusalem, Judea, Samaria, and the ends of the earth. Consider this approach to each of the four areas:

*Jerusalem.* Begin where you are. Look for ministry opportunities outside the walls of the church in your community and literally across the street from the church building. Remember that the church community itself is perhaps the church's most significant witness in Jerusalem. Everything we do—worship, Bible study, prayer, business meetings, and all types of ministry—is a witness to the surrounding community. Sometimes we fret about not doing enough at home and forget the ministry we offer right here where we live every week of the year: worship, Bible study, and prayer; a building and other resources; a community of faith often led by a trained ministerial staff; and, generally, 80 to 90 percent of the church's budget. The local church is a mission center in our community—our Jerusalem.

*Judea.* Judea could represent some area beyond your home community but still near you, perhaps another part of your state or country. For example, Lexington Avenue Baptist Church, Danville, located in the center of the state of Kentucky, felt God leading them to go east to Appalachia, working through Cooperative Baptist Fellowship's Together for Hope initiative. The goal of Together for Hope was to work alongside communities in the twenty poorest counties in the United States. Two of these counties are in the mountains of Eastern Kentucky, within a two-hour drive of the church.

*Samaria.* Tom Ogburn, in *Missions Ministry in the Missional Church: Developing a Local Church Missions Strategy*,[4] says that Samaria refers to any place or people that take you "beyond your cultural or religious comfort zones" or "those who are a stretch for you." "Samaritans" may be found within our Jerusalem, Judea, or the ends of the earth. Samaria could be represented by any number of groups:

- Those you have difficulty liking
- Those who are oppressed or neglected by society—minorities who are victims of prejudice and discrimination
- Those thought of as enemies
- Those who have been ostracized by the church, told that God's love is conditional

- Those who are of a culture, race, economic status, nationality, or religion different than our own, who might offer us a different perspective

A church that desires to follow Acts 1:8 could identify a place or people from one of the above groups and be intentional about loving these neighbors.

When my daughter joined a downtown church, someone from the new member committee came by to tell her about the ministries of the church. The ministry that got her attention was to those employed as strippers. A group of women in the church take food to these women in local clubs, befriend them, and offer care. "Stripper ministry" may seem odd on a church's nominating committee list next to "nursing home ministry," but it shouldn't if we follow Acts 1:8 and truly love our Samaritan neighbors. Walking through Samaria may make us feel uneasy, but that uneasiness is what makes it Samaria.

*The Ends of the Earth.* The ends of the earth for the disciples meant the Gentile world. Gentiles were not a part of their Jewish heritage and were certainly not familiar with the gospel of Christ. The ends of the earth could refer to those who have never heard the gospel or the most neglected people in our world.

Tom Ogburn tells this story to illustrate the importance of the ends of the earth:

> I vividly remember listening to Dr. Keith Parks describe the missions condition of our world. He drew from the latest missions research and explained to those of us gathered in that small room that the world could be divided into three parts. The first part, he offered, would be called World C. World C represented the Christian World, the 33% of the world's population where the majority of the population had already embraced the gospel message and had access to an ongoing living witness of the church. The church's missions efforts in its Jerusalem and Judea would represent its commitment to be a living witness to those in World C.
>
> The second global image he offered was World B. It represented the 43% of the world's population where the church was present and where a people had access to the gospel story, but where a majority of the population had not yet embraced Christianity. In this four-fold model for missions, World B would be represented by the work in Samaria. The people of your Samaria would call you to look beyond your location, language, cultural and religious comfort zones and move out as a witness

to those places where the church is present but not yet a significant movement in the life of its community.

The third global image he offered was World A. It represented the 24% of the world's population that has little or no access to the gospel. Traditionally, 91% of the missionaries serve in a World C setting, 8% in a World B setting and only 1% focus their efforts on World A peoples. I was recently sharing these numbers with a youth group and when I had finished there was a moment of silence in the room and then one young girl spoke up and said, "that just ain't right." She was right.[5]

What do we do with Acts 1:8? How do we as a church respond to Jesus' command to be witnesses to those near us and far away—to those like us and those unlike us and those we may not even like? Do we ignore Acts 1:8 as unrealistic or not applicable to us? Do we only give money to missionary-sending agencies and pray for missionaries? We could accept the challenge to go and witness in a way that is consistent with Acts 1:8. In addition to sending money and prayer, we could seek to become directly involved in each of the four areas as directed in Acts 1:8.

## Choosing Acts 1:8 Partnerships

How does a church go about choosing an Acts 1:8 partnership? Here are some questions that may help:

- When we pray, where do we discern God is leading us?
- Which community is most neglected?
- Which community has the fewest number of churches partnering with them?
- Where is our money already going? Could we follow up our financial support by becoming directly involved?
- Do we have any natural connection with a community? For example, are there people from this community who live in our area? Do we have a special relationship or connection with field personnel in an area? Do our church members have unique gifts, skills (for example, speak the language), and interests that fit well with this community?
- Are there people or churches in the field through whom we can work? How willing are they to partner with us?
- How accessible is the community? Are we able to travel there? How much does it cost? (Reaching the ends of the earth is difficult, but we should not avoid a challenge; otherwise, we may never leave the comfort of our own

church building. That, after all, is part of the point of "the ends of the earth": it is difficult to get there and the people are not easily accessible. Reaching the ends of the earth costs more.)
- If our church does not reach out to this community, who will?
- Is there a community that has knowledge, experience, culture, or resources that would benefit our faith community or broaden our perspective?
- Is there a community with specific challenges that our church is equipped to assist with—for example, poverty, housing, hunger, education, jobs? (Note: This should not be a disqualifying criterion. We need to learn how to recognize the value and significance of prayer and relationships as a missions activity, whether or not we are able to meet a physical need.)

## Neighborhood Ministry

An approach to ministry in our Jerusalem, which we might call "neighborhood ministry," begins by asking, with Luke 10:25-37, "Who is my neighbor?" Neighborhood ministry identifies an area small enough for a church to relate to every person or business in the area. Draw a circle around your church and seek to build a relationship with every person (or business) within the circle. Ministry and relationships could take a variety of forms such as block parties, backyard Bible clubs, Bible studies, friendships, bread delivery, a business lunch and devotion, or anything else you can imagine.

### An Example of a Neighborhood Ministry Planning Process

Every church and every neighborhood is different, so each church's approach to neighborhood ministry would be unique. The experience of First Baptist Church, Hopkinsville, Kentucky, is one example of how a neighborhood ministry planning process might work.[6]

First Baptist Church is a predominately white, middle- to upper middle-class congregation in a unique location: to its north lies the downtown business district; to the east is a predominately lower-income neighborhood (about 70 percent Black, 30 percent white); to the south, the street is lined with large historic homes occupied mostly by middle- to upper middle-class white families; to the west is a mixture of all of the above—businesses and medical offices, apartments and low-income homes, and large homes, all in proximity to each other.

With few of its church members residing in these areas, some church leaders asked, "How can we love our neighbors?" A neighborhood ministry leadership team of about ten members met for ten weeks to answer the question and develop a neighborhood ministry plan for the congregation.

The church used a four-step planning process:

*(1) Get to know the neighbors.* The group gathered demographic data, talking with community leaders like social workers, police officers, and the director of the planning commission to learn more about the neighborhood. By far the most effective way of learning about the neighborhood was through personal visits. Teams of three visited residences and businesses, saying something like, "We are from First Baptist Church. We're your neighbors. We just want to know how we can be better neighbors. Do you have a few moments to talk with us, and can we come back later after you have had some time to think about it?" The team members were able to share some of their preliminary ideas and get feedback and listen for more ideas. The team was apprehensive when they began, afraid of having doors slammed in their faces, but they found that their approach was disarming and they were welcomed everywhere they went. These neighborly conversations on front porches, in living rooms, and in businesses were rewarding experiences. The team felt that just by asking the question, "How can we be a good neighbor?" they were already being a neighbor.

In one living room conversation they asked a neighbor, a Black woman, what they could do to be a neighbor. She said, "We could have a Bible study in my home. I could get some of my neighbors to come over and you could bring some of your group and we'd have a beautiful, colorful bouquet like God intended." They followed through with a Bible study in her home.

*(2) Evaluate our resources.* The team named all the ways that First Baptist Church was already ministering to its neighbors. They listed all the resources of the church that could help them love their neighbors: the members' gifts, time, and money; mission groups; the Sunday school organization; and the church-owned recreation center. The team surveyed the congregation to discover interests in various areas of neighborhood ministry.

*(3) Consider community resources.* The team sought to avoid duplicating what others were doing. They contacted local churches, government assistance agencies, and other helping agencies in the community to see what was already being done.

*(4) Develop a ministry plan.* Finally, they used all of this information to develop a plan that would involve the church in ministry with its neighbors.

As a result of this planning process, a number of ministries and relational activities were developed, such as a monthly business lunch; an annual neighborhood block party in the church parking lot; a beautiful new playground and children's area created in a vacant neighborhood lot; Bible clubs; worship; deliveries of loaves of bread to residential neighbors and brownies to business neighbors; and eventually a tutoring ministry for neighborhood schoolchildren.

## *Christian Community Development*

Asset-based community development begins with the assets, or gifts, of a community rather than focusing on needs and weaknesses, and follows the lead of the people who live in the community. Community development seeks to work "with" and not just "for" the community in a way that empowers the community to deal with its own challenges. Asset-based community development contrasts with the all-too-common approach where churches, government agencies, or other helping organizations enter a community from the outside and act as if they are the only ones with skills and solutions to help the community. This "caseworker" mentality, as Perkins calls it, can lessen the community's sense of dignity and foster dependence.[7] Community development is about listening and learning from the community and then offering expertise, labor, and resources as needed. The goal of community development is not to place bandages on the most visible problems from the perspective of the outsider but to develop with the residents long-term systemic solutions for the difficulties of living in an "at-risk" community. Community development supports a community's desire for quality life, including meaningful work; the ability to provide for basic needs such as food, housing, and clothing; health care; safety and security; education; entertainment; dignity and purpose; and a sense of belonging.

Christian community development shares the objectives and many of the practices of asset-based community development, but it adds a spiritual dimension and is church-based. John Perkins writes, "Christian community development begins with people transformed by the love of God, who then respond to God's call to share the gospel with others through evangelism, social action, economic development, and justice."[8]

The three Rs of Christian community development as proposed by the Christian Community Development Association (CCDA) are reconciliation, redistribution, and relocation.

*Reconciliation.* Second Corinthians 5:18-21 reads, "All of this is from God, who reconciled us to himself through Christ and has given us the ministry of reconciliation; that is, in Christ God was reconciling the world to himself, not counting their trespasses against them, and entrusting the message of reconciliation to us." Reconciliation is the gift of our loving God to us and a message to share with our neighbors. Perkins notes that reconciliation moves in two directions: people to God and neighbor to neighbor:

> Reconciliation is at the heart of the gospel. Jesus said that the essence of Christianity could be summed up in two inseparable commandments: love God and love thy neighbor.
>
> First, Christian community development is concerned with reconciling people to God and bringing them into a church fellowship where they can be discipled in their faith.
>
> But can a gospel that reconciles people to God without reconciling people to people be the true gospel of Jesus Christ? Our love for Christ should break down every racial, ethnic, or economic barrier.[9]

In order for true Christian reconciliation to occur, we must love and be reconciled to God, move beyond surface friendliness with our neighbors, honestly acknowledge the differences that divide us, submit to God and to each other, and commit to loving our neighbors and working for reconciliation long term.

*Relocation.* Jesus, the incarnation of God, gave us the ultimate example of relocation. God, in Jesus, was born and lived among us, taught God's love by word and example, suffered as we suffer, and was killed. Relocation answers the call to "go therefore." According the CCDA, "being a vested member of the community one is called to serve is an important key to effectiveness."[10] Relocation is becoming a part of the community, sharing your Christian values, enrolling your children in local schools, experiencing the same risks as everyone else in the community, using your communication skills to advocate for the community, and being a next-door neighbor.

We are accustomed to missionaries relocating. Imagine a group of families from your church moving into a low-income community that your church is seeking to love. They buy, build, or renovate homes in the community. They become a part of the community, going to church there, relating to neighbors, conducting their business there, enrolling their children in local schools, and volunteering for the parent-teacher organization.

When the schools are inadequate or essential goods and services are not available, they utilize their communication and confrontational skills and knowledge of how the system works to help organize the community to bring about change. Perhaps they start businesses to support themselves, to provide jobs for the community, and to keep money flowing within the economy of the community. They mentor neighbors, sharing leadership and life skills as they also receive the gifts of their neighbors. Members of CCDA have learned from experience that "when connected neighbors share the influence they have in the marketplace, the church, the educational institutions, and the political systems, the flow of resources begins to spread into places long ago shut off. Relocated neighbors end isolation."[11]

*Redistribution.* Redistribution is empowering the community through economic and leadership development. Redistribution is working on all fronts to raise the standard of living—in business, education, health, housing, and the spiritual life. This means developing leaders from within the community, not so they can escape to a better life somewhere else but so they can stay to strengthen the community. Redistribution involves economic development, which keeps most of the community's money from leaving the community, offers jobs, and provides needed goods and services to the community. Economic developments may proceed in a variety of ways:

- Start up enterprises and operate them, primarily as a way to create jobs in the community.
- Act as a broker-developer for a site as a place to stimulate business in the community.
- Train people for existing jobs, micro-enterprises, or self-employment.
- Assist in start-up and expansion of local businesses through technical support and by providing access to below-market interest rate loan funds.
- Participate in a community-wide effort of other churches and/or community development groups.
- Invest in a company in order to bring in jobs, income, and services.[12]

## *The Mission of Christian Advocacy*

Christian advocacy addresses the root, systemic, and political causes of injustice against the most vulnerable in society. Christian advocacy is being prophetic and crying out on behalf of those least able to do so for themselves, in the tradition of Isaiah, Jeremiah, Amos, Micah, and Jesus.

Christian advocacy is lifting up the voice of the voiceless so that they may be heard.

Stephen Reeves, in his book *The Mission of Advocacy: A Toolkit for Congregations*, says that advocacy is "to speak out on behalf of another, to take their concerns as your own and use your voice to help change that problem or situation," and he adds that "we should help empower them to advocate for themselves as well."[13] According to Reeves, advocacy is rooted in the church's mission and the commandment to love your neighbor as yourself. When churches engage in missions, feeding the hungry, helping pay rent for a family about to be evicted, repairing homes, visiting the local jail, or ministering to migrants, they may wonder, "Why are these people in this situation to begin with?" Love for the people we come in contact with through our mission calls us get to the root of the problems. Reeves writes, "We can commit to resisting politics motivated by fear and scarcity, toward one rooted in God's abundance of love. If we're loving our neighbors just as we love ourselves, our voices and actions as citizens will show it. We're often reminded that we serve as the hands and feet of Christ in this age, but how might we serve as his voice?"[14]

In a handwritten sermon outline titled "The One-Sided Approach of the Good Samaritan," Martin Luther King Jr. has an interesting and helpful take on the Good Samaritan:

> Now, without a doubt Christian social responsibility includes the sort of thing the good Samaritan did. So we give to the United Appeals, the Red Cross, to all types of unfortunate conditions. In the midst of such staggering and appalling conditions we cannot afford to "pass by on the other side." Like the good Samaritan we must always stand ready to decend to the depth of human need. The person who fails to look with compassion upon the thousands of individuals left wounded by life's many roadsides is not only unethical, but ungodly. Every Christian must ply the good Samaritan.
>
> But there is another aspect of Christian social responsibility which is just as compelling. It seeks to tear down unjust conditions and build anew instead of patching things up. It seeks to clear the Jerico road of its robbers as well as caring for the victims of robbery.[15]

So in the case of the Samaritan on the Jericho road, advocacy might mean clearing the road of robbers or, as King suggests earlier in his sermon outline, investigating the lack of police protection or improving public roads so that the next traveler doesn't end up half-dead on the side of the road.

Political and social advocacy is a mission some churches may be reluctant to embrace. Why would we want to bring polarizing political debate into the church? We don't, but maybe we want to bring prayerful and constructive dialogue into the church about how the political systems of which we are a part affect the poor and oppressed we call our neighbors and to plan ways we can use our influence to promote more just systems.

The following story is a simple example of how advocacy worked in one small community. Residents were told that a government grant had been allocated to bring a public sewer system to the community. Some in this town had septic systems, but most still used outhouses. Despite the promise of a public sewer system, the neighbors were skeptical, to say the least. "We were promised a sewer system before," they said, "but when grants for that purpose were awarded to the local government, they spent it on something else." They had resigned themselves to complaining and never having the promised and much-needed sewer system, until Rhonda Abbott, the Associate for Missions of the Kentucky Baptist Fellowship, guided them to become advocates. She called a town meeting to discuss the issue. They agreed on and implemented a strategy. They would call another meeting and invite public officials to report on their plans to install the public sewer system. A different resident each week would send an email until work on the system began. Others would call periodically. Residents knew how to get angry and complain, but not always in the most productive ways. Without an adequate understanding of how political systems work, their angry criticism was often directed toward the wrong people and in a way that was too easily dismissed. So Abbott guided them to effectively and appropriately express their concerns and ask questions. Since the sewer system was promised by the person whom the community felt had let them down in the past, instead of complaining they praised this public official in the local newspaper in advance for bringing a public sewer system to their community. Their public adulation, in a nice way, applied pressure on the government to follow through. Several months after carrying out their plan, the sewer system was installed. It's hard to say how much difference their efforts made in getting the job done, but the community was empowered and learned about how to advocate for themselves.

Churches with members who are connected and know how the system works can use that influence to help those who are treated unfairly by our public policies. This is Christian advocacy for justice.

## Interfaith Dialogue

*This section was written by Kelsey Stillwell, Associate Pastor for Youth and Missions, First Baptist Church of Christ, Macon, Georgia.*

The parable of the Good Samaritan can teach us something about interfaith dialogue, which can inform and strengthen our mission.

As was Jesus' style, there is a lot packed into the parable of the Good Samaritan, multiple dimensions to discover in a seemingly simple story. Every time you visit it, something different grabs you. I found more depth in this parable when a part of the story that had always been there was first named for me. A profoundly simple truth that should have been so evident and clear was brought to light and added a new dimension I had been missing.

At a conference for youth ministers, one of the evening sessions was an interfaith dialogue between a minister and an Imam. They talked about their friendship and shared their thoughts on the importance of interfaith work. Not long into the conversation, the Imam starting referring to our Scriptures, saying, "You have an interfaith story in your Bible. It's right there in the parable that Jesus tells of the Good Samaritan." The Imam elaborated, their conversation continued, and his insight has stuck with me ever since—a statement that was so simple and so true, I couldn't believe I hadn't seen it myself.

Jesus not only uses a character that is of a differing faith in his story, but this character teaches us what it means to love our neighbor. The Good Samaritan is an interfaith story; it's that simple. People of other faiths have something to teach us; it's that profound. It is not a mistake or slip of the tongue. Jesus is being deliberate. The priest and the Levite are characters Jesus' followers would relate to, "church folk," but they are antagonists in the parable, passing by the wounded man on the other side of the road. The Samaritan, the one who is of a different faith, is the one who shows mercy and demonstrates neighborly, godly love.

This parable goes beyond loving one's neighbor simply for the sake of doing what God asks of us. It makes a connection that we might miss or choose to ignore. Learn from your neighbor. There is something to learn about caring for one another from people of different cultures and differing faiths.

Find yourself in the story. When you feel tempted to cross by on the other side of the road, look for how you might learn from someone else, someone who has different beliefs from you and much to teach about love.

Cross back over the road. Join them and work with them. And when you are the one in need of care, hoping someone will show mercy, be ready to receive hospitality from someone else, someone who may have different beliefs from you and much to teach you about receiving hospitality.

It is simple and deliberate. Jesus teaches using an interfaith story. Learn from your neighbors of differing faiths, they have much to teach you. There is much we can do together. Go and do likewise.

### Matthew 25: God Cares for "the Least of These"

"'. . . I was hungry and you gave me food, I was thirsty and you gave me something to drink, I was a stranger and you welcomed me, I was naked and you gave me clothing, I was sick and you took care of me, I was in prison and you visited me.' Then the righteous will answer him, 'Lord, when was it that we saw you hungry and gave you food, or thirsty and gave you something to drink? And when was it that we saw you a stranger and welcomed you, or naked and gave you clothing? And when was it that we saw you sick or in prison and visited you?' And the king will answer them, 'Truly I tell you, just as you did it to one of the least of these who are members of my family, you did it to me.'" (Matt 25:35-40)

Any church that would seek to engage in missions must take seriously Jesus' love and care for those he called "the least of these." God has a heart for those the world has forgotten or abused: the poor and hungry, the sick and imprisoned, the homeless or the immigrant, the lonely and hurting, the outcasts. "The least of these" is another name for Samaritans. Samaritans were despised, yet they were the focus of Jesus' special love and attention, which angered many of Jesus' own people. Throughout the Bible, God's care for the marginalized is emphasized. Our mission efforts should reflect that priority.

### Bible Study and Missions

Many Bible study groups incorporate service and missions into the plans and activities of the class. This practice should be affirmed. Missions and Bible study—action and reflection—go hand in hand. The Bible is not something we simply analyze, study, and learn about. The Bible is to be experienced and lived. We go to the Bible to experience God, and God calls us to gather in community and to go out to love our neighbors. Therefore, Bible study should be a springboard for mission activity and a place to reflect on how we have served God by serving others.

Bible study calls us not only to come together as a community but also to go together into the world. The Lord told Abraham that he was blessed so he would be a blessing: "Go from your country and your kindred and your father's house to the land that I will show you. I will make of you a great nation, and I will bless you, and make your name great, so that you will be a blessing" (Gen 12:1-2). The prophet Micah asks, "What does the LORD require of you but to do justice, and to love kindness, and to walk humbly with your God?" (Mic 6:8). Jesus calls us to "Go therefore and make disciples of all nations, baptizing them in the name of the Father and of the Son and of the Holy Spirit, and teaching them to obey everything that I have commanded you" (Matt 28:19-20). Jesus also says, quoting Isaiah, "The Spirit of the Lord is upon me, because he has anointed me to bring good news to the poor. He has sent me to proclaim release to the captives and recovery of sight to the blind, to let the oppressed go free, to proclaim the year of the Lord's favor" (Luke 4:18-19). These Scripture passages call us to go, and when we truly experience the word of God in Bible study, we will go.

### Missions Balance Sheet

As we evaluate our church in the area of missions, here are some things we might look for. Think of this as a "Missions Balance Sheet." Instead of simply answering "yes" or "no" to each area, we may consider how well we are doing at each.

(1) Age groups: Are all age groups involved? Children? Youth? Young, middle, and senior adults?

(2) Acts 1:8: Are we Jesus' witnesses in Jerusalem, Judea, Samaria, and the ends of the earth?

(3) Witness and Proclamation: Do our mission efforts include sharing the testimony of our faith, the good news of Jesus' life, death, and resurrection, and the story of God's reconciliation?

(4) Missions education: Do we offer missions education and training to increase our understanding of the field personnel and mission causes we support and to train us for our own mission work?

(5) Financial/Material: Do we support missions with our church budget and offerings? Do we offer resources for missions such as clothes, building materials, food, etc.?

(6) Prayer: Does our support include prayer?

(7) Direct involvement: Are we engaged in hands-on, face-to-face, relational missions?

(8) Matthew 25: Do we care for the "least of these"? Do we feed the hungry and provide drink to the thirsty? Do we welcome strangers? Do we provide clothes for those without? Do we visit the prisoner? Do we visit the sick?

(9) Holistic Ministry: Through our mission involvement, do we relate to people as whole individuals—spiritual, emotional, physical, and mental?

(10) Empowering: Do our mission efforts empower others to deal with the challenges they face? Are we engaged in community development? Are we teaching others how to fish as well as giving them a fish and even helping them to own the pond? Does our action maintain the dignity of those we relate to?

(11) Advocacy: Do we address the systemic causes of poverty and other forms of injustice and become advocates for equality, justice, and solutions that address systemic causes?

(12) Missional church: Do we have mission programs, or are we a missional church? Is our church community, and the way we live and relate to each other, an example of life as God intends and a witness to the world? Do we offer an alternative way of relating, conducting business, making decisions, and dealing with conflict? Are we engaged in God's mission?

(13) Other: Can you think of other ways to measure and evaluate our mission involvement?

## Missions Resources

Benson, Peter L., and Eugene C. Roehlkepartain. *Beyond Leaf Raking: Learning to Serve/Serving to Learn.* Nashville: Abingdon, 1993.

Bosch, David, J. *Transforming Mission: Paradigm Shifts in Theology of Mission.* New York: Orbis Books, 2009.

Caes, David, ed. *Caring for the Least of These: Serving Christ among the Poor.* Scottsdale, PA: Herald Press, 1992.

Cooperative Baptist Fellowship of South Carolina. *PilgriMission: Transforming by Being Transformed.* Decatur, GA: Cooperative Baptist Fellowship, 2016.

Crocker, David W. *Operation Inasmuch: Mobilizing Believers beyond the Walls of the Church.* St. Louis: Lake Hickory Resources, 2005.

Ehlig, Bill, and Ruby Payne. *What Every Church Member Should Know about Poverty, Revised.* Highlands, TX: Aha! Process, Inc., 2005.

Groome, Thomas H. *Christian Religious Education: Sharing Our Story and Vision.* San Francisco: Harper & Row, Pub., 1980.

Kretzmann, John P., and John L. McKnight. *Building Communities from the Inside Out: A Path Toward Finding and Mobilizing a Community's Assets.* ACTA Publications, 1993.

Krile, James F., with Gordon Curphy and Duane R. Lund. *The Community Leadership Handbook: Framing Ideas, Building, Relationships, and Mobilizing Resources.* New York: Fieldstone Alliance, 2006.

Mather, Michael. *Having Nothing, Possessing Everything: Finding Abundant Communities in Unexpected Places.* Grand Rapids: Eerdmans, 2018.

Littrell, Donald W., and Doris P. Littrell. *Practicing Community Development.* University of Missouri Extension, 2006.

*Maximizing Your Church's Mission Engagement.* Decatur, GA: Cooperative Baptist Fellowship.

Missional Church Network, "What is Missional?" www.missionalchurchnetwork.com/what-is-missional.

Newbigin, Lesslie. *Foolishness to the Greeks: The Gospel and Western Culture.* Grand Rapids: Eerdmans, 1986.

———. *The Gospel in a Pluralist Society.* Grand Rapids: Eerdmans, 1989.

Norman, Matt, and Michelle Norman. *Pivot: Turning Teams Toward God's Mission Near and Far.* Decatur, GA: Cooperative Baptist Fellowship, 2016.

Ogburn, Tom. *Missions Ministry in the Missional Church: Developing a Local Church Missions Strategy* (unpublished paper), 2001.

Perez, Javier, and Jason Coker, eds. *Deep Soil.* Published by Together for Hope with the Cooperative Baptist Fellowship. (Still in development at the time of this publication, *Deep Soil* is a resource for churches, practitioners, and nonprofits engaged in assets-based community for poverty alleviation in rural spaces.)

Perkins, John M., ed. *Restoring At-Risk Communities: Doing It Together and Doing It Right.* Grand Rapids: Baker Publishing, 1995.

Reeves, Stephen K., and Rev. Katie Ferguson Murray. *The Mission of Advocacy: A Toolkit for Congregations.* Macon: Nurturing Faith Inc., 2020.

Sherman, Amy L. *Restorers of Hope: Reaching the Poor in Your Community with Church-Based Ministries that Work*. Wheaton, IL: Crossway Books, 1997.

Stillwell, Keith. *Neighborhood Ministry and An Action/Reflection Bible Study on Luke 10:25-37*. Doctor of Ministry Project, Baptist Theological Seminary at Richmond, VA, 2000.

Together for Hope. The Cooperative Baptist Fellowship. hope.cbf.net.

Younger, Carol, and Kevin Pranoto. *CBF Global Missions: Small Group Bible Study*. Atlanta: Cooperative Baptist Fellowship, www.cbf.net/missions.

## Notes

1. In John M. Perkins, ed., *Restoring At-Risk Communities: Doing It Together and Doing It Right* (Grand Rapids: Baker Publishing, 1995), 119–20.

2. Groome, *Christian Religious Education*, 41.

3. Mennonite Missions Network, "What Is Missional?" www.missionalchurchnetwork.com/what-is-missional.

4. Tom Ogburn, *Missions Ministry in the Missional Church: Developing a Local Church Missions Strategy*, unpublished paper.

5. Ogburn, *Missions Ministry in the Missional Church*.

6. Keith Stillwell, *Neighborhood Ministry and an Action/Reflection Bible Study on Luke 10:25-37*, Doctor of Ministry project, Baptist Theological Seminary, Richmond, VA, 2000.

7. Perkins, *Restoring At-Risk Communities*, 119–20.

8. Perkins, *Restoring At-Risk Communities*, 21.

9. Perkins, *Restoring At-Risk Communities*, 22.

10. Perkins, *Restoring At-Risk Communities*, 75.

11. Perkins, *Restoring At-Risk Communities*, 86.

12. Perkins, *Restoring At-Risk Communities*, 145–48.

13. Stephen K. Reeves and Rev. Katie Ferguson Murray, *The Mission of Advocacy: A Toolkit for Congregations* (Macon: Nurturing Faith Inc., 2020), 13.

14. Reeves, *The Mission of Advocacy*, 22–23.

15. Martin Luther King Jr. Papers Project, November 20, 1955, 240. Martin Luther King Jr.'s original handwritten sermon notes. See https://stanford.app.box.com/s/rxjnkl701cyft7h2ssiodbq3e1jkm7r5.

*Chapter 6*

# Witness

## Conversations with Mary and Sam on Missions

As the three of us sat quietly, mulling over our previous conversation, the church bells began ringing out their version of "How Firm a Foundation," skipping a note occasionally where there was no bell to sound that particular note.

Mary sat up in her seat, tilting one ear up toward the ceiling. "Wow! What is that?"

Sam sat up too, his eyes searching the ceiling for the source of the sound.

"It's beautiful," Mary complimented.

"And loud," Sam added.

"Those are our church bells."

By now Sam was standing, looking around. "Where are they?"

"Up in the steeple, or we call it the bell tower."

"Can we go see them?"

"Well, maybe. I've only been up there once. You have to go up in the attic and climb a shaky ladder to get there."

"I'm okay by that. Sounds interesting."

"Yes, it is interesting but a little scary. Mary? Do you want to climb to the bell tower?" I hoped, and expected, that Mary would refuse.

"Sure, let's go."

"Okay." Nervously, I led my friends up the stairs toward the attic, hoping not to be responsible for any serious or even not so serious injuries to Mary or the Good Samaritan. On the third floor, I pulled down the attic door and unfolded the stairs. We climbed the stairs into the hot attic.

"That wasn't as bad as you made it sound," Sam noted as we reached the top.

"We aren't there yet. That wasn't the wobbly ladder."

Once in the attic, we walked single file across the plywood walkway to the center.

Sam shook the homemade ladder as he stared up to where it led into an opening at the peak of the ceiling above the sanctuary attic. "Now, that's a wobbly ladder. You were right."

I led the way, and one by one we scaled the rickety ladder up through a small hatch in the roof and out into the bright sunlight. From the landing, the bells, some twice the size of our heads, hung above and beside us. The final note of Luther's great hymn had finished playing well before we got there, or we would have gone deaf. After admiring the bells, we turned and enjoyed a beautiful bird's-eye view of the town. Downtown Main Street, businesses, the hospital, the college, and many houses stretched out in front of us.

"Seeing my town below reminds me of Jesus' commissioning in Acts 1:8: 'You shall be my witnesses in Jerusalem, Judea, and Samaria and to the ends of the earth.' This is our Jerusalem," I said.

Mary stretched out both hands toward the city. "I'm sure it can feel like an overwhelming task."

I nodded in agreement.

"So how do you witness to Jerusalem?" Mary pointed to the neighborhood just to our right and below us.

"Growing up, I was taught how to share the plan of salvation, like the Roman Road, Four Steps to Peace with God, or the ABCs."

"Can you elaborate?"

"For example, the ABCs are admit you are a sinner, believe that Jesus died to save you from you sins, and commit your life to Christ."

"Sounds simple," Sam said.

"Maybe too simple," Mary cautioned. "I've never heard that before. Is that from a Bible passage I don't remember?"

"It's a collection of verses from here and there in the New Testament."

"From everywhere but nowhere?" Sam wondered.

"I struggled with the whole idea of salvation as a child," I admitted. "I was obsessed with the question coming out of my tradition: 'Is walking forward during the invitation hymn and joining the church necessary for salvation?' I was not one who liked being in front of people, exposing my private self. I wanted to be a Christian without anyone knowing about it. I'm kind of embarrassed, but I heard the story of Gideon's fleece and decided to set up a test for God to answer the question."

After a pause, Sam said, smiling, "You can't stop there. What kind of test did you give God?"

"Okay, but remember I was a kid. The test was this: 'God, if I see a crayon drop on the floor today, then that means I have to join the church to be saved.' I was happy that we didn't even use crayons that day. So the next day, like Gideon, I switched it around. 'God, if I don't have to join the church today, then let me see a crayon drop on the floor.' We had an assignment involving crayons that day, and I was amazed when the girl a couple of seats in front of me spilled her whole box of crayons on the floor."

Sam roared with laughter. "Ha! That is so funny. I didn't think you had it in you."

"Are you making fun of me?"

"No! No! I'm proud of you. That was so bold for a kid to put God to the test—a kid too shy to ask an adult. So how'd that work out for you?"

"Not so well."

"The answer didn't satisfy you, did it?"

"No. Not really. I realized my test didn't matter. I think I just saw what I wanted to see. I still didn't understand."

Mary entered the conversation. "You were asking about the minimum you must do. Following Jesus is about giving the maximum. Following Jesus is about giving your whole self—body, mind, heart, and soul—to God's control. When you ask about minimum requirements or try to reduce the gospel into three concise points, ABCs, or four steps, you have missed the point from the start.

"Being a Christian is a relationship, a journey," she continued. "The call to salvation is an invitation to participate in God's story. There's no simple answer to 'How do I find eternal life?' To the expert in the law Jesus said, 'Love God with all your heart, soul, strength, and mind and your neighbor as yourself, and be like Sam. Break cultural barriers and help your neighbor in a ditch.' To the rich man, Jesus said, 'Sell all you have, give the money to the poor, and follow me.' To the woman at the well, Jesus said, 'Drink living water from the well that never runs dry.' To Peter and Andrew, Jesus said, 'Come follow me, and I will make you fish for people.' To Nicodemus the Pharisee, he said, 'You must be born again,' and 'Whoever believes in me will not perish but have eternal life.'"

"So, Mary," I said, offering my hand to the neighborhood below, "what does witness look like for these neighbors?"

Mary leaned over, looking down at the people walking along sidewalk. Then she stood and patted me on the shoulder. "That's for you and your church to figure out."

Sam laughed again. This time I'm sure he was laughing *at* me.

I looked at my watch. "Let's get out of here before these bells chime again."

## Witness

"You are witnesses," Jesus tells his disciples just before he ascends into heaven (Luke 24:44-49; Acts 1:3-8). We refer to this passage as Jesus' commissioning of his disciples, but we can't say exactly that Jesus "commanded" his disciples to be witnesses. Jesus is simply making a statement of the reality: "you are witnesses" and "you shall be my witnesses." By virtue of the fact that they were his followers, intimately involved with his life, they were witnesses. They heard him teach and pray on many occasions. They watched him heal the sick, feed the hungry, perform miracles, and cast out demons. They observed his interaction with all kinds of people, the despised and the privileged. They endured his rebuke and enjoyed his love and forgiveness. They watched him die and now they stood in his resurrected presence. They were witnesses to "these things."

What exactly are "these things"? What are the disciples, and then the church, to bear witness to? Luke writes, "Then he opened their minds to understand the scriptures, and he said to them, 'Thus it is written, that the Messiah is to suffer and to rise from the dead on the third day."

Jesus explains to this crowd of followers what he has already explained many times before, that he is the Messiah and that he must suffer and rise from the dead, but this time is different. Before, they didn't understand. Now, in the presence of the risen Jesus, they experience a transformative moment. They understand what Jesus is saying, and what the Scriptures meant, with real clarity for the first time. Being in the presence of the resurrected Jesus made the difference then as it does now. In communion with Christ, the truth becomes clear.

The disciples and many in Israel anticipated a Messiah. *Christ* is the Greek translation of the Hebrew "Messiah," which means "anointed one" or "God's anointed," the title given to Jesus. Isaiah prophesied,

> For a child has been born for us, a son given to us; authority rests upon his shoulders; and he is named Wonderful Counselor, Mighty God, Everlasting Father, Prince of Peace. His authority shall grow continually, and

there shall be endless peace for the throne of David and his kingdom. He will establish and uphold it with justice and with righteousness from this time onward and forevermore. The zeal of the LORD of hosts will do this. (Isa 9:6-7)

The disciples understood that God would send a messiah as king to rule over them. It's just that Jesus didn't fit their understanding of a conquering messiah who would restore the political kingdom of Israel and rule the nations on earth. Jesus' death confirmed, in their minds, that Jesus was not the messiah they had hoped for (Luke 24:21).

The resurrected presence of Jesus changed everything. Their minds were opened to understand the Scriptures and all that Jesus had shown and taught them. What they needed to know was there all along. The Messiah must suffer, not conquer. Jesus was the expected Messiah, coming in an unexpected way. Now it was beginning to make sense in light of Scripture and, most importantly, in the presence of God in Christ Jesus the King, the Messiah, the anointed one of God.

## The Messiah of the Kingdom of God

What the disciples were to bear witness to—what we are to bear witness to—is that, indeed, Jesus is the King, the long-awaited Messiah. Now Jesus' followers must rethink what that kingdom is all about, because it's not what they thought it was and it may not be what we think it is. The life, death, and resurrection of Jesus reteaches us the nature of the kingdom, of the reign of God, of life as God intends. It will take nothing less than repentance—a complete turnaround in our thinking and acting—in order for us to live into this new but old reality. Now we must hang on every word that comes from the mouth of Jesus and recall every act of Jesus and allow Jesus to completely transform our community into one submitted to the reign of God. Evidently the disciples heard many words from Jesus, as we are told that Jesus spent many days with them "speaking about the kingdom" (Acts 1:3).

This is what is to be "proclaimed in his name to all nations" (Luke 24:46-47): repentance and forgiveness of sin. We repent of our sinful loyalties to other kings—selfishness, greed, nationalism, fear, hate, or any number of other worldly rulers—and proclaim that Jesus is our King. We know this because he suffered, died, and rose again. We can trust what he said and did as the pattern for shaping our communities of faith. Jesus the

Christ showed us life as God intends. Jesus himself preached the good news of the kingdom of God (Luke 4:43; 8:1; 9:11; 16:16).

## Good News

The proclamation we make to all nations, we are told, is good news. When the angel announced the birth of Jesus to the shepherds, the angel said, "I am bringing you good news of great joy for all the people: to you is born this day . . . a Savior, who is the Messiah, the Lord" (Luke 2:10-11). Jesus is good news. "These things" we witness are good news. "Gospel" means "good news" or "good tidings," thus the stories of Jesus as told by Matthew, Mark, Luke, and John are called Gospels—the good news. An evangelist is one who shares the good news.

## What Is the Good News?

Let us explore this good news more thoroughly, since it is so important that it should be proclaimed to all people. What is the good news? The angel announced that good news was a baby born in a manger for all people, a Savior and Messiah. The good news is Jesus who lived, died, and was raised to new life.

The resurrection is certainly an important part of the story of Jesus, but it is not the whole story. Maynard-Reid points out that when a replacement apostle was sought, one of the requirements was that he had been with Jesus from the time of Jesus' baptism by John until his resurrection.[1] Luke and the other Gospel writers make the resurrection of Jesus the focus of their narrative, but they include much more of Jesus' life, words, and actions. Thus, the whole ministry of Jesus is good news to be proclaimed.

When attempting to summarize the gospel story, there is always the danger of oversimplifying. Condensing the gospel into the ABCs of Salvation, Four Spiritual Laws, or a Roman Road risks truncating the narrative of Jesus' life, death, and resurrection, and in many cases it oddly leaves out the story of Jesus altogether, except for the mention of his name. Any time we attempt to summarize the story from four Gospels, selecting passages and themes and choosing to emphasize those events and teachings we deem most important, we cannot help being influenced by our own contexts, biases, presuppositions, and life's experiences. The four Gospels themselves were written from the perspectives of the authors to a particular people, time, place, and situation. Thus we will attempt to note some key themes from the gospel of Jesus, doing our best to be fair and true to the gospel message of Jesus, in our case specifically the Gospel of Luke. We are looking for themes that show us what the kingdom of God looks like and how the church is to act, think, and believe as witnesses.

Let us keep in mind that this is, in part, the kingdom of God we proclaim. This is the good news we share. These are "these things" of which we are witnesses. This is the life we embody as a community, witnessing by example.

## The Kingdom of God Is . . .

*(1) The kingdom of God is a place where the poor and all who are marginalized are lifted up and where the rich are challenged to give up their riches for the sake of the poor.*

We can start with Jesus' own mission statement in Luke 4:16-21. Jesus read from the prophet Isaiah, "The Spirit of the Lord is upon me, because he has anointed me to bring good news to the poor. He has sent me to proclaim release to the captives and recovery of sight to the blind, to let the oppressed go free, to proclaim the year of the Lord's favor" (4:18-19), and then he declared that he was the fulfillment of Isaiah's prophecy. Jesus' mission was political, social, and economic. He didn't just say he came to love the poor but also said he came to act on their behalf—to proclaim "release to captives," "recovery of sight to the blind," and freedom for the oppressed.

Again and again, Luke emphasizes Jesus' concern for social and economic justice. Jesus said, "Blessed are you who are poor, for yours is the kingdom of heaven," but he also said, "Woe to you who are rich" (6:20, 24). In the parable of the sower, Jesus warns that God's word cannot bear fruit in some because "they are choked by the cares and riches and pleasures of life" (8:14). When Jesus sent out the seventy in pairs, he instructed them, "Carry no purse, no bag, no sandals" (10:1-12). The parable of the rich fools, as the title suggests, is an unflattering portrayal of a rich man building bigger barns to hoard his vast wealth (12:13-21). Jesus said, "None of you can become my disciple if you do not give up all your possessions" (14:33), "You cannot serve God and wealth" (16:13), "It is easier for a camel to go through the eye of a needle than for someone who is rich to enter the kingdom of God" (18:25). Jesus encouraged his flock not to be afraid, "for it is your Father's good pleasure to give you the kingdom. Sell your possessions, and give alms. . . . For where your treasure is, there your heart will be also" (12:32-34). If giving away our possessions does not sound like good news, perhaps that tells us where our hearts are.

The story of Zacchaeus illustrates how a rich man can enter the kingdom of heaven. Luke (and the children's song) tells us that Zacchaeus was a wee little rich man, the chief tax collector of Jericho. After Jesus stayed in his home, Zacchaeus gave half of his possessions to the poor and promised to pay back four times as much to everyone he had defrauded. Jesus affirmed Zacchaeus's actions by saying, "Today salvation has come to this house." Unfortunately, another rich man was not so easily parted from his wealth. When the rich ruler asked, "What must I do to inherit eternal life?" Jesus said, "Sell all you own and give the money to the poor." He turned away sadly because he was "very rich" (18:23). Before we get too comfortable in our condemnation of the rich, we might want to consider our own financial status relative to that of the rest of the world. We may find that we too are among the rich. In these two examples, "salvation" is tied to the men's response to the poor.

The kingdom of God has a social, political, economic dimension that is often at odds with that of culture.

*(2) Within the kingdom of God, people experience repentance, conversion, forgiveness, and salvation.*

After his resurrection Jesus says, "Repentance and forgiveness of sins is to be proclaimed in [the Messiah's] name to all nations" (24:47). True to Jesus' commission, this message is preached in the missionary sermons of Acts. Peter in his Pentecost sermon proclaims, "Repent and be baptized every one of you, in the name of Jesus Christ, that your sins may be forgiven" (Acts 2:38; also 3:19; 5:31; 8:22; 10:43). Paul too preached the message of repentance and forgiveness for all people, including the Gentiles (Acts 13:38; 17:30; 20:21; 26:18, 20). In one sermon, Paul recounts his own dramatic conversion experience and the mission Jesus gave him: "I am sending you to open their eyes so that they may turn from darkness to light and from the power of Satan to God, so they may receive forgiveness of sins and a place among those who are sanctified by faith in me" (Acts 26:12-18).

*Repentance, Conversion, and Forgiveness.* If repentance is a conversion and a turnabout, what are we turning from and what are we turning to? For what sin are we to be forgiven?

A quick survey of Jesus' teaching in Luke describes both the life we are turning from and the renewed life we turn to—the behaviors, attitudes, and ways of life that Jesus condemns and those he praises: do not judge but forgive (6:37); no good tree bears bad fruit, nor does a bad tree bear good fruit (6:43-46; 13:6-9); do not receive the word of God and then let the world distract you, but hear God and obey (8:4-15); do not strive to be the greatest, but welcome children (9:46-48); follow Jesus above all others, even family (9:57-62; 14:25-33); woe to those who reject Jesus and do not listen to him (10:13-16); pray (11:5-13); justice and love of God is better than legalism (11:37-52); do not store up riches on earth but strive for the kingdom of God (12:13-31); do not be caught unprepared but be ready (12:35-40); when you have a feast do not invite friends, relatives, and rich neighbors, but invite the marginalized, the poor, those with disabilities (14:7-14); be good stewards, honest and faithful with what God has given you (16:1-13; 19:11-27); and love God and your neighbor as yourself (10:27). The stories Jesus told and his encounters with others illustrate sin, repentance, and forgiveness and also the rejection of the way of God and the refusal to repent.

Zacchaeus was a sinner because he cheated others to make himself rich (19:1-10). Repentance for Zacchaeus meant giving half of his possessions to the poor and repaying fourfold if he had defrauded anyone. Jesus' response to Zacchaeus's conversion was forgiveness and salvation: "Today salvation has come to this house. . . . For the Son of Man came to seek out and to save the lost" (19:9-10). On the other hand, when a rich ruler asked Jesus what he must do to inherit eternal life, Jesus first told the man to follow "the parts of the Ten Commandments which relate people with people,"[2] and when the ruler said that he did obey the commandments, Jesus added, "Go sell all that you own and distribute the money to the poor, and you will have treasure in heaven; then come, follow me" (18:22). The rich ruler, though he was obedient to the Ten Commandments, chose his possessions over following Jesus. The prodigal son's sin was greed, immoral living, and dishonoring his father. Repentance involved recognizing his lowly state, returning to his father, repenting, and asking forgiveness: "Father, I have sinned against heaven and earth and before you" (15:18). The sin of the obedient yet unrepentant elder brother in the story was in not loving his neighbor by refusing to accept his brother. In Jesus' parable of the Good Samaritan, the priest and the Levite, even though they have the benefit of a high level of religious teaching and should know better, walk right by a beaten man without offering assistance. A Samaritan, considered to be a sinner of the worst kind, is the one who offers extraordinary compassion. Thus it is the Samaritan and not the religious leaders who offer the example of a repentant lifestyle.[3]

Sin is refusal to follow Jesus, arrogance and pride, greedy accumulation of wealth while the poor suffer, oppression of outcasts, favoring the rich and those just like me over the stranger and the dispossessed, failure to show compassion, immoral living, acts of injustice—in short, a lack of love for God and neighbor.

As we have seen, repentance and conversion are not just turning from sin but also turning to Jesus. Maynard-Reid writes, "Conversion is a 'paradigm shift,' to borrow Thomas Kuhn's term, a change of perspective in which one enters a new personal relationship with Jesus and joins him and his community in the task of transforming the world," and "transformation involves the pursuit of justice and equity in society."[4] Bosch notes that conversion is communal: "it moves the individual believer into the community of believers and involves real—even a radical—change in the life of the believer, which carries with it moral responsibilities that distinguish Christians from 'outsiders' while at the same time stressing their obligation to those 'outsiders.'"[5] Conversion is submitting to the reign of God, joining God's mission for the world.

*Salvation.* Repentance and forgiveness lead to salvation. For many, "salvation" is used almost exclusively to refer to an individual soul's rescue from the deadly consequences of sin to eternal life in heaven. While there is the idea of a person moving from "darkness to light," as Paul says (Acts 26:18), salvation is more comprehensive than an individual's spiritual justification. So how are we to understand salvation in Luke? In Zechariah's prophecy at the birth of John, salvation sounds political. Filled with the Holy Spirit, John's father says that God "has raised up a mighty savior for us, in the house of his servant David" and "that we would be saved from our enemies" (1:69, 71). Salvation includes the casting out of demonic forces and physical healing, often thought of as one in the same. When the Seventy returned from a successful mission of healing the sick and proclaiming the kingdom of God, Jesus said, "I watched Satan fall from the sky" (10:1-20). After announcing in the synagogue that his mission included "release to the captives and recovery of sight to the blind" (4:18), Jesus went down to Capernaum where he cast a demon out of a man (4:31-37) and healed Simon's mother-in-law and many others (4:38-41), while "Demons also came out of many" (4:41).

Salvation is not simply physical health; it is also spiritual healing. To the blind beggar, Jesus said, "Receive your sight; your faith has saved you" (18:42). Jesus healed ten lepers. One returned to say, "Thank you." Jesus said, "Your faith has made you well" (17:19). We might say nine lepers were healed and one was saved. Salvation—eternal life—for the lawyer meant loving God and neighbors, even despised neighbors, with concrete sacrificial acts of caring. Bosch notes that "Salvation involves the reversal of all the evil consequences of sin, against both God and neighbor."[6] And Maynard-Reid writes, "Salvation for Luke is wholistic. It is the transformation of body, soul, and spirit."[7]

Salvation is centered on Jesus. Jesus called Zacchaeus down out of his tree, "for I am going to your house today" (19:5), and at Zacchaeus' pledge to give half of his possessions to the poor and to repay those he had defrauded fourfold, he said to him, "Today salvation has come to this house" (19:9). The prodigal son was restored to his father (representative of God) and given an elaborate feast. To the repentant thief on the cross, Jesus said, "Today, you will be with me in Paradise" (23:43). Most importantly, salvation means being present with Jesus, God, and the Christian community both now and forever.

How we receive this salvation resists our simple formulas. The lawyer was to love God and Samaritan neighbors through acts of compassion. Zacchaeus and the rich ruler were asked to give their riches to the poor. The beggar cried out, "Son of David, have mercy on me." Jesus frequently asked people to "follow me." The healed Samaritan leper returned to Jesus to thank him. The prodigal son came to his senses and returned to the father asking forgiveness. The thief on the cross admonished the other thief, telling him he "should fear God" and confessing that he deserved his punishment. The woman at the Pharisee's house anointed Jesus with perfume out of love, and her faith saved her.

*(3) The kingdom of God is a banquet to which everyone is welcomed and barriers of race, nationality, and socioeconomic status are removed.*

Jesus says in his commissioning statement, "repentance and forgiveness of sins is to be proclaimed in his name to *all* nations beginning from Jerusalem" (24:47), and "you will be my witnesses in Jerusalem, in all Judea and Samaria, and to the ends of the earth" (Acts 1:8). All people, from all nations, are welcome at God's banquet table.

In Luke's Gospel, McKinnish Bridges points out, "Jesus is constantly either going to a meal, at a meal, or coming from a meal. Place Jesus at a dining room table filled with all kinds of folk whom the religious tradition had rejected, and you will see Luke's portrait of Jesus clear and undiluted."[8] In eating with anyone and everyone, Jesus showed that the kingdom was for all, including especially those rejected as unclean.

Three of Jesus' feasts illustrate how Jesus' invitation to the table is offered to dispossessed Jews. On one occasion, Jesus accepted an invitation to a banquet with tax collectors, hosted by Levi the tax collector (Luke 5:27-32). Tax collectors were despised as traitors and were considered dishonest and unclean. The scribes and Pharisees asked, "Why do you eat and drink with tax collectors and sinners?" On another occasion, Jesus ate at the home of a Pharisee. While they were eating, a woman, described as a sinner, entered. The fact that a woman entered a room full of men uninvited was scandalous enough, but then she bathed Jesus' feet with her tears and dried them with her hair, creating a murmur of disapproval. Jesus accepted the woman at the table and said, "your sins are forgiven. . . .Your faith has saved you. Go in peace" (7:36-50). Later, Jesus was invited to share a Sabbath meal with a leader of the Pharisees, along with others who "were watching him closely" (14:1-24). Observing how the guests were jockeying for positions of honor at the table, Jesus admonished the guests to seek the "lowest place" and the host to expand the guest list: "When you give a luncheon or a dinner, do not invite your friends or your brothers or your relatives or rich neighbors, in case they may invite you in return, and you would be repaid. But when you give a banquet, invite the poor, the crippled, the lame, and the blind" (14:12-13). Then Jesus told the parable of "the great dinner," which suggested that the lawyers and Pharisees with whom Jesus was eating were refusing God's invitation to the kingdom of God and that the doors were now open wide to the uninvited—"the poor, the crippled, the blind, and the lame" (14:21).

Jesus' concern for Samaritans further illustrates how the kingdom of God has no boundaries. Samaritans were at the lowest end of the purity scale in Jewish reckoning, after Israelites with slight blemishes, Israelites with grave blemishes, and Gentile slaves.[9] On one occasion, Jesus was denied passage through Samaria, angering James and John. Yet Jesus elevated Samaritans and welcomed them into the kingdom community. He made a Samaritan the hero of his parable about loving neighbors—the one we call the parable of the Good Samaritan. When Jesus healed ten lepers, the lone Samaritan was the only one who came back to thank him. While most Jews took the longer route around Samaria, Jesus went directly through Samaria.

The book of Acts is the story of how the gospel extends to the Gentiles and the ends of the earth. After some struggle, the church continues Jesus' mission and welcomes Gentiles into the kingdom community, thanks to the guidance of the Holy Spirit and to the stubbornness and determination of Paul.

Thus, God's banquet table is large enough to seat Jews, Samaritans, Gentiles, women, lepers, tax collectors, sinners, prostitutes, rich and poor, the outcasts, and all people, from Jerusalem to the ends of the earth. God's house has a big table.

*(4) God's kingdom is peace, not vengeance. It is God's kingdom, not nationalism.*

The first few chapters of Luke have references to the mission of Jesus that sound political, expressing hope for the restoration of the nation of Israel (see, for example, 1:46-55; 1:68-79; 2:29-32). When Jesus reads from the prophet Isaiah in the synagogue, the response is initially positive. Isaiah was writing to the exiles in Babylon, prophesying the "year of the LORD's favor" when Babylonian domination would end and Israel would return to Jerusalem to control their own destiny. These verses resonated with a people under Roman rule. They were pleased that Jesus chose to read this Scripture. However, Jesus left out a key phrase—"the day of vengeance of our God"—and his commentary makes it clear that political and military revolution was not his desire. When Jesus says, "Today this scripture has been fulfilled in your hearing," the people expect from Jesus patriotic nationalism and revenge on Israel's enemies, especially Rome. But Jesus has no room for vengeance. Instead, he proclaims compassion for those enemies by citing examples of Gentile foreigners who received God's blessings. Jesus is "wholly different from what has been expected," according to Bosch. "He is the Anointed of God who will announce a year of favor for both Jews *and* their opponents."[10] This story serves as a caution to any of us who would seek to create a Christian state or to place allegiance to state above that of God's reign. The kingdom of God is not a nation state over against other nations. Love of enemies, not vengeance, is the way of the kingdom of God.

When a Samaritan village refused to receive Jesus, James and John wanted to call down fire from heaven on them in retribution. Jesus quickly rebuked them, and they went on to another village. Jesus would not take vengeance on his enemies.

Jesus' arrest, trial, and death are the ultimate examples of the peaceful nonviolent way that Jesus chose for himself and modeled for the church. When Judas betrayed Jesus with a kiss, one disciple cut off the high priest's slave's ear with a sword, and the rest were ready to take up swords to defend Jesus from the authorities (22:47-53). Jesus said, "no more of this," healed the slave's ear, and surrendered himself to the officials. Jesus was beaten, mocked, falsely accused, flogged, and crucified, and his response to all of this was not hatred and revenge but peaceful submission and these words: "Father, forgive them; for they do not know what they are doing" (23:34).

Contrary to our human instincts, Jesus teaches us to forgive when wronged rather than exacting revenge. "Luke," according to Bosch, "presents [his audience] with a challenge: Jesus and his powerful message of nonviolent resistance and above all loving one's enemy in word and deed. The peace that comes with Jesus is not won through weapons, but through love, forgiveness, and acceptance of one's enemies into the covenant community."[11]

*(5) God is present within the kingdom through the Holy Spirit. The Holy Spirit empowers the kingdom.*

Though Jesus is no longer physically present with the Christian community after his ascension into heaven, Jesus remains present within the community in the form of the Holy Spirit. Jesus said, "I am sending upon you what my Father promised; so stay here in the city until you have been clothed with power from on high" (Luke 24:49), and "you will receive power when the Holy Spirit has come upon you" (Acts 1:8). The life of the kingdom community is guided and empowered by the Holy Spirit. Thus, prayer and discernment characterize the kingdom community, looking within for the inspiration and guidance of the Spirit of God.

The Holy Spirit initiated the mission and witness of the church. They were to wait until the Holy Spirit came upon them and empowered them. At Pentecost, as promised, the Holy Spirit was poured out on the believers. The church was born and commissioned. Peter preached the new church's first sermon: "This Jesus God raised up, and of that all of us are witnesses" (Acts 2:32). As a result, the church received its first converts (2:37-42).

Empowered by the Spirit, the disciples went from hiding in fear to speaking the message boldly, risking and suffering persecution, imprisonment, beatings, and death. Peter, who not so long ago had denied that he even knew Jesus, now fearlessly confronted his fellow Jews with the message of Jesus. Luke frequently uses the words "boldness" and "speaking boldly" when referring the witness of the believers and says "they were all filled with the Holy Spirit and spoke the word of God with boldness" (4:31; see also 4:13, 29; 9:27; 13:46; 14:3; 18:26; 19:8; 28:30-31). The book of Acts is the story of how the church, empowered by the Holy Spirit, was able to accomplish amazing things and witness powerfully to kingdom of God come in Christ Jesus.

Not only does the Spirit initiate and empower the mission of the church; the Spirit guides the missionaries. Bosch notes several examples in the book of Acts:

> Philip's encounter with the Ethiopian eunuch, for instance, is through the agency of the Spirit (Acts 8:29). Of special importance for the understanding of Luke's second volume is the conversion of Cornelius. The acceptance of this Gentile (without circumcision!) into the Christian fold is confirmed when a second Pentecost is enacted: the Spirit is poured out even on a Gentile and his family (Acts 10:44-48). In his report to the Jerusalem community, Peter explains that it was the Spirit who told him not to hesitate but to go to Cornelius (Acts 11:12). Again, the ratification by the Jerusalem Council of the decision to baptize Gentiles without prior circumcision is also described as having taken place under the impulse of the Spirit (Acts 15:8, 28) (cf Zingg 1973:207; Senior and Stuhlmueller 1983:275). Similarly, it is the Spirit who charges the worshiping and fasting church of Antioch to set Saul and Barnabas apart for a special task (13:2), as it is the Spirit who sends them on their way (13:4). The Spirit prevents Paul from going deeper into Asia (16:6): through the vision of a man from Macedonia the Spirit directs him to Europe (16:9). In all these narratives the emphasis is on the Holy Spirit as catalyst, guide, and inspirer toward mission.[12]

Certainly, Luke's emphasis on the Holy Spirit tells us that, as a church, we should listen and be aware of God's presence. For the community, time in prayer, reflection, and discernment is essential to the church's witness so that we might learn the Spirit's direction and boldly follow God's leading.

*(6) The kingdom of God is a journey.*

Jesus called his disciples to follow him and they did. To Levi (or Matthew) the tax collector Jesus said, "Follow me" (5:27-28). Jesus said to the fisherman Peter, who was with James and John, "from now on you will be catching people" (5:10-11). In both instances Luke adds that they "left everything and followed him." In Luke's Gospel, this journey carried the disciples through Galilee on their way to Jerusalem, the place of Jesus' passion—his suffering, crucifixion, and death. Along the way they listened to Jesus' teaching and observed his actions and became his community. At Jesus' ascension the disciples learned that the journey continues for them, and the Christian community today, from Jerusalem to Judea and Samaria and to the ends of the earth.

The kingdom, or salvation, is not a onetime event of repentance and conversion but a life of following Jesus with the Christian community—learning, growing, and living out the teachings of Jesus.

## The Message of the Kingdom

In a chapter on witness, you may have expected a list of steps to salvation, like the ABCs of how to become a Christian, the Roman Road to Salvation, or Steps to Peace with God. Instead of simple steps to an end, though, Jesus gives us a kingdom to proclaim. Jesus offers a way of life to which we invite others to become a part—a life marked by concern for the poor; repentance, conversion, forgiveness, and salvation; diversity; peace; God's presence through the Holy Spirit; growth; and more. Jesus said, "You are witnesses of these things" (Luke 24:48).

The message we proclaim is not merely that, if we agree intellectually with certain statements about Jesus, such as "Jesus died and rose again to save me of my sins," then we will gain heaven and avoid hell. The message we proclaim is an invitation to be a part of the Christian community, following Jesus and submitting to the reign of God, where we love God with all our being and love our neighbors as we love ourselves, where the poor and all who are marginalized are lifted up, where those who have more than they need give it up for those who have less than they need, where neighbors are treated with fairness, where barriers of race, socioeconomic status, and nationality are torn down and everyone is welcome at God's banquet table, where vengeance is set aside and love for enemies, forgiveness, and peace are the norm, where the old sinful way of life is totally transformed into new life through repentance and forgiveness, where we live in communion with Jesus the Christ, led by and empowered by the Holy Spirit—now and forever.

Lee C. Camp in *Mere Discipleship* offers this synopsis of the good news we bear witness to:

> God created a good creation in order to be in relationship. In rebellion, we rejected the offer of relationship, made a hell of God's good creation, and find ourselves enslaved to those things created for our good. In God's mercy, God consistently pursued covenant relationship and sought to redeem the rebellious creation. God offered in Jesus a new beginning, the kingdom of God, the new creation. We rejected him again and killed the Son. Yet our rebellion did not have the last word, for Jesus' obedience even unto death unmasked the rebellious powers of this world for what

they are—weak, paltry, concerned only with their own pitiful self-existence. Thus the Father raised him from the grave—and offers that same power of renewal to be at work in his covenant people, embodying the new creation. We may receive the Good News (which comes with the same suffering experienced by Jesus, for the world lives yet in rebellion) and trust that we shall be vindicated and blessed beyond measure by fellowship with God. Or we may continue in our rebellion, left to our own peril, self-centeredness, loneliness, and hell.[13]

## *How Do We Witness?*

So how does a church bear witness to the kingdom? We can think about the witness of the church in terms of four overlapping ideas: community, proclamation, the practices of the church, and the example or life of the church.

Many of us have been trained to see evangelism as a solo act—one individual Christian sharing the message of Christ with a lost person. This may be a piece of evangelism, but witnessing is the work of the church community. Even when an individual shares the good news with another, they do so as part of the larger Christian community, which points to the kingdom, helping to embody the good news and making it easier for another to grasp. When one comes to faith in Christ, they become a part of that Christian community where they are nurtured in the faith. The "you" in "you shall be my witnesses" (Acts 1:8) is plural, as is the "you" in "you are witnesses of these things" (Luke 24:48).[14]

The church (plural) in word and deed bears witness to the kingdom. The proclamation of the church, its practices, and the example of community life point to the kingdom, already come but not yet fully realized. The church is not the kingdom. The church is a glimpse of what the kingdom is like. The church is not a perfect representation of the kingdom, but even in imperfection the church can demonstrate the reconciliation, forgiveness, and growth found in God's kingdom.

Our teaching, preaching, and everyday conversations proclaim Jesus' life, teachings, suffering, and resurrection. Our words declare the good news of the kingdom of God. Our actions show what that can look like in real life.

The practices of the church bear witness to the kingdom: prayer, missions, worship, care, and teaching. These key functions of the church and others are demonstrations of kingdom life. As a community we offer praise and thanksgiving to God in worship, thereby showing to the world where our loyalties lie. Our sacred symbols and symbolic acts in worship—Communion, baptism, the cross, the Bible, and others—embody and share the message. Kingdom people talk to God and listen to God and hold up the concerns of the world in prayer. When we engage in missions and care for one another, we continue the work of Christ who taught us to love our neighbors. The task of teaching shows that we continue to follow and learn from Jesus as disciples. All of these functions proclaim in concrete and symbolic ways what it means to be a Christian community. The witness of the church is not limited to "official" church practices. Everything we do as a church can bear witness to the kingdom or confuse the message.

Lee Camp, in *Mere Discipleship*, asks a challenging question: "The gospel proclaims that the coming reign of God has already broken into human history. But why should the world believe this?" The evidence of history would dispute this claim. "Since the time of Jesus, war-making continues, greed consumes, injustice pervades."[15] If Jesus was the Messiah, where is the promised era of peace?

How does the church answer these challenging questions? Justin Martyr, one of the early Church Fathers, answered this way:

> For from Jerusalem there went out into the world, men, twelve in number, and these illiterate, of no ability in speaking: but by the power of God they proclaimed to every race of men that they were sent by Christ to teach to all the word of God; and we who formerly used to murder one another do not only now refrain from making war upon our enemies, but also, that we may not lie nor deceive our examiners, willingly die confessing Christ. For that saying, The tongue has sworn but the mind is unsworn, might be imitated by us in this matter. (First Apology 39)

Justin was confident enough to say, "You want proof that Jesus is the Messiah of peace? Look at our community." Could we be so bold as to say to the world, "Look at us for an example of life as God intends it, a life of love, forgiveness, reconciliation, and peace"? Whether or not we say, "Look at us," the world does look at us, and what they see is either a witness to the kingdom or a lie. So everything we do is important. Do we conduct our business in a discerning, loving, and prayerful manner or simply according to a win-lose business-style bottom line? Are we accepting of people who are not like us? When a member of the community sins, do we ostracize them, or do we seek reconciliation and offer forgiveness and grace? Are we honest and just in our dealings? Do we care about Jesus' "least of these"? Are the words of John 13:35 true for us: "By this everyone will know that you are my disciples, if you have love for one another"? The life of our community is, or should be, our witness. Camp said it well:

> If the Good News is the presence of the kingdom of God, then "evangelism" is much more than "saving souls." Evangelism means sharing and showing to the world how to realistically, faithfully, and creatively respond to the real needs of a world laboring under ongoing rebellion. Evangelism means living according to the ways of the kingdom of God and inviting others to join us on the way. Evangelism is not selling Jesus, but showing Jesus; evangelism is not mere telling about Christ, but about being Christ.[16]

In large part, Saint Patrick and his missionary Christian community was able to reach the Celtic people by "being Christ" in their presence. Patrick's missionary teams established monastic communities near tribal settlements so that the day-by-day Christian way of life could be observed. The Celtic people were invited to belong to the community and participate in Christian practices of ministry, prayer, worship, Bible study, and conversation. After seeing and belonging, they came to believe and practice the Christian faith in a form indigenous to their culture.[17]

In Jesus' parable of the Good Samaritan, helping the man on the side of the road is witnessing to the kingdom. The Good Samaritan, by his actions, is witnessing to life as God intends: a life where people are not beaten and left on the side of the road; where race is not discriminated against; where we love God and neighbor, especially the neighbor who has been forgotten and abused.

## Putting Witness into Practice

Following are some specific approaches a disciple community might take for bearing witness to the kingdom and proclaiming the good news. Certainly there are other ways for a church to be faithful in its witness, depending on its unique calling and context.

### The Celtic Way of Evangelism

In *The Celtic Way of Evangelism*, George Hunter describes how Saint Patrick's Christian community reached the supposedly unreachable Barbarians of Ireland. After years of having lived among the Celtic people, learning their language and understanding their culture, Patrick reached out to them with the gospel. Patrick would approach a tribal settlement with a team of twelve or more and, with permission, set up camp adjacent to the settlement. Here seekers could observe how the Christians lived day by day. The "team would meet the people, engage them in conversation and in ministry, and look for people who appeared receptive. They would pray for sick people, and for possessed people, and they would counsel people and mediate conflicts." In addition,

> They would engage in open air speaking, probably employing parable, story, poetry, song, visual symbols, visual arts and, perhaps, drama to engage the Celtic people's remarkable imaginations. . . . The apostolic band would probably welcome responsive people into their group fellowship to worship with them, pray with them, minister to them, converse with them and break bread together. . . . The church that emerged with them would have been astonishingly indigenous.[18]

Patrick's approach was based on his deep understanding of the people: their love for heroic stories, their use of imagination and visual symbols, their appreciation of ambiguity and paradox, and their respect for nature. This understanding informed his message. For example, the Celtic people were comfortable with paradox and "were aware that Ultimate Reality was mysterious and complex." They also had a fascination for the number three. So perceptively, "when Irish seekers ask Patrick how Christianity understands God, he withdraws, from the bank of Christian doctrine, the doctrine of the Trinity." Thus the "doctrine of the Trinity became the foundational paradigm for Celtic Christianity."[19] The familiar shamrock is one of many ways this doctrine was symbolized in Celtic Christianity.

Not everything in the culture could be incorporated into the Christian faith and practice. The Celtic Christians were "Trinitarian Monotheists," while the native religious tradition included the worship of many local gods and idols. These other gods were challenged and their idols were not accepted as a part of Christian faith, though many of their symbols and sacred places were transformed into Christian symbols.

Five themes summarize the Celtic approach to evangelism: (1) Evangelism works best with a team approach. In contrast to "'Lone Ranger' one-to-one evangelism," they engaged in "friendship, conversation, ministry, and witness" in community. (2) The community prepared people to "live with depth, compassion, and power in mission." The community was formed spiritually through a combination of solitary isolation, time with a "soul friend" and with a small group, participation in the "common life, meals, work, learning, biblical recitation, prayers, and worship" with the whole community, and ministry observation and experience. (3) Imaginative prayer played a role in all settings. Celtic prayers are well known for their poetry and connection to everyday life. "Christ in my lying, Christ in my sitting, Christ in my rising" is a line from one of Patrick's more popular prayers. (4) The community had a hospitality ministry with seekers, visitors, and refugees. (5) The seeker's experience was respected within the Christian community in the process of conversion. In contrast to the more Western approach of believing and then joining the fellowship, in the Celtic tradition belonging usually precedes believing. Participation in the life of the Christian community leads to belief.[20]

## Learning from Patrick and the Celtic Way of Evangelism

Hunter contends that within Western culture there is a significant population of what he calls "New Barbarians." He notes these similarities to the situation in Patrick's Ireland and significant parts of Western culture today: (1) The "New Barbarians" are secular. Many have no church background, and we cannot assume that they are influenced, to any large degree, by Christianity. (2) Postmodern culture is similar to that of the Celts in its suspicion of authority, emphasis on what you see, touch, and experience over what you hear, trust in intuition and not just logic, and desire for community. (3) Most churches assume, or at least behave as if, the postmodern so-called "New Barbarians" are unreachable. Many, if not most, church members are uncomfortable with the language, dress, behavior, and values of these "New Barbarians" and are not sure they want them in their churches.

Thus, the following approaches, similar to those used to reach the Celtic peoples, could be effective for the Western church attempting to reach postmoderns with no church background:

(1) Witness through the life of the community. Everything we do—worship, baptism, Communion, Bible study, prayer, ministry, sharing meals, and conducting our business—we do before a watching world.

(2) Send missionary teams. Smaller communities within the church could go out to live among people and immerse themselves in the dress, language, and customs of the culture when not inconsistent with their Christian faith.

(3) Teach and encourage private prayer.

(4) Offer "soul friends" for encouragement and accountability in the Christian journey. "Soul friends" are prayer partners and more, sort of like mentors, but the friends mentor each other equally.

(5) Involve seekers in small groups like home fellowship groups, Bible study groups, and special interest groups, where the Christian life can be embodied.

(6) Remember that "belonging can come before believing." This is not uncommon in churches today. Few people profess faith in Christ after a presentation of the gospel and then join a church. Most come to believe after being involved in a small group, worship, or ministry in the church where they develop friendships, engage in conversations, and observe how Christians live.

(7) Cultivate a concern for the everyday. For example, a book of contemporary Celtic-style prayers includes prayers for a new job, the kitchen, going to school, travel, a new bicycle, a pet, or for a variety of illnesses.[21] A church, in an effort to reach out to the local business community, could develop a prayer for downtown businesses written by church members who work there.

(8) Extend hospitality to all. This requires intentionality regarding visitors to our church who do not look and act like us, to make sure they are noticed and made to feel welcomed. For those who typically do not attend our church—whose dress, language, and customs are not like ours—we may need to discern God's mission for our church and recommit ourselves to that mission. We will have to get out of our comfort zones, sometimes in dramatic ways.

(9) Use imagination, story, poetry, art, music, and drama in communicating the gospel message.

(10) Empower the laity. All Christians are gifted and called for ministry, not just paid church staff ministers.

(11) Use community practices. Incorporate appropriate music styles, stories, symbols, celebrations, and customs of the people in your neighborhood.

(12) Live in contrast to the cultural norms that are contrary to the Christian faith. Not everything in a given culture is relevant and consistent with the kingdom of God. Some cultural values should be challenged and not absorbed.

## Lifestyle Evangelism

The premise of "lifestyle evangelism" advocated by Helen T. Boursier,[22] Jeffrey Johnson,[23] and Bill Hybels and Mark Mittleberg[24] is that we each have different personality types, so it is best to use, primarily, a style of evangelism that fits our personality. This should come as a relief to most of us whose primary style is not "confrontational." When we think of evangelism and evangelists, the confrontational style may come to mind. Lifestyle evangelism expands the idea of what it means to be evangelistic and how to go about sharing the good news. Each of the above-named authors has a slightly different but very similar way of labeling evangelism styles. Basically, five styles could be identified: (1) assertive/confrontational, (2) analytical/intellectual, (3) storytelling/testimonial, (4) relational/interpersonal, (5) invitational, and (6) incarnational/servant.

### Assertive/Confrontational

Often when we think of evangelism, we think of a confrontational approach. Some people are comfortable talking to strangers and find it easier than most to talk directly about matters of faith. Johnson says, "Assertive personalities engage life with a verbal directness," and "they tend to be competitive, confident, bold, decisive, and direct; they have very definite, often passionate, opinions."[25]

Peter's Pentecost sermon is an example of the assertive style. When observers questioned what the events of Pentecost meant, Peter immediately launched into a sermon. Luke says, "Peter stood with the eleven apostles and spoke in a loud and clear voice to the crowd . . . 'listen carefully what I have to say.'" Peter proclaimed that Jesus was the fulfillment of prophecy, confronted his fellow Jews for having Jesus put to death, announced that Jesus had been raised from the dead, and implored the people to repent, be baptized, and receive forgiveness. As a result of Peter's confrontational sermon, Luke tells us, 3,000 people believed and were baptized.

### Analytical/Intellectual

The analytical person is logical, studied, and needs for things to make sense. Johnson writes that analytical people are "inquisitive, often well educated . . . They enjoy discussions about controversial issues. They enjoy debating topics and issues," and "they like to dig into the underlying reasons people hold certain opinions and beliefs."[26]

Paul is one who used an analytical or intellectual approach. Acts 17:1-4 provides an excellent example:

After Paul and Silas had passed through Amphipolis and Apollonia, they came to Thessalonica, where there was a synagogue of the Jews. And Paul went in, as was his custom, and on three sabbath days argued with them from the scriptures, explaining and proving that it was necessary for the Messiah to suffer and to rise from the dead, and saying, "This is the Messiah, Jesus whom I am proclaiming to you." Some of them were persuaded and joined Paul and Silas, as did a great many of the devout Greeks and not a few of the leading women.

## Storytelling/Testimonial

Story is powerful. We can relate to a good story. The best stories touch on basic themes and experiences common to all people. Our testimony of how God has worked in our lives and what Jesus means to us may connect with the life experiences of others. Hearing such a testimony may help a neighbor imagine how they could relate to God in a similar way. The honest testimony of another may give me comfort in knowing I'm not the only one who struggles at times. Your story can become my story, my story can become your story, and the gospel story can become our story. Some people are especially gifted as storytellers. Johnson describes the storytelling personality this way: "Storytellers are entertaining, engaging people. . . . Their verbiage is more descriptive and their gestures more demonstrative. . . . They are able to make you feel that you are reliving the experience with them."[27]

The story of the blind man healed by Jesus, found in John 9, is an example of the testimonial approach. When confronted by religious leaders seeking a simple answer with which to condemn Jesus, the formerly blind man told the story of how Jesus had healed him. This was not what they wanted to hear, so they asked him again, and he shared his story concisely: "All I know is, I used to be blind, but now I can see!" (John 9:25).

## Relational/Interpersonal

Johnson notes that the first three evangelism styles are word based, while the relational style is the first of the works-based evangelism styles for those whose actions speak louder than words. "Relational individuals," Johnson states, "are available, trustworthy, attentive to others, transparent, connective, and very loving. They are genuine, sympathetic, unconditional, nonjudgmental, and patient. They believe in shared experiences."[28] Relational evangelists make friends, invite people to their homes, and take time to listen to other people's joys and hurts.

Matthew (or Levi) is an example of relational evangelism. After he became a follower of Jesus, Matthew hosted a big dinner for Jesus and invited many of his fellow tax collectors and others (Luke 5:29). Matthew brought together friends and coworkers so they could meet Jesus, relate to Jesus, and experience Jesus as he had. Matthew shared Jesus, literally, with those with whom he had built relationships.

## Invitational

Perhaps the invitational style is the one used most often by Christians. Many of us are accustomed to inviting others to church worship services, Sunday school class, or other church events. Rather than specifically sharing the gospel, we invite neighbors to church, where they will hear the message proclaimed and taught and see it lived out by other Christians. "Invitational people are hospitable," according to Johnson. "They are inclusive. They are constantly thinking about others. They do not even go to the store without thinking about someone else going along."[29]

The Samaritan woman at the well used the invitational approach. After her encounter with Jesus at the well in Samaria when Jesus told her everything she had ever done and offered her living water, she immediately ran back into town to invite everyone to meet Jesus. "Come see a man who told me everything I have ever done! Could he be the Messiah?" (John 4:29). John writes that everyone did come and see. As a result of the woman's invitation to her town, Jesus stayed among them a couple days, and when he left they said, "We have faith in Jesus because we have heard him ourselves" (4:42). Those who use the invitational style don't necessarily share the message themselves but invite people to places where they can hear the message.

## Incarnational/Servant

The incarnation of God was God with us in the bodily form of Jesus. The incarnational approach embodies the message of Christ through service after the example of Jesus. Christians and the church are incarnational when they live among people as an example of the Christian life. The life of the Christian community at worship, home, work, and leisure is a living witness to the good news of Jesus. Acts of service of all types are ways of demonstrating the love of God and being with people. Johnson states that the incarnational style of evangelism "involves linking up with people and walking alongside them—not for minutes, not for hours, not for days or even weeks—but months that literally spill over into years."[30]

Dorcas is an example of the incarnational style. It was said of her that "She was always doing good things for people and had given much to the poor" (Acts 9:36). Jesus is the ultimate example of the incarnational style: "Let the same mind be in you that was in Christ Jesus, who, though he was in the form of God, did not regard equality with God as something to be exploited, but emptied himself, taking the form of a slave [servant], being born in human likeness. And being found in human form, he humbled himself and became obedient to the point of death—even death on a cross" (Phil 2:5-8).

Johnson offers a personal assessment[31] to help people discover the evangelism style that best fits their personality. Chances are, though, most people probably know which style or styles they are most comfortable with. The point of evangelism styles is that Christians are unique, and there is more than one way to share the good news with the world. We can find an evangelism style that fits our personality.

## Servant Evangelism

The days when a church member could knock on a stranger's door and expect to be invited in for a long conversation about the church and salvation are long gone. Few people today feel they have time or that their home is ready for unexpected guests, even friends. Certainly, no one invites a stranger into their home. No longer can it be assumed that the family behind the door has some Christian background or that, if they are not a church member now, deep down they know they ought to be. Many people have a negative impression of Christians and the church.

How does the church overcome skepticism and negative stereotypes in order to share the good news of the kingdom? Steve Sjogren, in *Conspiracy of Kindness*, advocates servant evangelism, which is "demonstrating the kindness of God by offering some act of humble service with no strings attached."[32] Sjogren's church members regularly offer service or gifts of kindness such as car washes, cleaning toilets in businesses, shoe shines, soft drinks, Christmas gift-wrapping, raking leaves, or gum. When the recipients of these acts of kindness ask, "Why are you doing this?" they answer, "We just want to show you God's love in a practical way."

I joined Sjogren's Vineyard Fellowship on a Saturday for one of their Servant Evangelism outreach efforts. I was placed in a group that visited a nursing home. After introductions, an explanation of our purpose, and prayer, we visited the nursing home residents. Some visited residents in their rooms, offering gum, playing cards, and sometimes painting women's fingernails. I was with a group that visited Alzheimer's patients, engaging in conversation and batting a balloon up in the air back and forth. Their purpose truly was to demonstrate God's love in a practical way. There was little chance the church would gain new members from among these nursing home residents.

Sjogren looks to Jesus' ministry as the example of servant evangelism: "Jesus was a bringer of God's love to the broken world."[33] Jesus claimed the words of Isaiah 61 as his mission statement: "He has sent me to bring good news to the poor," "sight to the blind," "to let the oppressed go free," and "to proclaim the year of the Lord's favor" (Luke 4:18-19). The goal of servant evangelism is to "bring the kingdom of God to this city through acts of love and mercy. Everything in the Christian life flows out of the first commandment: to love God with our heart, soul, strength, and mind. That *vertical love*, from God to us, lays the foundation for any other love. *Horizontal love* for our neighbor overflows out of the love of God."[34] Sjogren believes that Jesus was especially interested in the poor, and we should be too. He writes, "Though Jesus loved everybody, he apparently *enjoyed* some people more than others. His heart especially went out to the poor, the sick, and the lost."[35] Jesus' parable of the Good Samaritan provides a model for servant evangelism. By reflecting on the actions of the priest, Levite, and Samaritan, Sjogren suggests, we can learn several principles: "Be 'with the people'"; "Step out of your comfort zone"; "Bring the kingdom"; "Begin to care"; and "Make yourself available."[36]

I have been a part of churches that have attempted to reach out to neighbors and businesses across the street from the church by delivering brownies to businesses and home-baked loaves of bread, tea, devotion books written by members, and children's books to residential neighbors, in addition to offering neighborhood block parties, fall festivals, and health fairs on the church grounds. Church sports teams have given water bottles and sports drinks to opponents. Though on rare occasions someone may rudely close the door on church members offering one of these acts of kindness, the response of our neighbors has been overwhelmingly positive. Acts of kindness with no strings attached are disarming. One of our volleyball opponents, after he was given one of our colorful volleyball water bottles, said, "Now that's the gospel with skin on it." He expressed very well what we hope to accomplish with servant evangelism.

One of the acts of kindness Sjogren refers to that intrigues me is "toilet cleaning" for businesses. It is no doubt a humbling and dirty job, the work of servants. I can't help but think of toilet cleaning as a contemporary equivalent of the foot washing that Jesus demonstrated and implored his disciples to emulate.

## Hospitality Evangelism

"Welcome! We are glad you came." Perhaps the first thing that comes to mind when we hear the word "hospitality" in the context of church is the way we greet guests who come to our church services. The goal of hospitality to church visitors is to make them feel welcomed. We do this in a number of ways that will vary from one church to the next, but here are a few practical considerations:

- Do we greet guests with a smile, a handshake, and a kind word that comes from a genuine love for people and a desire to welcome them into the church family?
- Is everyone welcome?
- Will a guest know where to park, and can they find a parking spot near a usable door?
- Church buildings can have many doors. Can a first-time guest find their way to the right door?
- Is our facility accessible to people with disabilities and to the elderly?
- Are there members present in the parking lot, at entry doors, and in classrooms when guests enter to greet and direct them?
- Can guests find their way around our building to restrooms, classes, the fellowship hall, and the sanctuary? Are there maps, clear signs, and, preferably, members to guide them? Are rooms and directions clearly marked?
- How do we welcome guests to small groups, suppers, worship, or special events?
- Do we have a way of minimizing or explaining the church language, customs, inside jokes, and abbreviations that we are accustomed to using among ourselves but that may be difficult for outsiders to understand? For example, from the pulpit we might say something like "this is a hymn or Scripture we all know," but a guest may not, or after reading Scripture the reader may say, "This is the word of the Lord," and the congregation responds, "Thanks be to God," without being prompted. Unexplained practices could feel awkward for guests.
- Do we have a system that ensures that no one enters and leaves our services and events without being greeted?
- Do we follow up with guests after they visit our church?

Christian hospitality includes our casual greeting of guests and the important considerations listed above, but it goes much deeper than saying "hello!" to new but familiar faces. Christian hospitality, as we learn from the parable of the Good Samaritan, includes the stranger and far more care than a simple greeting.

The kind of hospitality Jesus practiced may demand more of our churches than we are comfortable with or accustomed to offering. The sheep and the goats, according to Jesus in Matthew 25, will be divided based on who did and did not extend hospitality to the hungry by feeding them, the poor by clothing them, prisoners and the sick by visiting them, and the stranger by welcoming them. Hospitality involves personal, face-to-face involvement with those normally outside our circle of friends and family.

Christine D. Pohl in her book, *Making Room*, describes the depth of welcome offered by Christian hospitality:

> Gracious welcome to those with significant needs and vulnerabilities (e.g., homeless people, refugees and migrants, and persons with severe disabilities) includes material and physical help, inclusion in community, and a respect for them that values their identities, stories, and contributions. Hospitality to such persons, especially if welcoming involves more than an individual or single family in need, often requires the resources of a community organized around hospitality.[37]

Hospitality is often associated with the shared meal, and for good reason. Pohl notes, "Offers of food or a meal together are central to almost all biblical stories of hospitality, to most historical discussions of hospitality, and to almost every contemporary practice of hospitality," and "in most cultures, eating together expresses mutuality, recognition, acceptance and equal regard."[38]

Linda McKinnish Bridges notes Luke's use of the common meal as a key setting in Jesus' ministry.[39] In one example, Jesus shook up the status quo at a meal hosted by a leader of the Pharisees. "When you give a luncheon or a dinner," Jesus said, "do not invite your friends or your brothers or your relatives or rich neighbors, in case they may invite you in return, and you would be repaid. But when you give a banquet, invite the poor, the crippled, the lame, and the blind. And you will be blessed, because they cannot repay you" (Luke 14:12-14). Jesus made room for everyone at the table who had no places of rank and status. So bring on the church potluck dinners as a practice of hospitality, but be careful that they don't become places where some are neglected and status and rank are reinforced, as happened with the early church. (The first deacons were enlisted to help with the problem of widows being neglected at the fellowship table; see Acts 6:1-6.)

The kind of hospitality Jesus taught was subversive in the prevailing culture. Recognizing and honoring those the culture dishonors can bring scorn, shame, and even violence from society. Consider the anger wrought against many White churches that welcomed Black members into their fellowship in the sixties. What groups would not receive a warm welcome at your fellowship meals? Jesus said, "Invite the poor, the crippled, the lame, and the blind." He was often rebuked for the people he ate with, people the Pharisees called "sinners and tax collectors," but Jesus welcomed all people, especially those shunned by society.

True Christian hospitality is living out God's kingdom on earth: "Thy kingdom come." Pohl writes, "Sometimes, by the very acting out of welcome, a vision for a whole society is offered, a small evidence that transformed relations are possible."[40] The church can be a witness to the welcoming kingdom, leading the way in welcoming people the culture rejects and making it easier for the rest of society to welcome them. Too often, the church follows the culture in welcoming the unwelcome only when it is safe to do so, after the culture as a whole has come to accept them. For example, many churches were not open to Black members until most other social institutions had ended discrimination against Black people.

Both the Israelites throughout their history and the early Christians knew what it was like to be a persecuted minority and an alien in a strange land. This experience was often given as the reason people of God should extend hospitality to the stranger. "You shall love the alien as yourself, for you were aliens in the land of Egypt," states the law of Leviticus (19:34; also Exod 22:21 and Deut 10:19). They knew the discomfort, fear, and sometimes suffering that came with being an outsider and should not want anyone else to experience that pain.

Christine Pohl shares the touching story of her grandmother's empathetic concern for the lonely,

> "I was an orphan at thirteen. No one should ever be alone." These two simple sentences provided a window into my ninety-one-year-old grandmother's determination that, once again, we would take Christmas dinner to an elderly acquaintance of hers who lived several towns away. For all of her long life, my grandmother welcomed countless acquaintances and

strangers, but never before had she or I connected this consistent practice of hospitality to her own childhood experience of having been left alone, raised in an unfamiliar and sometimes unkind household. Her distant but still vivid memory of having been an orphan and stranger sustained a lifelong passion for hospitality.[41]

Hospitality evangelism recognizes that hospitality is a cornerstone to how we understand our witness as a church. Our welcome is our witness. The church resource *Hospitality Evangelism: Sharing the Bread of Life* asks these important questions about reaching out through hospitality:

> What would our evangelism look like if we considered a stranger—someone not like us, someone who did not believe like us, someone whose life was very different than ours, someone whose opinions were strange to us, someone whose appearance or language or economic status was foreign to us—as a guest of Christ? Or even as Christ himself? What would our evangelism look like if we saw our role as that of host?[42]

So let us serve as host to a world that needs the bread of life, and let us humbly allow our neighbors to be hosts to us. Let us be a witness to the kingdom by our hospitality.

## *Listening*

The title of Ronald Johnson's book asks a pertinent question when it comes to our witness to the world: *How Will They Hear If We Don't Listen?*[43]

People are busy—too busy, perhaps. There was a day when a salesperson or evangelist might knock on your door in the evening or on a Saturday expecting to be allowed in to make a lengthy presentation. I cannot imagine that today. I would never feel that my house was ready or that I had the time, and even if I did, I wouldn't want to spend it listening to a sales pitch.

Sharing our faith today will most often happen in the context of relationships, in the give and take of dialogue, in listening as well as speaking. Guiding our neighbors in the faith requires a great deal of listening, understanding, and empathy. When the lawyer asked Jesus, "What must I do to inherit eternal life?" Jesus put the question back to the lawyer and listened to his answer. In Luke, the great commandment to love God, neighbor, and self is on the lips of the lawyer. Only after a brief dialogue does Jesus tell his story of the Good Samaritan. If we want to be heard, we must listen. Paul R. Dekar says it well:

> All things being equal, effective evangelism is a result of listening. It is unlikely that we will hear God's voice unless we have contact with God, God's people, and the rich diversity of God's world. Moreover, it is unlikely we will share the gospel of Jesus Christ with others or do anything about the conditions that adversely shape their lives unless we have listened to them. People will pour themselves out to those who have loving hearts and ears to listen.[44]

I think most Christians would agree that we should do to others as we would have them do to us, that we should be honest and fair and not lie, and that we should show respect to other people. These seem like obvious, reasonable ways of relating to others. Yet, when it comes to people of other religious faiths, Christians often do not adhere to these ideals. Too many times I have heard Christians distort and misrepresent other religions in ways that would anger us if a Muslim, Jew, Hindu, Buddhist, atheist, or agnostic misrepresented Christianity in the same way to us. If Christians would have any hope of sharing with people of other religions about our faith in Christ, we must treat them as we would like to be treated. If we would like for people to listen to our faith story, we must be willing to listen to theirs. We might even learn something from them that could strengthen our own faith. If we would like others to treat Jesus and our faith with respect, we should show respect to others and their perspectives. If it angers us to hear the teachings of Christ mischaracterized, then we should not denigrate another's religion in an effort prove the superiority of Christianity. We must be willing to listen respectfully because it is the neighborly thing to do, especially if we would like for our witness to be heard.

## Witness Resources

Abraham, William J., and Donald English. *The Art of Evangelism: Evangelism Carefully Crafted into the Life of the Local Church*. Eugene, OR: Wipf & Stock, 2011.

Abraham, William J. *The Logic of Evangelism*. Grand Rapids: Eerdmans, 1989.

Bosch, David. *Transforming Mission: Paradigm Shifts in Theology of Missions*. New York: Orbis Books, 1991.

Boursier, Helen T. *Tell It with Style: Evangelism for Every Personality Type*. Downers Grove: InterVarsity Press, 1995.

Bowen, John P. *Evangelism for "Normal" People: Good News for Those Looking for a Fresh Approach*. Minneapolis: Augsburg Fortress, 2002.

Bridges, Linda McKinnish. *The Church's Portraits of Jesus*. All the Bible. Macon: Smyth & Helwys, 1997.

Camp, Lee C. *Mere Discipleship: Radical Christianity in a Rebellious World*. Grand Rapids: Brazos, 2008.

Dekar, Paul R. *Holy Boldness: Practices of an Evangelistic Lifestyle*. Macon: Smyth & Helwys, 2004.

Field, David N. *Our Purpose Is Love: The Wesleyan Way to Be the Church*. Nashville: Abingdon, 2018.

Field, David N. Leader Guide by Barbara Dick. *Our Purpose Is Love: The Wesleyan Way to Be the Church, Leader Guide*. Nashville: Abingdon, 2018.

Hunter, George G. *The Celtic Way of Evangelism: How Christians Can Reach the West . . . Again*. Nashville: Abingdon, 2000.

———. *The Recovery of Apostolic Ministry and Evangelism*. Nashville: Abingdon, 2003.

Hybels, Bill, and Mark Mittleberg. *Becoming a Contagious Christian*. Grand Rapids: Zondervan, 1994.

Jeremias, Joachim. *Jerusalem in the Time of Jesus*. Philadelphia: Fortress Press, 1969.

Johnson, Jeffrey. *Got Style? Personality-Based Evangelism*. Ed. Patricia G. Duckworth. Valley Forge: Judson, 2009.

Linn, Jan G. *Reclaiming Evangelism: A Practical Guide for Mainline Churches*. St. Louis: Chalice, 1998.

Maynard-Reid, Pedrito U. *Complete Evangelism: The Luke Acts Model*. Scottsdale, PA: Herald Press, 1997.

Nall, Phill, and Mark Price. *Hospitality Evangelism: Sharing the Bread of Life, Leaders Guide*. Atlanta: Cooperative Baptist Fellowship, 1999.

Pohl, Christine D. *Making Room: Discovering Hospitality as a Christian Tradition* (Grand Rapids: Eerdmans, 1999.

Simpson, Ray. *Celtic Blessings: Prayers for Everyday Life*. Chicago: Loyola Press, 1998.

Sjogren, Steve. *Conspiracy of Kindness: A Refreshing New Approach to Sharing the Love of Jesus with Others*. Ann Arbor, MI: Vine Books, 1993.

Wilson, Jonathan R. *Why Church Matters: Worship, Ministry, and Mission in Practice*. Grand Rapids: Brazos, 2006.

## Notes

1. Pedrito U. Maynard-Reid, *Complete Evangelism: The Luke Acts Model* (Scottsdale, PA: Herald Press, 1997), 60–61.

2. Maynard-Reid, *Complete Evangelism*, 103.

3. See Bosch's excellent treatment of sin, repentance, forgiveness, and salvation in Luke: David Bosch, *Transforming Mission: Paradigm Shifts in Theology of Missions* (New York: Orbis Books, 1991), 104–108.

4. Maynard-Reid, *Complete Evangelism*, 119.

5. Bosch, *Transforming Mission*, 117.

6. Bosch, *Transforming Mission*, 107.

7. Maynard-Reid, *Complete Evangelism*, 109.

8. Linda McKinnish Bridges, *The Church's Portraits of Jesus*, All the Bible (Macon: Smyth & Helwys, 1997), 68.

9. Joachim Jeremias, *Jerusalem in the Time of Jesus* (Philadelphia: Fortress, 1969), 352–58.

10. Bosch, *Transforming Mission*, 111, and see 108–13 for more on this.

11. Bosch, *Transforming Mission*, 112.

12. Bosch, *Transforming Mission*, 114.

13. Lee C. Camp, *Mere Discipleship: Radical Christianity in a Rebellious World* (Grand Rapids: Brazos, 2008), 59.

14. Jonathan R. Wilson, *Why Church Matters: Worship, Ministry, and Mission in Practice* (Grand Rapids: Brazos, 2006), 76–77.

15. Camp, *Mere Discipleship*, 187.

16. Camp, *Mere Discipleship*, 192.

17. George G. Hunter, *The Celtic Way of Evangelism: How Christians Can Reach the West…Again* (Nashville: Abingdon, 2000), 53–55.

18. Hunter, *The Celtic Way of Evangelism*, 21–22.

19. Hunter, *The Celtic Way of Evangelism*, 82.

20. Hunter, *The Celtic Way of Evangelism*, 47–54.

21. Ray Simpson, *Celtic Blessings: Prayers for Everyday Life* (Chicago: Loyola Press, 1998).

22. Helen T. Boursier, *Tell It with Style: Evangelism for Every Personality Type* (Downers Grove: InterVarsity Press, 1995).

23. Jeffrey Johnson, *Got Style? Personality-Based Evangelism*, ed. Patricia Duckworth (Valley Forge: Judson, 2009).

24. Bill Hybels and Mark Mittleberg, *Becoming a Contagious Christian* (Grand Rapids: Zondervan, 1994).

25. Johnson, *Got Style*, 21.

26. Johnson, *Got Style*, 41.

27. Johnson, *Got Style*, 55.

28. Johnson, *Got Style*, 71.

29. Johnson, *Got Style*, 85.

30. Johnson, *Got Style*, 97–98.

31. Johnson, *Got Style*, 111–15.

32. Steve Sjogren, *Conspiracy of Kindness: A Refreshing New Approach to Sharing the Love of Jesus with Others* (Ann Arbor, MI: Vine Books, 1993), 17–18.

33. Sjogren, *Conspiracy of Kindness*, 40–41.

34. Sjogren, *Conspiracy of Kindness*, 106.

35. Sjogren, *Conspiracy of Kindness*, 106.

36. Sjogren, *Conspiracy of Kindness*, 88–92.

37. Christine D. Pohl, *Making Room: Discovering Hospitality as a Christian Tradition* (Grand Rapids: Eerdmans, 1999), 101.

38. Pohl, *Making Room*, 73.

39. McKinnish Bridges, *The Church's Portraits of Jesus*, 68–75.

40. Pohl, *Making Room*, 64.

41. Pohl, *Making Room*, 104.

42. Phill Nall and Mark Price, *Hospitality Evangelism: Sharing the Bread of Life, Leaders Guide* (Atlanta: Cooperative Baptist Fellowship, 1999), 4.

43. Ronald Johnson, *How Will They Hear If We Don't Listen? The Vital Role of Listening in Preaching and Personal Evangelism* (Nashville: Broadman & Holman, 1994).

44. Paul R. Dekar, *Holy Boldness: Practices of an Evangelistic Lifestyle* (Macon: Smyth & Helwys, 2004), 81.

*Chapter 7*

# Care

## Conversations with Mary and Sam on Care

The three of us sat quietly in my office. After a while, Mary, noticing the faraway look in my eyes, asked, "What's on your mind?"

"I have a question for Sam."

"Go ahead," Sam said.

"As I think about you walking down that road to the man in the ditch, beaten half-dead, I wonder what that must have been like for you. I mean, from what I understand, this road was notoriously dangerous and had plenty of hiding places, so robbery was common. You had to wonder if the robbers were still around, waiting for the next person to beat up. You could have ended up in the ditch with the other man. That must have taken a lot of courage to stop and help."

Sam furrowed his brow for a moment, then answered, "Maybe. But to be honest, I didn't feel courageous. I didn't think about it. I just couldn't pass by him and leave him there to suffer and die. If you were in my place, wouldn't you do the same?"

"Well, maybe. I hope so. Maybe I would run in the other direction."

Sam pressed, "What if that was your daughter dying on the side of the road? Would it take courage to stop and help? Wouldn't you do everything for her that I did for that man on the side of the road?"

"Yes," I answered without hesitation. "No doubt. I would do anything for her. But you didn't even know him."

"True," Sam replied, seeming a bit perplexed. "But what does that matter?"

The question made me uncomfortable. I searched for a response.

Sam didn't wait for one. "So you don't love strangers?"

Mary added, "Aren't we all God's children?"

"Ouch," I said. Their questions stung. "You ask tough questions." I squirmed in my seat, searching for a comfortable position and finding none.

"Yes, I would like to think I love all people—though, honestly, maybe I love some more than others."

Sam pressed on. "So maybe you don't love all your neighbors as you love yourself, or as you love your daughter."

"Yes, that's probably true," I answered, slumping in my seat. "I'm sorry to say it."

Sam paused, allowing me some time to process this, then declared thoughtfully, "Maybe it doesn't take courage to care as much as it takes love."

"Yes," Mary continued, "that's what we've been talking about in all of these conversations, love God and . . . ." Mary paused.

Sam looked to me to finish her sentence.

"Love your neighbor as yourself," I finished.

"Good for you," Mary affirmed.

"Thanks for reminding me."

After letting all of this sink in for a moment, I said, "Since we're talking about caring, I want you to meet my friend James Stillwell."

"Your brother?" Sam asked.

"Uh, yes, but we're not related."

I stepped to the office door and invited James into my office.

Sam laughed. "How convenient that he just happened to be standing outside your office."

"Yes. Thanks, James, for always being there for me." We shook hands and hugged. "James, meet my friends, Mary and Sam."

"What an honor to meet both of you," James said excitedly. "I have read so much about you and heard many sermons about you. Preached a few myself."

I introduced James as they greeted one another. "James is a counselor, a longtime church minister and teacher, and is known for his divorce recovery workshops. He is a caring guy who has helped many people, including me. So that's why I wanted him to join us for this discussion."

I turned to James and explained, "We've been talking about the ministry of care."

"Important topic," James said. "I have found in my ministry that many people are 'hanging on by a thread.'"

Sam noted, "The man on the side of the road certainly was."

Mary nodded in agreement.

James continued, "So Keith tells me you have been talking about loving God and neighbors as yourself. That's what care is all about."

"Obviously caring for others is about loving your neighbor, but talk to us about how caring for others is about loving God," I said.

"Remember," James responded, "Jesus said, 'If you have done it unto the least of these, you have done it unto me.'"

"Yes," Sam agreed. "I find that I need 'God with skin on.' When I saw the man on the side of the road, it was like seeing God."

James explained, "Like the homeless guy with his homemade sign. Or the Alcoholic Anonymous group meeting in the church basement. Or the group meeting to talk about the loss of a spouse. Or the divorce recovery workshop that meets in the fellowship hall. Or the elderly man in a nursing home. When we love our neighbors, we are loving God."

"Yes," Mary said. "We pray, and then we put our prayer into action. We care."

James continued, "I think that's what the coming of Jesus was all about. I also think that's what the ascension and Pentecost are all about: the Son went up, the Spirit came down, and now we can all go out and show that we care."

"Yes, yes, yes," the three of us agreed.

"James, thanks for joining us. Can you hang around and talk with us some more about the ministry of care?" I asked.

"Sure! I would love to. The ministry of care is one of my favorite subjects."

## Care

When Jesus told his story of the Good Samaritan, he might have just said, "A Samaritan was going down that road. He did not pass by on the other side, but he stopped and helped the man on the side of the road." But Jesus had much more to say about the Samaritan's assistance. First, the Samaritan saw the wounded man, and then he was moved with pity. The Samaritan had a caring heart before he ever walked down that road. He looked with empathy and saw a fellow human being in pain. Before he acted, he saw and he cared. His ability to empathize and to love his neighbor led to action. The care given by the Good Samaritan, the unlikely caregiver, was extravagant. Let's count the ways: (1) He poured oil on the wounds, which softened them. (2) He poured wine on the wounds, cleansing them. (3) He bandaged the wounds. (4) He put the hurt man on his own animal. (Imagine what it would have been like to lift a half-dead man onto your donkey. That's not something you can do without getting dirty and bloody.)

(5) He brought the wounded man to an inn. (How far?) (6) He took care of the man until the next day. (7) He gave two denarii to the innkeeper to care for the man. (Two denarii were equivalent to two days' wages.) (8) He promised to come back and pay any additional expenses incurred by the innkeeper. These are eight actions beyond what most would have expected. But remember, it began with seeing and caring.

*Note: The following sections were written by James Stillwell.*

## Care in the Life and Ministry of Jesus

*Care in Jesus' Mission Statement.* Jesus' mission statement, announced at his hometown synagogue as he began his public ministry, was all about care: care for the poor, the prisoners, the blind, the wounded, and those burdened by debt (Luke 4:18).

*Care for those Considered Unclean.* Jesus was willing to touch the "unclean" (Luke 5:12-14). The kosher laws of the Bible were meant to remind people of their reliance on God. They were not intended to keep people away from God's love (see Jonah 4:11; Acts 10).

Christians are often taught not to "get their hands dirty" through direct contact with the world. Like the kosher laws of the Jews, holiness codes followed by some Christians can keep them separated from people in need. If we're not careful, something that the Holy Spirit guides us to do as part of our personal discipleship can be impeded by legalism that blocks the flow of God's love to those in need. What people groups have sometimes been treated as "unclean" by churches? These are the very ones for whom Jesus calls us to show care.

Peter had an experience in which God directly told him not to avoid Gentiles (Acts 10). Later, Paul had to confront Peter for not being willing to share table fellowship with Gentiles (Gal 2:11-14).

*Care for Those Who Need to be Carried.* On one occasion, four friends brought to Jesus a man who was paralyzed, and finding the home too crowded to enter, they dramatically tore a hole in the roof and lower their friend down on a mat to Jesus (Luke 5:17-25). Forgiveness is mentioned in this passage, implying that the man's needs were emotional and spiritual as well as physical. Without the help of his four friends, the paralyzed man likely would have never found healing and wholeness. Who are the "four to carry you" that you could call at 2:00 a.m. if you had an emotional emergency? How can our church community act like the four friends caring for others' emotional, spiritual, and physical wellness and carrying others to Jesus for healing and wholeness?

*Care for Those Who Seem to be Out of Control.* Many New Testament scholars today believe that while demonic activity may be a reality that can be discussed in spiritual terms, often what shows up in our world today is best understood and treated as mental illness.

One example is the demon-possessed man in Luke 8:26-39. Mental illness can often be effectively treated in our day through counseling, medicine, and support groups. Counselors, psychiatrists, and support group leaders can be the "hands and feet of Christ" in the lives of people who in the past were simply dismissed as possessed by evil spirits.

If we encounter someone who is obviously "out of control," it is helpful to get that person to a trained clinician. When the right resources are available, it is a blessing to be able to steer that person toward healing. When that person experiences wholeness, often in community, it definitely has spiritual implications, for something of a miracle has taken place.

*Care for Women.* Luke 8:40-56 tells two stories about women: one at the onset of puberty and the other who was dealing with an ongoing issue of nonstop menstruation.

The young girl at the beginning of the passage was likely at the common age of child marriage and probably scared that her life as a little girl would soon be over. How did Jesus deal with the young girl after she was healed? There is a need in our day for caring ministry to those who have lost their innocence too young, whether by sexual abuse, trafficking, child marriage, or other such trauma. What can you or your church do to make a difference in these situations?

The woman with the "issue of blood" was courageous more than we in the modern world realize. She was willing to make Jesus ceremonially unclean in order to find healing for her condition, for the laws of Leviticus would have prevented him from having physical contact with her (see Lev 15:10). Ask yourself, "Am I a safe person for someone to open up to with painful details about their life? Do I know a counselor to recommend who is trained to deal with people's intimate life details that they might not be ready to share with others?"

What resources are available to people in your community who need counseling or health care, perhaps at a reduced financial cost? Where can people get help in a safe way from difficult situations (such as a women's shelter)?

*Care at the Same Time and Place as Worship and Teaching.* Can care happen at the same place or the same time as worship or your faith community's religious education? For some in Jesus' day, the answer was no. But for Jesus, care can happen in the same place and even at the same time as worship or religious instruction (see Luke 13:10-17, especially verse 13). In the synagogue and on the Sabbath, Jesus cared for a woman who was unable to stand up straight. Jesus placed his hands on her back and healed her. Immediately, she stood up straight and praised God. What sort of healing interactions can happen when your faith community is gathered for worship or instruction? How can worship itself be healing?

*Care as a Consequence of Being "On the Way."* Is care an inside job (for church members) or an outside job (for the unchurched)? The life and teachings of Jesus would indicate that it is for both (see Luke 14:21).

Think of one of our two characters for this whole series, the Good Samaritan. What do you think he would say about ministry while you're "on the way"? The participle Jesus used when he said "Go" in Matthew 28:19 literally means "as you go."

Some have found it helpful to think of "pathways of life" in order to develop caring relationships in your whole life. The idea is to go to the same restaurant, the same post office, the same grocery store, etc., in order to develop relationships and to care for people more effectively.

Jesus demonstrated this when he was "on the way" to Jerusalem for the most stressful, momentous, and difficult week of his entire life. Perhaps that was one reason that he rode at a donkey's pace rather than galloping into town on a stallion. He was able to slow down to touch and heal someone who was "on the way." How can you more intentionally structure your life to be a blessing to others?

Jesus cared for others even in the midst of his death on a cruel Roman cross (see John 19:25-27). How can we interact with others even in their time of dying to help them the way Jesus did in that moment?

## Care in the Life of the Early Church

The history of the church can be marked as beginning with the coming of the Holy Spirit to empower all believers who were present at the festival of Pentecost (Acts 2). These people knew that the job of sharing the good news was not limited to the Apostles or even to the Palestinian Jews who first made up those we think of as Jesus' disciples.

As the church grew and diversified, it meant that natural preferences towards one's own group might impede the flow of ministry to those of other ethnicities and cultures. It was discovered that Gentile widows were going hungry and being overlooked in the daily distribution of food. Acts 6 records how the Apostles dealt with this problem. The church selected enough people to distribute food in order to take care of the Gentile widows among them, and they held high standards in order to assure quality of care.

Apparently, this need continued into the next generation of the church, for in the letters we call the "pastoral epistles," there are two groups of leaders mentioned who required a high degree of character—elders and deacons. The word for deacon in the New Testament literally means "servant." Those in the early church given the task of waiting on tables for widows who had been neglected were called "deacons." In some ways, the qualifications for deacons are more restrictive than those for elders, for deacons are to be in close interaction with people in need.

In this simple arrangement in the early church, we can see elders for teaching and leading the congregation and deacons for closer care of church members—an organizational tactic that can serve as a model for churches today.

## Care Based on Specific Needs

Other churches may decide that the best way to express care is to develop specialized ministries of care based on need. The following are some examples, but every congregation will have different needs arise and different spiritual gifts and experiences in its available leaders. Churches can have specific ministries to take care of

- families with expectant mothers, babies, and young preschoolers.
- families that include elementary-age children and their caregivers.
- families of teens.
- college students, students who are away, those in military or other types of service.
- single adults in need of community through all the stages of life.
- married couples through the stages of marriage.
- those going through marital separation or divorce.
- those adjusting to remarriage and stepfamilies.
- adults whose partners have died.
- senior adults and those who are aging.
- the dying and those in palliative care.
- those who are sick and/or hospitalized.

- those struggling with mental illness.
- all who desire confidential and professional counseling.
- those who desire to be married, engaged couples, and the newly married, including those who are not married but cohabitating.
- those who have experienced miscarriage, death of a child, or infertility.
- those who are grieving.
- those undergoing job loss or under-employment.
- LGBTQIA+ people of all ages.
- parents of LGBTQIA+ people.
- those addicted to substances.
- those in relationship to people addicted to substances.
- those who are in or coming out of abusive relationships.
- those coming out of the military or who have experienced trauma in military service.
- first responders, both military and civilian.
- refugees and displaced people from other countries.
- those dealing with food insecurity.
- those dealing with environmental disaster in their neighborhoods.
- victims of rape and sexual assault.
- prisoners and inmates and those being released.
- families dealing with dysfunctional family members.
- people with disabilities.
- people experiencing homelessness.

And the list could go on.

Dr. Robert Schuller in the 1970s and 1980s built a ministry based on the philosophy, "Find a need and fill it, find a hurt and heal it." Every year, he would take two weeks off from preaching and focus on knocking on doors within two miles of the church to ask people what they believed were the greatest needs in the community. He then set out to develop ministries to meet those needs.

After identifying what needs require attention, the church should prioritize needs and then build an infrastructure to meet those needs. Schuller emphasized that "God owns the cattle on a thousand hills," so no one church or individual is limited to its own means of meeting those needs. It is often possible to network and partner with other resources in the community in order to be a part of the solution.

People often look up to God and ask "Why?" when faced with societal problems. It probably makes more sense to think about God looking down to God's people and asking us why we are not part of the solution.

A popular Christian song in recent years asked the question, "If we are the body, then why aren't we reaching . . . ?"

We are the body of Christ. Christ depends on us to be his hands and feet in this world. That is true both inside and outside the church.

We are called to care.

## Putting Care into Practice

### Care for the Entire Church

Many churches have a deacon ministry plan where deacons are assigned tasks related to various aspects of member care.

In some churches, there is an organization known as Stephen Ministries that trains church members for the ministry of caring. Stephen ministers are in close contact with church members to take care of spiritual and other needs, making sure that no one is neglected or suffering from an unmet need.

These two possibilities, deacon ministry and Stephen Ministries, are designed to care for the whole church. In churches that have a strong Sunday school ministry, the classes can be organized in such a way as to help facilitate care for all church members.

### Listening

The early church, much like churches today, had to deal with conflicts between people. People are imperfect, have their own opinions, and can easily be more focused on their own interests than the interests of others. Therefore, listening is hard.

When we don't listen, we set ourselves up for unnecessary conflict. When we don't listen, we find ourselves unable to help others resolve conflict. The words of James 1:19 form a great outline for this topic. Let everyone be (1) quick to listen, (2) slow to speak, and (3) slow to get angry. Easier said than done, for sure!

In order to facilitate this process, know that you are a psycho-spiritual-physical human being with "triggers." You, like all psycho-spiritual-physical human beings, can "flip out" and be overtaken with anger or other strong feelings before you know what's going on.

If the apostle James were here today, he might recommend something we call "mindfulness." That is, be in a "noticing" mode instead of a "reactive" mode. Take a deep breath. Use your five senses. Put on your psychic armor so you are not easily offended. Then you are able to do what James said in his letter to first-century churches because you are coming from a calm place rather than a place of anxiety and wariness. Using the apostle James's outline might go like this:

(1) Seek to understand more than to be understood. Use "active listening," which is paraphrasing the speaker's words and meanings until the speaker lets you know they feel heard.

(2) Be deliberate. Trust your best, loving self to come up with words wrapped in kindness when it is your turn to speak. Jesus talked about the Holy Spirit giving us words when we need it. Don't panic. Trust God. Keep your words few rather than many.

(3) Be slow to anger. This comes largely out of the mindfulness mindset described earlier. A good rule is to "assume good will." If at all possible, see the best in the other person. If anger is inevitable or provoked before you realize what's going on, remember it is okay to "agree to disagree" and to walk away. It's not about convincing someone else. Just take care of your own equanimity and the responses of others will likely take care of themselves.

## Caring in Times of Grief and Loss

Everybody goes through tough times. Sadness is the appropriate response. When someone is sad and working through the "what now?" struggles that go with any major loss in life, they need your presence more than anything else.

When you have a chance, read through the story of Job and his friends. Job lost just about everything in his life. The book of Job is rather long because it has speeches of Job talking with his friends about the meaning and purpose of suffering. God finally has to come into the picture and remind them of the mystery of it all. This tells us a few important things about loss and grief.

We need to be able to allow the grieving person to ask their painful and difficult questions out loud in front of others. The best thing Job's friends did for him was show up and be quiet in their first several days of sitting with him. It was when they began to draw conclusions that only God is qualified to draw that they stepped over the line. Their gift, before they started talking, was to give Job their presence. When God speaks at the end of the book, he insists on mystery and holds the prerogative of things we will never know. People think they need answers, but they more often need to know someone cares. Give your presence.

Any major life change is difficult because it is a change of identity and a loss of the presence of a person or people who were a regular part of life before the loss. It takes time to heal. Be patient and remind the grieving person that as they go around the calendar, they will get better, they will have a new normal, and they will put together a new world of meaning over time. Be a good listener as they work through this process.

Any major loss is like having a huge jigsaw puzzle that you've been working on for years suddenly blown all over the room, and the pieces don't seem to make sense anymore. We can be part of the constants in someone's life where change seems to be coming way too fast.

## Hospital Visits

In Matthew 25:36, Jesus says, "I was sick and you visited me." These words are mostly in reference to hospital visits but could also work for most home visits, including nursing homes.

Life, as singer/songwriter Sting says in one of his most beautiful songs, is "fragile."[1] When we are healthy, we forget "how fragile we are." Dr. M. Scott Peck, bestselling author of *The Road Less Traveled*, used to talk about the miracle of grace that we're not all deathly sick all the time.[2] We seem to be able to miss most sickness "bugs," but eventually we will all be unwell. And when someone is not well, they have both physical, practical needs as well as psychological, spiritual needs for the support of others.

How important is it to visit, call, send cards, and make contact via social media when people are suffering from sickness? It's so important that Jesus told a story about the great kingdom banquet that's coming. One key to our participation, according to Matthew 25, will be that we realize that in caring for the sick, we are ministering to Jesus himself. And when we miss out on those opportunities, it is as if we are missing out on ministering to Jesus. It's that important.

What are some practical ideas about visiting with the sick? Here are a few:

(1) Call ahead if possible and make sure it's a good time. Make sure your visit is "timely," for example, not when they're undergoing procedures where your presence might not be appropriate.

(2) Err on the side of brevity and quiet rather than overstaying your welcome or being too boisterous. The sick person may naturally be a "people pleaser" and may feel an obligation to offer hospitality when they're not up to it. Respect their need for respite and that they don't have to entertain you.

(3) Ask if they would like you to share a brief reading or brief prayer. Take something with you, such as a Bible, that is marked for an appropriate reading. Always ask permission. Even those who are religious might not want to hear that. Those who are not religious may fear your motives if you come on too strong. Prayer and Bible reading can be distinctively Christian ways of caring and are often appreciated, but don't assume. A prayer from a representative of the church can be powerful and is encouraged by Scripture (Jas 5:13-15). God uses our prayers for healing, for encouragement, and for expressing love.

(4) When not able to visit, send a card. Thoughtful "thinking of you" notes are often kept and displayed during lonely times when it seems that no one cares or that everybody is busy. They mean a lot.

(5) If people want to talk and need you to listen, be open to that. Sometimes the deepest thoughts come when we realize our fragility the most, and having a trusted friend to share these thoughts with can be a treasure.

### Caring for the Orphans and Widows and Those in Distress

James 1:27 tells us to "Visit orphans and widows and those who are in distress."

Who were the orphans and widows in the first century? They were people who were utterly abandoned, had no safety net, and were at risk of abuse or death. They were people who were utterly dependent on someone else to care for them, but then the person who cared for them died. They were therefore in great distress.

Who is in that situation in your world? Perhaps it is someone in your faith community. Perhaps someone in your neighborhood. Perhaps someone in your circle at work or your daily routine.

When someone is in distress, if at all possible, connect them to resources. First Baptist Church in Frankfort, Kentucky, for example, has long been known as a place where people can get medical help when they otherwise could not afford it. The church has a free medical clinic housed within the building. Ministries like that are a powerful witness to the community that the church cares about more than itself.

Churches often have a list of people in distress that they share when they have a midweek prayer gathering. They pray for the sick, both the homebound and those in hospitals. They pray for the grieving. They send cards to the sick and the grieving. Sometimes an offering is gathered to meet the needs of someone in a dire situation.

Churches often are less sensitive to those who have lost a spouse to divorce or lost a family member through family conflict. It also may not be on the church's "radar" when someone loses a job or their life is otherwise disrupted. Also, those dealing with addictions or mental illnesses are often ignored.

For many of these needs, leaders in your faith community can have a targeted, specific ministry or program for taking care of people, such as

• Divorce recovery workshop. A six- to eight-week series using material such as *Growing through Divorce* by Jim Smoke[3] or *A Time for Healing* by Harold Ivan Smith[4] can give people going through this extremely difficult life change a place to regroup, heal, and find redirection for life.

• A support group for those who have lost a spouse or partner. Those who have lost a loved one to death can benefit from regular, perhaps monthly meetings with mutual support and educational programs about grief or single living. One example of this is a monthly gathering on the same day each month. One such group called itself "Second Chapter," as it marked a new chapter in life with people who understand.

• Alcoholics Anonymous and other twelve-step groups. These groups are often looking for churches who will be open to hosting them. A church that is open to supporting sobriety is a tremendous asset to a community.

• Other caring connections such as connecting with refugees in a community. Kentucky Refugee Ministries is one example of a group that actively seeks to partner with churches to help some of the most vulnerable new guests and potential citizens who have lost everything in their home country.

• Those in your church who cannot easily leave their homes. This might include those who are are elderly or who have a physical disability or mobility issue. Talk to church leadership about how you might help bring joy to someone who may be isolated at home.

The possibilities are endless. May this list prompt you to think of others and to follow God as God leads you to care for those who need it.

## Self-care Is Not Selfish

"Love your neighbor as you love yourself" assumes that you will not completely burn yourself out and make yourself sick as you care for others. Jesus said the Sabbath was created for our renewal. Jesus regularly took time out to pray and then to get away by himself or with his closest associates. If Jesus needed to practice self-care in order to do his ministry, so do we.

The model might be the childhood of Jesus himself: "Jesus increased in wisdom and in years, and in divine and human favor" (Luke 2:52, Contemporary English Version). In other words, Jesus grew mentally, physically, spiritually, and socially. Are you regularly involved in your own development? After all, you have no blessings to pour out to others if you are not regularly pouring into yourself. Let's use this verse as an outline for self-care:

(1) Grow mentally: Attend to your mental self-care. Read good books and articles. Watch good television and movies. Have regular times for quiet, even silence. The old computer phrase "garbage in, garbage out" means we need to care about what we're putting into our minds. In his letter to the Philippians, Paul says, "Whatsoever things are excellent . . . think on these things."

(2) Grow physically: Get out of your chair and stand. Get up and walk, run, dance, bicycle, canoe, swim, and move around. The body is not intended for long, uninterrupted times of sitting. It's deadly. Take regular breaks and move!

(3) Grow socially: Motivational experts say you become like the five people you spend the most time with, so who is a part of your weekly or monthly support system? Where do you find mutual encouragement and care? This can be done around meals or coffee, but the important thing is the regularity and mutual support.

(4) Grow spiritually: Spiritual growth is self-care. Read spiritual books, including the Bible. Participate in regular worship experiences where you can receive both the word (preaching, teaching, spiritual singing, and other forms of uplifting music) and sacrament (the Lord's Supper). Have a prayer and devotional life. Take regular time-outs for retreats.

Allow yourself to have growth experiences. You'll be better able to care for others.

## *Caring Like Jesus Cared*

These stories from the life of Jesus can help a church, small group, care committee, or leadership team reflect on the many ways Jesus cared for others and how a church community might show care in a variety of circumstances they may not have considered.

(1) Jesus' mission statement, announced at his hometown synagogue as he began his public ministry, was all about care: care for the poor, prisoners, the blind, the wounded, and those burdened by debt (Luke 4:18). How can my church or small group make an impact on the various groups mentioned by Jesus? Brainstorm!

(2) Jesus was willing to touch the "unclean" (Luke 5:12-14). What people groups have sometimes been treated as "unclean" in the lives of people or churches? Peter had an experience in which God directly told him not to avoid Gentiles (Acts 10). Later, Paul had to confront Peter for not being willing to share table fellowship with Gentiles (Gal 2:11-14). What was the solution in Acts 6 when a certain ethnic group was being neglected?

(3) Read Luke 5:17-25. What do you notice about the paralyzed man? Who are the "four to carry you" that you could call at 2 a.m. if you had an emotional emergency?

(4) Forgiveness is mentioned in the passage. How is it true that sometimes we need someone else to help carry us to a place of forgiveness?

(5) How do you resolve the paradox of Galatians 6:2, which tells us to carry one another's burdens, and Galatians 6:5, which tells each of us to carry our own?

(6) Read Luke 8:26-39. How do we tend to react when someone enters our space and appears to be out of control? What can be one outcome when someone experiences dramatic healing that positively affects their mental health? (Luke 8:35)

(7) How does the Twelfth Step of Alcoholics Anonymous (pass this teaching on to others) relate to Jesus' word to the formerly demonized? (Luke 8:39)

(8) What do you notice about the past of one of Jesus' closest female disciples (Luke 8:2)?

(9) Luke 8:40-56 tells two stories about women: one at the onset of puberty and the other who was dealing with an ongoing issue of nonstop

menstruation. How did Jesus deal with the young girl after she was healed? How can your church care for those who have lost their innocence too young through trauma?

(10) The woman with the "issue of blood" was willing to make Jesus ceremonially unclean in order to find healing for her condition. Are you a safe person for someone to open up and share with you painful details about their life? Do you know a counselor to recommend who is trained to deal with people's intimate life details that they might not be ready to share with others? What resources are available to people in your community who need counseling or health care, perhaps at a reduced financial cost? What places can people find where they can get help in a safe way from difficult situations, such as a women's shelter?

(11) Care in the same place or at the same time as liturgy or instruction (Luke 13:10-17, especially verse 13). Can care happen at the same place or the same time as the place or time for worship or your faith community's religious education? What sort of healing interactions can happen when your faith community is gathered for worship or instruction? How can worship itself be healing?

(12) Jesus cared for others even in the midst of his death on a cruel Roman cross. See John 19:25-27. How can we interact with others even in their time of dying to help them to cover such important bases as Jesus achieved in that moment?

## The Caring Role of the Deacon

*Note: This section was written by Keith Felton, pastor, First Baptist Church, Frankfort, Kentucky.*

Concerning the role first filled by the deacons in Acts 6:1-6, Luke writes, "Now during those days, when the disciples were increasing in number, the Hellenists complained against the Hebrews because their widows were being neglected in the daily distribution of food. And the twelve called together the whole community of the disciples and said, 'it is not right that we should neglect the word of God in order to wait on tables. Therefore, friends, select from among yourselves seven men of good standing, full of the spirit, and of wisdom, who we may appoint to this task.'" And Luke adds that this "pleased the whole community."

The initial task of the very first deacons was to care for widows who were one of the most vulnerable groups in the Greco-Roman world. This indicates to me that deacons should be primarily concerned with care for the community. The term for deacon literally means servant or slave. Through caring service, this officer of the church is charged to make sure the needs of their family of faith are taken care of. There were no special graces or authoritarian responsibilities bestowed on the first deacons. They were chosen as individuals of character and simply given their directive to care for those who needed a helping hand and compassionate heart.

Deacons are to lead in service to the community. Throughout church history, the role of the deacon has at times been erroneously expanded and wrongly understood as a "board of directors"—positions of power. Biblically, they are agents of care and extensions of the pastor's reach to those in need. They are set apart and ordained for this purpose. It is a critical role in the life of a local church. The ministerial staff cannot be multiple places at one time. The deacon has been called and blessed by the church to broaden the scope of care to the family of faith and even beyond to the larger community.

## Care Resources

### General Caring Churchwide

Aleshire, Daniel O. *FaithCare: Ministering to All God's People Through the Ages of Life*. Philadelphia: Westminster, 1988.

Bagby, Daniel. *Crisis Ministry: A Handbook*. Macon: Smyth & Helwys, 2002.

Coker, K. Jason. *Faded Flowers: Preaching in the Aftermath of Suicide*. Macon: Smyth & Helwys, 2020.

Hauk, Gary H. *Family Enrichment in Your Church*. Nashville: Convention, 1988.

Hightower, James E., Jr., ed.. *Caring for Folks from Birth to Death*. Nashville: Broadman, 1985.

Hinkle, Joseph W., and Melva J. Cook. *How to Minister to Families in Your Church*. Nashville: Broadman, 1978.

Lampe, Karen. *The Caring Congregation: How to Become One and Why It Matters*. Nashville: Abingdon, 2011.

———. *The Caring Congregation: Training Manual and Resource Guide*. Nashville: Abingdon, 2014.

Smith, Amy Luscher. *My Faith Sparkles: Memoir of a Cancer Survivor*. Kenosha, WI: Silver Linings Media, 2019.

Stephen Ministries. 2045 Innerbelt Business Center, St Louis MO 63114-5765.

Taylor, Barbara Brown. *Learning to Walk in the Dark*. New York: Harper-Collins, 2014.

## General Resources for Theological, Ethical, and Pastoral Care

Augsburger, David. *Helping People Forgive*. Louisville: John Knox, 1996 (grieving and forgetting, p. 69; griefwork loop, p. 70).

Clinebell, Harold. *Basic Types of Pastoral Care and Counseling*. Nashville: Abingdon, 1984 (use of religious resources, pp. 121–37; bereavement care, pp. 218–42).

Hartbauer, Roy E., ed. *Pastoral Care of the Handicapped*. Barrien Springs, MI: Andrews University Press, 1983 (when there has been a stroke, chapter 3; the family of the institutionalized, chapter 4; the amputee and the paralytic, chapter 8; the visually impaired, chapter 9; parents of the impaired child, chapter 10; communicative disorders, chapter 11).

Hunter, Rodney J., gen ed. *Dictionary of Pastoral Care and Counseling*. Nashville: Abingdon, 1990.

Kornfeld, Margaret. *Cultivating Wholeness*. New York: Continuum, 2011 (community, pp. 21–23; community care, pp. 74–79; preparing for community care, pp. 91–113; caring through the seasons of life, pp. 145–277).

Lester, Andrew D. *Anger: Discovering Your Spiritual Ally*. Louisville: Westminster John Knox, 2007.

Peck, M. Scott. *The Different Drum*. New York: Simon and Schuller, 1987 (stages of community making, pp. 86–106).

Rowatt, G. Wade, Jr. *Adolescents in Crisis: A Guide for Parents, Teachers, Ministers, and Counselors*. Louisville: Westminster John Knox, 2001.

## Accessible Premarital and Marriage Counseling for Pastors and Marriage Mentors

Apple, David, compiler. *I Take Thee to Be My Spouse*. Nashville: Convention Press, 1992.

Dunn, Dick. *New Faces in the Frame*. Nashville: LifeWay, 1997.

PREPARE-ENRICH. Life Innovations. Minneapolis, MN. Empowering Couples: Building on Your Strengths.

White, Ernest, and James E. White. *Counsel for the Nearly and Newly Married*. Nashville: Convention Press, 1992.

**Single Adults and Divorce Recovery**

Adler, Allan J., and Christine Archambault. *Divorce Recovery: Helping the Hurt Through Self-Help and Professional Support*. New York: Bantam Books, 1990.

Akamine, Hale. *Healing the Wounds: Teens Learning to Cope with Divorce*. Nashville: LifeWay, 1995.

Collier-Slone, Kay. *Single In the Church: New Ways to Minister with 52% of God's People*. Durham, NC: The Alban Institute, 1992.

Flanagan, Bill. *Developing A Divorce Recovery Ministry in Your Church*. Colorado Springs: David C. Cook, 2002.

Richards, Sue Poorman, and Stanley Hagemeyer. *Ministry to the Divorced: Guidance, Structure and Organization that Promote Healing in the Church*. Grand Rapids: Zondervan, 1986.

Smith, Harold Ivan. *A Time for Healing: Coming to Terms with Your Divorce*. Nashville: LifeWay, 1995.

Smoke, Jim. *Growing through Divorce*. Eugene, OR: Harvest House, 1995.

# Notes

1. "Fragile," *Nothing Like the Sun*, AIR Studios, 1987.

2. M. Scott Peck, *The Road Less Traveled: A New Psychology of Love, Traditional Values and Spiritual Growth* (New York: Touchstone, 1978).

3. Jim Smoke, *Growing through Divorce* (Eugene, OR: Harvest House, 1995).

4. Harold Ivan Smith, *A Time for Healing: Coming to Terms with Your Divorce* (Nashville: LifeWay, 1995).

*Chapter 8*

# Leadership

## Conversations with Mary and Sam on Leadership

Sam and Mary returned to my office and Mary addressed me. "Keith?"

"Yes?"

"Sam and I have been talking."

"About what?" I didn't know where this was going, but it seemed to be going somewhere new.

Mary answered, "The three of us have been discussing some important topics, like . . ."

"Community," Mary and Sam said in unison.

Mary continued, ". . . and worship, teaching, and prayer."

"And missions, witness, and care," Sam added.

"Yes," I agreed, still wondering where this was going.

"So what now?" Sam asked.

"Yes," Mary said, "how do you lead your church toward being a disciple community?"

"How do you equip a church to love God and neighbor?" Sam continued.

"Wow, those are big questions. But those are questions I think about often."

"So what are your thoughts?" Sam invited.

Mary and Sam took a seat and turned to me with a look of genuine interest. I felt that they were teaching me by listening.

"Obviously, leading a church in being a disciple community and equipping a church to love God and neighbor is a big task, and there are not three simple steps for all churches to follow," I began. "I think there are a number of things a church can do that will help it become the missional church God intends—more than we have time for today. But let me say this: the church needs to understand with a church is."

Mary asked, "Does the church not know what it is?"

"Sometimes I think we miss it. The church is not a business, a government agency, a sports team, or the local mall. Because these kinds of organizational models are so prevalent, it's not surprising that we might tend to mimic them. But our goals are different. We are God's church on God's mission. We are the body of Christ. We are, as the letter of 1 Peter says, 'a chosen race, a royal priesthood, a holy nation, God's own people.' Some say that we are a 'sign, foretaste and instrument of God's kingdom.'"

"Sounds like the church is important," Sam noted.

"Yes, we need to understand who we are and whose we are," I concluded.

Mary stood up. "You and your church have much to pray about."

Sam stood next to Mary and added, "Yes, and then you must get busy, putting it into practice."

"Okay, but why are you standing?"

"Keith," Sam said, walking over to me and putting a hand on my shoulder, "it's time for us to go."

"But we have so much more to talk about."

"There's more to talk about," Mary said, "but these are things for you and your church to talk about together."

"I'm going to miss you both," I said as I stood and hugged each of them.

"We will miss you too," Mary said.

"But we will be watching from afar. You have a faithful church, so we expect more good news," Sam encouraged as they moved toward the door.

"Goodbye!"

I was mentally drained, so I laid my head on my desk to rest a minute.

I must have dozed off, because I was disoriented when I heard a knock at my office door. I don't know how long I had been asleep.

"Yes? Sam? Mary?"

"Keith?" The voice from the other side of the door sounded familiar. "Are you going to stay here all night?"

"Sorry, come in."

In walked my pastor. "Who are Sam and Mary?" he asked. "Are you expecting visitors?"

I shook my head, surprised.

Laughing, he observed, "You look like you've seen a ghost."

"Wow! Yes, maybe I have seen two ghosts. I dreamed I was visited by Mary and Sam."

"Who?"

"Oh, never mind."

"Let's go home, friend. You can tell me all about it tomorrow."

"Yes, I can't wait to tell you all about it."

# Leadership

## A Lever Long Enough

Leadership is equipping, guiding, supporting, and facilitating the disciple community in the practices of community, worship, teaching, prayer, missions, witness, and care. Leadership is the process whereby the disciple community understands its identity as God's people, discerns God's vision, and opens itself to being transformed by God's vision and mission for the church.

When it comes to church leadership, I would suggest that certain key practices and assumptions could make a significant difference in the church's ability to carry out God's mission. These are aspects of the disciple community's life that might be neglected, dysfunctional, or simply not all they could be.

Archimedes is credited with saying, "Give me a lever long enough and a fulcrum on which to place it, and I shall move the world." Think of these practices as long levers than can help move the church toward becoming the missional church God intends.

### Loving God

"You shall love the Lord your God with all your heart, with all your soul, and with all your strength, and with all your mind" (Luke 10:27). Worship is our expression of love and devotion for a loving God, as is everything we do. The whole life and ministry of the church flows out of the church's total love for and obedience to God. Knowing God fully, we are guided in the way to serve, make disciples, witness to the good news, worship, pray, and live together in community. Loving God with our whole hearts will lead us to love our neighbors and to live faithfully as God's people.

Loving God is where Christian leadership begins. Loving God permeates every worship service and Bible study, every committee meeting and business meeting, every fellowship meal and hallway conversation, and every act of service with our neighbors. Loving God is the final aim of leadership.

*What difference does it make in the life of the disciple community when we are fully devoted to God in thought, word, feelings, and action?*

**Loving Neighbors**
"And you shall love your neighbor as yourself" (Luke 10:27). This second command goes hand in hand with the first command to love God. Similarly, 1 John 4:19-21 reminds us, "We love because he first loved us. Those who say, 'I love God,' and hate their brothers or sisters, are liars; for those who do not love a brother or sister whom they have seen, cannot love God whom they have not seen. The commandment we have from him is this: those who love God must love their brothers and sisters also."

Our God who first loved us commands us to love our neighbors in the same way God loves us. In the parable of the Good Samaritan, Jesus teaches us that our neighbors are not only those who look and act like us. Neighbor love is offered to all, no matter their ethnicity, nationality, gender, religion, economic status, sexual orientation, or political party. This radical hospitality is extended to all people, even those we might think of as enemies.

Loving neighbor as self is easier to do if we can see the world from our neighbor's perspective. Jesus' Golden Rule, "Do under others as you would have them do unto you" (Luke 6:31), is so self-evident that similar injunctions appear in many other religious and cultural traditions. One of Steven Covey's habits of highly effective people is "seek first to understand, then to be understood."[1]

The church community is called to be a community of empathy—an example to all people of what loving neighbor as self looks like. Neighbor love is demonstrated in the community when we welcome all people with no exceptions, when we relate to one another with unconditional love, forgiveness, and grace, and when we defend those who are hated and oppressed by others.

Discerning God's mission for our church includes the question, "Who are our neighbors, and how can we love them?"

*What difference does it make in the disciple community when we offer hospitality and love to all neighbors without discrimination?*

**What Is the Church?**
What is the church? What are our models for the church? So many organizational models compete for the church's attention: business or corporation, sports team, shopping mall, government, educational institution. If these models are accepted without evaluating or adapting in light of the gospel, then numbers, money, winning, success, consumerism, or individual satisfaction may become the ultimate goal rather than God's mission. Other biblical models provide a healthier image of the church as God intends:

sign, foretaste, and instrument of God's kingdom; holy nation; royal priesthood; God's own people; the body of Christ; the vine and the branches.

> But you are a chosen race, a royal priesthood, a holy nation, God's own people, in order that you may proclaim the mighty acts of him who called you out of darkness into his marvelous light. Once you were not a people, but now you are God's people; once you had not received mercy, but now you have received mercy. (1 Pet 2:9-10)

*What difference does it make in the disciple community when we understand our true identity and model our church after the biblical images of a holy nation, royal priesthood, God's own people, and the body of Christ?*

## All Christians Are Called and Gifted for Ministry

Who are the ministers? Many churches function as if it is the job of hired professional clergy to minister, while the laity are volunteers there to help or are the ones receiving ministry. Sometimes we act as if the church cannot carry out God's mission without hired ministers. We stress about finding the perfect pastor, as if a savior pastor will solve all of our perceived problems. However, Scripture passages like this one from Romans (Rom 12:3-8; see also Eph 4:11-13 and 1 Cor 12) would suggest a different understanding: "For as in one body we have many members, and not all the members have the same function, so we, who are many, are one body in Christ, and individually we are members one of another. We have gifts that differ according to the grace given to us."

The view that most church members are laity and volunteers whose role is to receive ministry and serve the church as they desire or when convenient is an obstacle to the church reaching its God-given potential. There is no real difference between clergy and laity. We are all members of the body of Christ, with different gifts and ministries working together on God's mission. All Christians are called by God to ministry. All are given spiritual gifts to use in carrying out God's mission. Imagine how much a church could accomplish if all of its members understood themselves to be called and gifted ministers.

*What difference does it make in the disciple community when all members see themselves as ministers called and gifted by God and are fully engaged in God's mission?*

## Discerning God's Vision Together

Often the church makes important decisions about vision, direction, practice, and the future using win/lose procedures like Robert's Rules of Order, preference surveys and votes, and business meetings disconnected from the Bible study, prayer, and worship life of the church. It's not about our favorite music styles for worship or what another church is doing to attract people. If the mission of the church is not our mission but God's mission, then our task is not to decide what we want but to discern God's vision. Together, through prayer, worship, Bible study, dialogue, and practice, we discern God's mission.

Every word in a church's process of "Discerning God's Vision Together" is important.

*Discerning.* This is a prayerful listening and learning process—a journey. Jesus' twelve disciples didn't catch Jesus' vision overnight. They followed him around, listened to his teaching, asked questions, and observed his actions. Still, it wasn't until after his death that they began to understand Jesus' radical mission for them. If we are to discern God's vision, it will take time, prayer, Bible study, dialogue with our church family, and discipleship.

*God's.* It must be God's vision. We are not polling our members to determine what most of them want. We are seeking nothing less than God's dream for our church. We must allow God to challenge our assumptions through the Bible, prayer, and other Christians in order to teach us God's way for us in this place at this time.

*Vision.* A vision can help us see more clearly to be the kind of church God wants us to be. A godly vision can inspire us and guide us into a great future. God's vision calls us to do what is not humanly possible and become more than we could ever dream. A godly vision challenges and excites us.

*Together.* God's vision is not determined by the pastor and staff alone, by a leadership team, or by an outside consultant. God's vision is imparted to the whole community of faith. We are the body of Christ, and each member is important. Therefore, we discern God's vision together. We are not perfect. Sometimes it is difficult for us to distinguish God's vision from our own traditions, biases, and cultural influences. With the leadership of trained pastoral ministers, we engage in prayerful dialogue and study the call of God in the biblical story to gather insights from all of God's gifted people. Together, we do the best we can to discern God's vision for our church.

This takes time. A series of key questions similar to the following can guide a discernment process: What is our heritage? What is our current context? What are the challenges we face? What are our assets and gifts? What is God's mission? What is God's unique mission for our church? How can we implement God's vision for our church? We would do well to make the process of discernment a pattern of the church's life. The wheel of action and reflection keeps turning, from listening to the Spirit in prayer, worship, Bible study, and community conversations to understanding the world around us, planning and then living out our faith as participants in God's mission, and again reviewing our life and work in the context of prayer, Bible study, and worship. This is not a task the church finishes, any more than the church gets finished worshiping or praying or studying the Bible.

*What difference does it make when the disciple community prayerfully discerns God's vision together with a passion for carrying out that vision?*

## The Kingdom of God

For many, the idea of the kingdom, if not completely ignored, is thought to refer only to heaven in the future and doesn't require anything of us. Yet we pray regularly, "Thy kingdom come, thy will be done, on earth as it is in heaven" (Matt 6:10). We have a role in building God's kingdom when we answer the call to join God in mission in the world. We are sent by God to share the good news by embodying life as God intends through our life together as a community. We live the kingdom "on earth as it is in heaven" in committee meetings and at fellowship supper, in worship and serving in the neighborhood, in our homes and in our careers. We demonstrate life as God intends when we share the "fruit of the spirit" within our church family, with strangers, and even with enemies. We actively work to bring God's kingdom by advocating for justice and engaging in ministry with the poor and oppressed. We are called to be a sign, foretaste, and instrument of God's reign. When we are faithful to God's kingdom call, we provide a glimpse of what God's future kingdom will look like (a sign), we offer a small taste of that kingdom now (a foretaste), and we act as the hands and feet God uses to bring the kingdom to the world (instrument).

*What difference does it make if the disciple community embodies life as God intends in word and action and relationship?*

## The Relationship of the Church to Culture

We all are influenced by our culture, often in ways we don't recognize. Some of these untested assumptions and perspectives could be unhealthy, hurtful, or erroneous if accepted without question as God given. For example, individualism, consumerism, competition, power, and numerical growth are cultural values adopted by churches without evaluating them in light of the life and teachings of Christ. It is natural and unavoidable that we would be influenced by our culture, since we live in it 24/7. At times we will stand in contrast to cultural norms, demonstrating another way of being and acting.

However, we should not use resistance to the negative influences of culture as an excuse to maintain our comfortable traditions to the neglect of the world around us—the world God so loved and the world we are called to engage. Sometimes the church figuratively closes its doors to its neighbors by saying, "This is who we are. This is our tradition. We will not change. We will not compromise the gospel." We should hold fast to the mission God has for the church and live as a church community with fidelity to the life and teachings of Christ. We resist chasing after the latest fads, whatever those may be, or surrendering to the values of a culture that idolizes growth, competition, and entertainment. But loving our neighbors means taking seriously our neighbors' traditions, values, and culture. Context matters. We share the gospel in the language of the people. Our worship, work, and fellowship take into account the surrounding culture without compromising God's mission for the church.

In order to be faithful in this time and place, we must, to the best of our ability, understand our culture and context and discern God's will for how we relate to our culture.

*What difference does it make when the disciple community understands its cultural context, appreciates the culture, and acts as salt and light in the culture?*

## Community

We live in a culture that values individualism and independence. America, as a nation, was formed out of a passion for freedom and independence. These values are deeply ingrained in our consciousness: independence, autonomy, individual rights and freedom, and the right to privacy. Baptist distinctives include autonomy of the local church and soul freedom. The emphasis is on the individual's right to approach God without an intermediary. There is something to be said for freedom and independence, but perhaps, for many, this means we don't need anyone else. We don't need community. Faith is a private matter between an individual and God alone. When the Bible says "you" plural, we may hear "you" (me) singular. Yet the Lord's Prayer says, "*Our* Father in heaven . . . Give *us* . . ." (Matt 6:9-13). At the creation, God said, "It is not good that man should be alone." The Trinity—God, the Son, and Holy Spirit—is community. Jesus gathered around him a group of disciples and was criticized for sharing meals with sinners and outcasts of society. The early church "had all things in common" (Acts 2:44). Paul referred to the church as the body of Christ: "the eye cannot say to the hand, 'I have no need of you'" (1 Cor 12:21). We are unique individuals with unique gifts, but each is an integral part of one whole body. We were created for community. We cannot be the church as God intends without mutual encouragement and support, accountability to the community, healthy conflict resolution, and openness to diversity. We cultivate Christian community by sharing a meal together, praying and worshiping, working together serving our neighbors, studying the Bible, visiting the sick and elderly, and making decisions with a committee. We cultivate Christ-like community by moving out of our comfort zones to offer hospitality to those who don't look or act like us.

*What difference does it make when the disciple community cultivates Christ-like community through service, fellowship, worship, prayer, and Bible study with the body of Christ and with those we might view as strangers?*

## Thinking Systemically

Churches are complex systems of interrelated and interconnected parts, such as leadership and decision-making processes, ministry teams and committees, theology and tradition (those of your church, denomination, and Christianity in North America), cultural context (local community and North American), missional vision and strategies, church groups, relationships, ministries (worship, study, fellowship, mission partnerships), and outcomes.

Change in one element of the system influences the others. Paul and Inagrace Dietterich describe how one element in a church system can affect others and how the system seeks equilibrium:

> Whenever something occurs that puts the system out of balance, the organization reacts and moves toward a balanced state. If one team or committee in a church suddenly increases its performance dramatically, it throws the rest of the system out of balance. This team or committee might increase demands on the church's budget. It would probably demand more time from top leaders. It would want more information.

Other groups would begin to feel the pressure of keeping up with this group. Before long, some actions would be taken to put the system back into balance. Either the rest of the church would change to become more productive and thus be back in balance with the single group, or more likely, actions would be taken to get the front-running group to slow down, to modify its behavior to be consistent with the levels of performance of the rest of the church system. The system would develop energy to move back toward a state of equilibrium or balance.[2]

So, while we are working to change one piece of the whole system, we may find that other parts of the system push back.

Change and growth work best when the whole system is involved. How many times has a pastor participated in a transformative conference, read an important book, or been inspired by a worship experience outside the local church that prophetically called the church to radical love for the world, only to be disappointed when church leaders did not share their commitment to change? Worship leaders make changes in the order of worship, the building committee engages in major facilities renovations, or a group goes on a life-changing mission trip, but the enthusiasm for real change may not last.

In an email conversation I had with Dale Ziemer, former Managing Director with the Center for Parish Development in Chicago, he described the systems approach to change compared to operational changes:

> In responding to a radically changed and changing world, leaders and members of local churches have attempted many different kinds of changes. Renewal usually implies change. But most changes that churches attempt are operational. Helpful renewal efforts today invite more strategic thinking to bring about system-wide change.
>
> Operational changes refer to those improvements that are focused on individual pieces or components of a church's work and ministry. These changes occur within the existing frame, mindset, and pattern of practices of a local church. They are more on the scale of fine-tuning or changing from one program, project, or worship style to another. They often serve to solve a problem that folks are experiencing or to make a perceived improvement.
>
> Other changes are strategic and systemic in their nature and in their approach. These changes are holistic and designed to impact most or all of the components of a church's work and ministry. This approach involves leaders and members together in a vibrant learning community of discovering afresh the current context, discerning God's calling for the

future, and living into that future faithfully and fruitfully. A whole system approach to change does not offer a self-study here or a write a mission statement there. Instead, with the whole system in mind, a comprehensive process that facilitates broad-participatory learning and renewal is facilitated among the congregation. As a result, the existing priorities and goals, vision and mission, attitudes and practices are altered. The difference it makes is palpable in the life of the church, as reflected in this observer's remarks: "The church is different now, I am not sure what it is; it just tastes and smells like mission!"[3]

Churches that look for overly simplistic answers to perceived problems without taking into consideration the multifaceted system as a whole may not get to the root of the issues the church faces in our everchanging world.

*What difference does it make if, instead of focusing on incremental change to individual programs or practices, the disciple community focuses on systemic change of the beliefs and practices of the church as a whole?*

## The Missional Church

When we speak of the missional church, we are not talking about the church engaged in mission projects or giving to mission personnel in faraway places, though these may be a part of what it means to be missional. The missional church movement has voiced the perspective, "The *church* does not have a mission. *God* has a mission. The church is God's mission to the world." The resurrected Jesus said to his disciples, who were hidden in a locked room, "As the father has sent me, so I send you" (John 20:21). The church is sent by God into the world as a witness to life as God intends. Everything we do as a church is our mission and witness to a world that is watching.[4]

Often the church has thought of itself as having a missions program that is somehow separate from other aspects of the church's life and work. The focus may be on what we want to do rather than on discerning our part in God's mission. As a result, we compartmentalize church. The purpose of worship and Bible study is to feed us, and it is judged successful by the number of people who attend. Completely separate from worship, Bible study, and prayer are business and decision-making processes. Thus, with that mindset, we may conduct business, handle finances, meet with committees, and make decisions using secular business practices without the benefit of biblical, spiritual discernment models. "Missions" (and witnessing or evangelism) may be thought of as yet another program of the church apart from the rest.

"Missions" is not one thing we do. It is everything, so that when we worship, study the Bible, pray, care, serve, relate, and make decisions, we are on God's mission. We incarnate, or embody, God's desire for creation in all that we say and do. Thus every aspect of the church's life is important to God's mission: How do we make decisions and handle conflict? Do we offer forgiveness or judgment to those who have failed? Do we worship God or entertain an audience? Are we making disciples? Do we extend hospitality to all, even those who are different? Do we love God and neighbors? What is the nature of our parking lot conversations? Do we cultivate Christ-like community? Is everyone welcome around our supper table? Do we care for the hurting and lift up the poor, outcast, and oppressed? At work, home, and leisure, do we see ourselves as the church in the world?

The missional church is the church sent by God, engaged in God's mission in community, worship, teaching, prayer, service, witness, care, and leadership.

*What difference does it make if, instead of the church having missions programs, the disciple community functioned as God's mission to the world?*

## Discipleship

What does it mean to be a disciple? Several passages in Luke would suggest that being a disciple is not easy:

- "If any want to become my followers, let them deny themselves and take up their cross daily and follow me. For those who want to save their life will lose it, and those who lose their life for my sake will save it." (Luke 9:23-24)

- "As they were going along the road, someone said to him, 'I will follow you wherever you go.' And Jesus said to him, 'Foxes have holes, and birds of the air have nests; but the Son of Man has nowhere to lay his head.' To another he said, 'Follow me.' But he said, 'Lord, first let me go and bury my father.' But Jesus said to him, 'Let the dead bury their own dead; but as for you, go and proclaim the kingdom of God.' Another said, 'I will follow you, Lord; but let me first say farewell to those at my home.' Jesus said to him, 'No one who puts a hand to the plow and looks back is fit for the kingdom of God.'" (Luke 9:57-62)

- "Whoever comes to me and does not hate father and mother, wife and children, brothers and sisters, yes, and even life itself, cannot be my disciple. Whoever does not carry the cross and follow me cannot be my disciple. For which of you, intending to build a tower, does not first sit down and estimate the cost, to see whether he has enough to complete it?" (Luke 14:26-28)

However, if instead of a discipleship model we use an attractional model, where the ultimate goal of the church is to attract people, then we may be tempted to make church sound as easy and attractive as possible. Is the goal to get more people attending church services, or is making disciples our calling? If attendance is *the* measure of success, would we say that some restaurants, malls, and sports teams are the best churches? If discipleship is the goal, then we need to be honest and acknowledge that the way of Christ will at times mean sacrifices and in some cases suffering. Discipleship means devoting our lives to following Christ, learning from Jesus, and emulating his example. Discipleship will demand our quality time and a reshuffling of priorities in our busy world. Discipleship requires that we consider what our idols may be—entertainment, wealth, career, sports, or perhaps even church attendance. Being a disciple means loving God and neighbor and modeling our ethic and lifestyle after those challenging teachings from the Sermon on the Mount. Being a disciple means engaging in discipleship practices: community, prayer, worship, Bible study, service, and sharing the good news.

In his book *Not a Fan*,[5] Kyle Idleman tells the story of a transformative moment he experienced as he agonized over what to preach on Easter Sunday. Since there were so many who only came to church on Easter Sunday, he thought, "I want to make sure they all come back. What could I say to get their attention? How can I make my message more appealing?" After reading the story of Jesus preaching to a large crowd (John 6) and observing that Jesus' sermon would likely have driven many of them away, he concluded that "it wasn't the size of the crowd Jesus cared about; it was their level of commitment." So in his Easter sermon, Idleman confessed, "Too often in my preaching I have tried to talk people into following Jesus. I wanted to make following him as appealing, comfortable, and convenient as possible." He continued, "I should tell you [that the journey of following Jesus] hasn't been easy."

What coach would say, "Come join my team. It will be easy. Just show up. You won't have to do anything"? Perhaps we will find that when we call people to join us in a great and worthy cause that demands commitment and our best effort, rather than being repelled, people will want to devote themselves to this mission of utmost importance—God's mission of love. It will not be easy, but it will be worth it.

*What difference does it make if instead of attracting people to church we cultivated disciples who follow Christ daily and sacrificially?*

## Organizational Structures and Decision-making Processes

Well-intentioned churches who love their neighbors and diligently seek God's leadership can still be hindered by ineffective organizational structures and decision-making processes. Does the organization serve the church and God's mission, or does the church serve the organizational structure? Do committees, councils, and leadership teams work with a clear understanding of God's mission for the church and how the work of their group fits into this mission? Are leadership groups representative of the diversity of the congregation? Is attention given to team building, conflict resolution, and constructive dialogue? Are decisions made primarily through democratic win/lose votes or through prayerful discernment and consensus building? Do leadership groups work collaboratively within the team and with other teams? Is there a free flow of information throughout the organizational structure? Are finances handled wisely, openly, and responsibly? Are members involved in the decisions that affect them, or, for example, are decisions about the church's youth ministry made by groups with no parents, youth, or youth leaders represented? Are leadership teams made up of people who are involved in the area for which the team is responsible? For example, are Bible study leaders included on the Spiritual Formation Leadership Team? Are members enlisted to serve based on calling and spiritual gifts or only to fill slots on the nominating committee list? Are worship, prayer, and study integral to the decision-making process, or are worship, prayer, and study divorced from the business, decision-making, and planning meetings of the church? Do we debrief and review previous activities to see what we have learned?

Our organizational structures and decision-making processes can help or hinder God's mission.

*What difference does it make if our organizational structures and decision-making processes are highly functioning and effective, using best practices and procedures?*

## Putting Leadership into Practice

How does a church practice "loving God and neighbor"? How can we be a disciple community? How do church leaders cultivate community and equip a church to worship, teach, pray, serve, witness, and care? How can we utilize the levers we have to move the church to become a sign, foretaste, and instrument of God's kingdom? How do we develop a missional culture and climate within the church body?

### *Foretaste: Leadership for the Missional Church*

Paul M. Dietterich address these questions in *Foretaste: Leadership for the Missional Church*,[6] a culmination of decades of study, reflection, and practice by the Center for Parish Development, drawing on extensive biblical/theological study, research in the social sciences, and practical work and reflection with congregations. Dietterich addresses four management systems and six leadership behaviors that build a missional climate in a church.

The climate of a church affects every aspect of the church's life—its culture, attitudes, behaviors, activities, decision-making, and relationships. Climate matters. "A church's climate can give people a foretaste of life in God's kingdom, or, conversely," Dietterich writes, "it can give people one more experience of life in today's dominant competitive and consumer culture (in religious garb)."[7]

### Management Systems

Management systems create climate. Dietterich describes four management systems that are more or less conducive to promoting a missional climate.[8]

<u>System 1: Coercive Management</u>

In a coercive management system, control is concentrated at the top. Leadership is authoritarian. Decisions are made by the leader (or council) and passed down in the form of directives. Communication does not flow up in the organization, nor is information shared among the members. Members serve the leader out of fear or guilt, with little sense of ownership or responsibility. As a result, the climate that is created is "Fearful, dependent, powerless, suspicious, distrustful, low motivation."[9]

### System 2: Competitive Management

In a competitive management system, policy and major decisions are made at the top, but some decisions about implementation are delegated to individuals and work groups. Most of the information flows down in the organization, though communication from some members and work groups does flow up to the leader. Members compete for funding, status, power, and attention. Information is hoarded or distorted and used to gain influence. In North American culture where competition plays such a prominent role in the way we conduct business, politics, education, and sports, competition can become the norm in the church. As a result, the climate that is created is "Suspicious, rivals, competing factions, energy devoted to winning instead of performing, distrustful."[10]

### System 3: One-to-One Consultative Management System

Major decisions are made by the leadership of the organization, but the leader is in a supportive role rather than a "top-down dominating position," and more decisions are made by work groups. Communication flows back and forth between the leader in a strong one-to-one relationship with each member and work group, which contributes to better-informed decision-making. There is some communication among group members and among leaders of groups, but the system lacks intentionality in fostering group decision-making, goal setting, and visioning. Communication among group members tends to focus on how to carry out broad organizational policies and goals decided on by leadership rather than on utilizing the gifts and wisdom of the group in developing the policies and goals. As a result, the climate that is created is "Inherently unstable because too much information is held by one person, limited but growing trust, increased cooperation."[11]

### System 4: Team Consultative Management System

The team consultative management system values the unique gifts, experience, knowledge, and insight of each member of the body. Decisions are made throughout the organization. Communication flows in all directions: with team leaders, with each member of the team, and laterally among the team members; and teams share information and decision-making with each other through "linking members" that overlap groups. Groups practice openness and receptivity to ideas. As a result, the climate that is created includes "High motivation, trust, team productivity, creativity, team cohesiveness. Information flows openly in all directions, safe and supportive environment."[12]

The Likert profile is an instrument that can help a church determine its current management style and the management style the congregation prefers. It can lead a church to understand its management style and how it could move to a more consultative management style.[13]

## Six Leadership Behaviors that Build a Missional Climate

Six leadership behaviors can help move a church toward a consultative and, hopefully, team consultative management system.

### (1) Support People's Dignity and Giftedness

The world needs the church, and the church needs leaders who see all people as God's good creation, members of the body of Christ who are given spiritual gifts by God for the work of ministry. Thus, all people are to be valued and treated with dignity. When we don't value the gifts and contributions of all members, we waste valuable resources that would help us be a sign, foretaste, and instrument of the kingdom of God. And we perpetuate a system that lifts the dignity of some while it pushes others to the margins. As an example, and a contrast to the surrounding culture, we offer "not domination, but service; not pride, but humility; not self-defense, but hatred overcome by love."[14]

Supportive leaders don't micromanage members and teams but equip them with the training, information, tools, and resources they need to use their gifts for God's mission.

### (2) Practice Receptivity

Supportive leaders view others as people of worth and dignity and therefore are receptive to their ideas, concerns, values, and goals. Rather than focusing on how to persuade others to accept the leader's point of view, they are open to sharing the visioning, goal-setting, and decision-making process with the group.[15]

### (3) Emphasize Performance

The pastor and congregation work together to carry out God's mission for the church, so any emphasis on performance involves the whole body—pastor, ministerial staff, coordinating council (whatever form that takes), leadership teams and workgroups, and all members of the church.

A first step in emphasizing performance is to identify the most important work to be done. Leadership asks the question, "What is the most important work our congregation must be doing in order to live as a faithful missional community?"[16] These most important things to be done are called "key result areas." Dietterich suggests the following key result areas as a good place for a church to begin: "worshiping community," "disciple community," "missionary community," "witnessing community," and "equipping community."[17] For example, a key result area for an equipping community might be, "to form a community whose leaders and members are cultivating and utilizing their diverse gifts in service to the ministry of God's people."[18]

The key result areas are not the end in themselves but guide the church in determining action steps, indicators to measure progress, action plans, training, and budgeting time and money so that the church achieves these results at a high level of performance.

### (4) Build Missional Leadership Teams

Dietterich states, "Wise missional leaders emphasize and invest time and energy in building church councils and other leadership groups into high performing missional teams."[19] High performing teams give careful attention to enlistment, purpose, roles, membership criteria, diversity, communication, and group maintenance.[20]

### (5) Facilitate Work

"Work facilitation in the church," according to Dietterich, "is the process of making it as easy as possible for church leadership groups to plan and accomplish their work in ways that are both faithful and fruitful."[21] But first, let's be clear about the work we want to facilitate. If the only work the church is about is building maintenance, overseeing programs and activities, and making sure we stay within the budget, then we are only focused on preservation, maintenance, or survival. Few people are inspired by the vision, "We don't want to die. We want to survive." Rather than focusing on organizational maintenance, Dietterich imagines a more challenging agenda focused on: cultivating a worshipping and learning community, cultivating a community that is aware of the cultural issues it is confronting and that stands in contrast to cultural norms that run contrary to God's vision for the world, and cultivating an equipping community.[22]

## (6) Practice Group Decision-Making

The church is called to be a contrast society, showing the world an alternative way of relating, working together, and making decisions based on Jesus' example, the Holy Spirit's guidance, and the teachings of Scripture. Too often the church merely reflects the world's cultural values and practices, even when in conflict with God's kingdom ways of being.

Dietterich notes that North American culture, "uses competitive and adversarial processes of decision-making. These processes lead to win/lose debates, parliamentary maneuvering, lobbying for special interests, majorities imposing their preferred solutions upon minorities, or both parties agreeing to solutions that represent the lowest common denominator." When we bring this style of decision-making into the church, we get winners and losers, division, defensiveness, and even hostility.

Dietterich offers an alternative to a competitive decision-making climate:

> In contrast, a supportive decision-making climate is marked by encouragement and freedom to behave spontaneously without fear of sanctions. Information is openly shared, energy is focused on the problem-solving task, creative options are proposed and examined . . . . With energy focused on the problem-solving task, members seek and receive information from each other more clearly. Everyone wins. One result of a more supportive climate is better decisions. Another result is a greater unity in the body.[23]

These six leadership behaviors are important tools for leaders moving toward a Team Consultative Management System for equipping the missional church.

## Becoming a Learning/Disciple Community

How does the church adapt to a rapidly changing world while remaining faithful to God's mission? Programs, schedules, and organizational structures put in place in one era often remain the rule, whether or not they make sense in a new cultural historical reality. A learning community, as described by Peter Senge, is one that has the organizational systems, practices, and climate in place to continually learn and adapt to change.[24] The five characteristics of a learning community, according to Senge, are (1) Personal Mastery, (2) Mental Models, (3) Shared Vision, (4) Team Learning, and (5) Systems Thinking.

The Center for Parish Development has adapted Senge's work from a biblical/theological perspective to help churches cultivate a learning community. They offer these five dimensions, or disciplines, of learning communities: (1) Generating Responsible Participation: Cultivates broad, responsible participation in collective learning, decision-making, planning, and leadership; (2) Identifying and Testing Interpretive Models: Provides opportunity, resources, and context for surfacing and testing underlying assumptions about the nature and purpose of the church; (3) Discerning Shared Vision: Practices the discipline of developing shared images of the future that foster enthusiasm and commitment; (4) Encouraging Commitment to Team Learning: Nurtures patterns of interaction through "dialogue" and "thinking together" that move beyond defensiveness and win/lose dynamics; and (5) Thinking Systemically: Focuses on the church as a whole system of interrelated and interdependent elements, processes, and relationships, not only a collection of separate components.[25]

So, to borrow (steal?) from Peter Senge and the Center for Parish Development, let me offer this.

## Five Characteristics of a Disciple (Learning) Community

*1. Spiritual Gifts.* Discover and use all members' spiritual gifts, which cultivates broad, responsible participation in collective decision-making, planning, leadership, and learning.

*2. Models.* Provide opportunities for the church to discover and evaluate the underlying assumptions about what it means to be the church: What is the nature of the church? What is the mission of the church? What is the biblical model of the church?

*3. Vision.* Discern God's vision together. As a community under the leadership of God, practice the discipline of developing shared images of the future that foster enthusiasm and commitment.

*4. Dialogue.* Encourage commitment to team learning. Nurture patterns of interaction through "dialogue" and "thinking together" that move beyond defensiveness.

*5. Body of Christ.* Think systemically. Focus on the church as a whole system (family system, body, community) of interrelated and interdependent elements, processes, and relationships, not just a collection of separate body parts.

## Missional Church Models to Consider

Each of the following books presents some excellent models (patterns, examples, practices) of missional churches. A church would do well to reflect on these, consider whether they are consistent with God's mission for the church and are relevant in your context, and evaluate your congregation's practice in light of them.

### *Treasure in Clay Jars: Patterns in Missional Faithfulness*[26]

The Gospel in Culture Network formed a research team that examined eight congregations and one cluster of related congregations. These diverse congregations were chosen based on recommendations from a wide range of people across North America. These were churches that modeled twelve indicators of a missional church: (1) proclaims the gospel, (2) is a community where all members are involved in learning to become disciples of Jesus, (3) sees the Bible as normative in church life, (4) understands itself as different from the world because of its participation in the life, death, and resurrection of its Lord, (5) seeks to discern God's specific missional vocation for the entire community and for all of its members, (6) is indicated by how Christians behave toward one another, (7) practices reconciliation, (8) holds people within the community accountable to one another in love, (9) practices hospitality, (10) views worship as the central act by which the community celebrates with joy and thanksgiving both God's presence and God's promised future, (11) has a vital public witness, and (12) recognizes that the church itself is an incomplete expression of the reign of God.[27]

These churches were not perfect, but, like a treasure in clay jars, they exemplified patterns of missional faithfulness. The research team found these eight patterns among the nine congregational groups they studied:

> *Pattern 1, Missional Vocation.* The congregation is discovering together the missional vocation of the community. . . .
> *Pattern 2, Biblical Formation and Discipleship.* The missional church is a community in which all members are involved in learning what it means to be disciples of Jesus. . . .
> *Pattern 3, Taking Risks as a Contrast Community.* The missional church is learning to take risks for the sake of the gospel. It understands itself as different from the world because of its participation in the life, death, and resurrection of its Lord. . . .
> *Pattern 4, Practices that Demonstrate God's Intent for the World.* The pattern of the church's life as community is a demonstration of what God intends for the life of the whole world. . . .

*Pattern 5, Worship as Public Witness.* Worship is the central act by which the community celebrates with joy and thanksgiving both God's presence and God's promised future. . . .

*Pattern 6, Dependence on the Holy Spirit.* The missional community confesses its dependence upon the Holy Spirit, shown in particular in its practices of corporate prayer. . . .

*Pattern 7, Pointing Toward the Reign of God.* The missional church understands its calling as witness to the gospel of the in-breaking reign of God and strives to be an instrument, agent, and sign of that reign. . . .

*Pattern 8, Missional Authority.* The Holy Spirit gives the missional church a community of people who, in a variety of ways and with a diversity of functional rules and titles, together practice the missional authority that cultivates within the community the discernment of missional vocation and is intentional about the practices that embed that vocation in the community's life.[28]

## *Shift: Three Big Moves for the 21st Century Church*[29]

The era in which the church held a position of favor and power in North American culture is ending. Churches organized for that era will continue to struggle. Mark Tidsworth writes, "the Christian Church as we have known it is radically shifting. Church-as-we-have-known-it is coming to an end. I do not mean that the Christian Church is ending. I believe great days are ahead for the Christian movement in God's world. Yet, I also clearly believe that the way we have been doing church during the Modern Era is drawing to a close."[30] Major shifts are needed.

Tidsworth recommends three big shifts the church should undertake:

*(1) Member Identity to Disciple Identity.* Shifting from a focus on the number of people who join the church as members of an organization *to* cultivating disciples who learn from Jesus and follow as a community in all aspects of life.

*(2) Attractional Church to Missional Church.* Shifting from a major emphasis of getting people to events on the church campus *to* an understanding of the church as God's sent people on mission.

*(3) Consumer Church to Sacred Partnering.* Shifting from an understanding of a church that distributes spiritual goods and services to people seeking to be fed *to* disciples coming together in relationship to form a community in sacred partnership with God and each other.

## *Images of the Church in Mission*[31]

John Driver writes, "The images with which the church understands its identity and roles are mostly drawn from surrounding society rather than from the church's rootage in true biblical tradition."[32] This book offers some "Biblical Images of the Church in Mission" for the church's self-understanding, listed in four categories:

<u>Pilgrimage Images</u>

*(1) The Way.* One of the Christian community's earliest self-designations (see, for example, Luke 19:9, 23; 22:4; 24:14, 22).

*(2) Sojourners.* "Stranger," "foreigner," "exiles," "pilgrims," and other similar terms (see, for example, Heb 11:9-13 and 1 Pet 2:11).

*(3) The Poor.* The early Christian community identified with, and saw themselves as, the poor (see, for example, the Beatitudes; Luke 6:20; and Rom 15:26).

<u>New-Order Images</u>

*(1) The Kingdom of God.* Jesus' mission and that of the church was to proclaim the kingdom of God through Jesus' presence among them (see, for example, Matt 10:7-8; Acts 1:3-5, 8; and the Lord's Prayer, Matt 6:10).

*(2) New Creation.* In Christ, God was restoring creation, and the church is a sign of that new creation (see, for example, 1 Cor 5:17-19).

*(3) New Humanity.* Christ brings together a divided humanity into one humanity in Christ (see, for example, Eph 2:13-18 and Col 3:9-11).

<u>Peoplehood Images</u>

*(1) The People of God.* The early Christian community understood themselves as God's chosen people (see, for example, Rom 9:26 and 1 Pet 2:9).

*(2) The Family of God.* Following Jesus' statement, "whoever does the will of my Father in heaven is my brother and sister and mother" (Matt 12:50), the Christian community thought of themselves as a family—siblings in faith (see, for example, 1 Pet 2:17; 5:9).

*(3) The Shepherd and the Flock.* The church is the flock following Jesus the Shepherd, who guides and cares for the flock.

## Images of Transformation

*(1) Salt, Light, and a City.* The Christian community as salt, light, and a city on a mountain is "called to live and witness radically under God's reign in the midst of the world"[33] (see Matt 5:13-16 from Jesus' Sermon on the Mount).

*(2) A Spiritual House.* Built on Christ, metaphorically the Christian community is a living spiritual house, or temple, a testimony of God's living presence among us (see, for example, 1 Pet 2:4-8).

*(3) A Witnessing Community.* The apostles experienced Jesus' life, death, and resurrection and bore witness to that experience with others. The Christian community experiences Christ through the Holy Spirit and bears witness (see, for example, Luke 24:48 and Acts 1:8).

### Going to the Root: Nine Proposals for Radical Church Renewal[34]

Many Christians agree that the church is in need of renewal. The problem with many approaches to church renewal is that they ask the wrong question. According to Smith, "Most begin by asking, 'What strategy or program will work best to revitalize this church?' Wrong question."[35] We need to dig deeper. We need a clear vision of what God intends the church to be. Radical renewal is required. Smith offers these nine proposals for the church to test and refine:

  1. *Build Intentional Christian Community.* "[Radical church renewal] begins with the conviction that the church should not be a place of casual acquaintanceships but of committed community."[36]

  2. *Do Church without Clergy.* "[Radical church renewal] calls us to shift ministry away from professionals and give it back to the ordinary people of God. To do this, we must rethink a key aspect of modern church life: the clergy."[37]

  3. *Decentralize Leadership and Decision-making.* "If Jesus taught anything concerning leadership and authority, it was egalitarianism."[38]

  4. *Open Up Worship Services.* "Structurally, the worship services of many churches are preplanned, clergy-oriented, and performance-oriented. Such characteristics profoundly shape our experience of worship and often undermine our best intentions. Radical church renewal asks us to reconsider the whole affair."[39]

  5. *Overcome the Edifice Complex.* "Going to the root challenges us to reconsider how we think about our church buildings. It calls us to reexamine our priorities and begin to explore more dynamic, flexible forms of

organization and structure that better symbolize and facilitate adaptability, humility, creativity, and good stewardship."[40]

6. *Cultivate Grace-ful Spirituality of Everyday Life.* "[Radical church renewal] summons us to learn and live a new spirituality of everyday life, one that is steeped in grace."[41]

7. *Practice Lifestyle Evangelism.* "The Bible makes it clear that the central and irreplaceable medium for communicating the gospel is the quality of believers' lives together."[42]

8. *Work for Social Justice.* "[Radical church renewal] seeks to transform the way we engage ourselves as churches with the fallen social order. Radical church renewal calls us to work for social justice."[43]

9. *Do Grass-Roots Ecumenism.* "Radical church renewal rejects the unnecessary divisions that separate and isolate Christians from each other. It calls believers to work for unity in the Spirit."[44]

## Conflict Resolution

Conflict in the church, as in life, is inevitable. The degree to which the church can handle conflict in a healthy way will affect its ability to cultivate community, facilitate transformation, and faithfully participate in God's mission. In my experience, churches are reluctant to engage in an intentional process of conflict resolution until the stress levels are so high that factions develop, views harden, members become defensive, issues become personal, anger takes over, and finding a resolution becomes difficult and feels impossible. But what if we learned and practiced conflict resolution before the battle lines were drawn? What if we learned and practiced the communication skills that would allow us to engage with difficult but important issues while anxiety is lower?

Many churches, as well as families and workplaces, would rather ignore seemingly minor differences and avoid controversial issues. What if instead we practiced our communication and conflict resolution skills intentionally around issues on which we may disagree but in which we are not as heavily invested, to prepare us for more difficult and consequential issues? Churches that seek to discern God's vision will naturally encounter differences in how members understand that vision, and there will be differences in biblical interpretation and theology. These differences, communicated with respect for one another and a willingness to listen, can be constructive. Being a contrast community that is a sign, foretaste, and instrument of God's kingdom is not easy and will often lead us to confront injustice and inequality. Conflict resolution can help a church boldly pursue God's mission.

So what does a healthy process of conflict resolution look like? Organizations that are experienced and skilled in conflict resolution can help guide a church through a process of conflict resolution, much like a process for discerning God's vision. I recommend taking advantage of their experience and expertise.

## Times of Disagreement

The Presbyterian Church (USA) provides a helpful guide titled "Seeking to Be Faithful Together: Guidelines for Presbyterians in Times of Disagreement."[45] This document includes guidelines such as, "Treat each other respectfully so as to build trust, believing that we all desire to be faithful to Jesus the Christ"; "Focus on ideas and suggestions instead of questioning people's motives, intelligence, or integrity"; and "Indicate where we agree with those of other viewpoints as well as where we disagree." Ideally a document like this could be presented to a congregation with no particular conflict in view, but could be offered to a group prior to the discussion of a controversial topic or a difficult decision.

## The Jerusalem Council Deals with Conflict

The early church, as recorded in Acts 15, was faced with the highly controversial issue of whether or not to accept uncircumcised Gentiles into the fellowship of the church. Some taught that, "Unless you are circumcised, according to the custom of Moses, you cannot be saved" (15:1). Paul and Barnabas had "no small dissension and debate with them" (15:2). The church did not take this decision lightly. Luke describes in detail the decision-making process, a process that churches can learn from today. Some key elements of that process can be noted:

1. Prior to the conflict, Peter had a change of heart after a vision from God. Cornelius, a Gentile, was converted after Peter visited him. The gospel was preached to Gentiles, the Holy Spirit was poured out on them, and they were baptized.

2. Paul and Barnabas, and some of the others, brought their disagreement to the apostles and elders who met together to consider the matter (15:2, 6).

3. They engaged in much debate (15:7).

4. Peter told the story of how Gentiles had heard the message and believed and how God had given them the Holy Spirit (15:7-11).

5. "The whole assembly kept silent and listened" (15:12).

6. James shared Scripture that prophesied "from long ago" that "even all the Gentiles" would seek the Lord (15:13-18).

7. "With the consent of the whole church," the apostles and elders sent a letter to the believers in Antioch that "no further burden" should be placed on the Gentile believers (15:22-29).

8. "For it seemed good to the Holy Spirit and to us" (15:28).

The decision to accept Gentiles into the body of Christ, and uncircumcised Gentiles at that, was as polarizing as any church will face today. It was a decision that opened the doors of the church to Gentiles, like me and perhaps you too. Addressing the conflict was worth it and led to a more inclusive church. What important decisions deserve your church's attention and some bold and loving conflict resolution?

## *Leadership Team Basics*

Committees and leadership teams sometimes have a bad reputation, or at least we like to make fun of them. I often begin leadership team orientation sessions with cartoons poking fun at poorly functioning church committees. These cartoons are not hard to find. One cartoon, and a joke that is used frequently, labels the camel as "a horse designed by a committee." However, one member of a leadership team turned the illustration around: "This team destroys the old joke about a camel is a horse that was built by a committee. I think we ought to turn that one around and say that a horse was a camel before this team got hold of it."[46] But why should we be so hard on the camel? What an amazingly adapted creature, perfectly designed for its challenging environment—a marvel from head to toe to hump (and sometimes another hump). If a camel is built by a committee, then wow, what a brilliant and creative committee. Truly our committees, or leadership teams, are necessary and important. Healthy, effective leadership teams discern God's inspiring vision, make important decisions, do the work, and help the church accomplish God's mission for the church. Let's all stand now, wherever we are, and give leadership teams the standing ovation they deserve (and hoorah for the camel).

Here are a few basic considerations for church leadership teams (many more could be added):

- Form leadership teams based on the tasks that need to be accomplished in order for the church to fulfill God's mission. When a leadership team has completed its work, or it no longer fits the priorities of the church, then disband the committee.
- Use leadership teams. Give them authority, release them, trust them, and hold them accountable.
- Orient and train leadership teams.
- Do not divorce worship, prayer, and Bible study from the decision-making processes of the church. Leadership teams will be more missional when they engage in worshipful work. Serious prayer and study are integral to the work of leadership teams, not a waste of time. Worshipful work leads to more faithful, effective work.
- Think about how long leadership team members will serve and how they will be selected and enlisted. Consistency, experience, and knowledge of the work are obviously important. For some leadership teams, it may be fine to allow members to serve for as long as they feel called. For other leadership teams, consider using a rotation system, especially for teams with the potential to attract members who may want to exert power or press a narrow agenda (for example, the finance committee).
- Who makes decisions about the overall vision and mission of the church? Pastor? Staff? Deacons? If that responsibility doesn't rest with the pastor, staff, or deacons, then with whom? Many pastors desire to share decision-making with a more representative group of church leaders and would like deacons to be a servant leadership body. However, if no coordinating council or leadership team is in place that is made up of people linked to key groups within the church, members will take their questions or concerns to staff members, deacons, or the parking lot. Members need a place to share their ideas, worries, and vision for the church. That should be to a group with the makeup and authority to effectively consider such input, preferably not only the professional staff or deacons.
- Leadership teams need a linking person to facilitate communication with the coordinating council, pastor, staff, and other teams. When the coordinating team makes decisions, the people strategically linked to other teams in the church should be in the room and part of the conversation.

## Leadership Resources

Barrett, Lois Y., ed. *Treasure in Clay Jars: Patterns of Missional Faithfulness.* Grand Rapids: Eerdmans, 2004.

Bugg, Charles B. *I'm Trying to Lead . . . Is Anybody Following: The Challenge of Congregational Leadership in the Postmodern World*. Macon: Smyth & Helwys, 2014.

Center for Parish Development. Chicago, IL. www.missionalchurch.org (consulting and a large variety of resources supporting the church in mission based on decades of research, training, and practice in the church).

Chawla, Sarita, and John Renesch, eds. *Learning Organizations: Developing Cultures for Tomorrow's Workplace*. Portland, OR: Productivity Press, 1995.

Covey, Stephen R. *The Eighth Habit: From Effectiveness to Greatness*. New York: Free Press, 2004.

———. *The Seven Habits of Highly Effective People: Powerful Lessons in Personal Change*. New York: Simon & Schuster, 1989.

Dietterich, Paul M. *Foretaste: Leadership for the Missional Church*. Eugene, OR: Cascade Books, 2019.

Driver, John *Images of the Church in Mission*. Scottsdale, PA: Herald Press, 1997.

Field, David N. *Our Purpose Is Love: The Wesleyan Way to Be the Church*. Nashville: Abingdon, 2018.

———. In Leader Guide by Barbara Dick, *Our Purpose Is Love: The Wesleyan Way to Be the Church, Leader Guide*. Nashville: Abingdon, 2018.

Galindo, Israel. *The Hidden Lives of Congregations: Applying Positive Deviance for Effective Leadership*. Herndon, VA: The Alban Institute, 2004.

———. *Perspectives on Congregational Leadership: Discerning Church Dynamics*. Educational Consultants, 2009.

Gray, Joan S. *Sailboat Church: Helping Your Church Rethink Its Mission and Practice*. Louisville, KY: Westminster John Knox, 2014.

Guder, Darrell L, ed. *Missional Church: A Vision for the Sending of the Church in North America*. Grand Rapids: Eerdmans, 1998.

Idleman, Kyle. *Not a Fan*. Grand Rapids: Zondervan, 2016.

Kotter, John P. *Leading Change*. Boston: Harvard Business School Press, 1996.

Likert, Rensis, and Jane Gibson Likert. "The Likert Profile of a Church." Questionnaires. Center for Parish Development, www.missionalchurch.org.

McKim, Mark G. *Countercultural Worship: A Plea to Evangelicals in a Secular Age.* Macon: Smyth & Helwys, 2016.

McSwain, Stephen B. *The Giving Myths: Giving Then Getting the Life You've Always Wanted.* Macon: Smyth & Helwys, 2007.

Senge, Peter M. *The Fifth Discipline: The Art and Practice of the Learning Organization.* New York: Doubleday, 1990.

———, Art Kleiner, Charlotte Roberts, Richard B. Ross, and Bryan J. Smith. *The Fifth Discipline Fieldbook: Strategies and Tools for Building Learning Organizations.* New York: Doubleday, 1994.

Smith, Christian. *Going to the Root: Nine Proposals for Radical Church Renewal.* Scottdale, PA: Herald Press, 1992.

Tidsworth, Mark E. *Farming Church: Cultivating Adaptive Change in Congregations.* Chapin, SC: Pinnacle Leadership Press, 2017.

———. *Forty Days of Prayer: Preparing Ourselves for God's Calling.* Pinnacle Leadership Press, 2012.

———. *Making the Shift Field Guide: Implementing the Three Big Shifts.* Pinnacle Leadership Press, 2016.

———. *Shift: Three Big Moves for the 21st Century Church.* Pinnacle Leadership Press, 2015.

Vestal, Daniel. *Being the Presence of Christ: A Vision for Transformation.* Nashville: Upper Room Books, 2008.

Ziemer, Dale A. "Cultivating a Learning Community." *Transformation* 2/3 (Summer 1995).

## Notes

1. Steven Covey, *The Seven Habits of Highly Effective People: Powerful Lessons in Personal Change* (New York: Simon & Schuster, 1989).

2. Paul Dietterich and Inagrace Dietterich, *A Systems Model of the Church* (Chicago: Center for Parish Development, 2002), 19.

3. Dale A. Ziemer, former Managing Director with the Center for Parish Development, Chicago, IL, personal email to author, 2020.

4. See Darrell L. Guder, ed., *Missional Church: A Vision for the Sending of the Church in North America* (Grand Rapids: Eerdmans, 1998).

5. Kyle Idleman, *Not a Fan* (Grand Rapids: Zondervan, 2016), 7–8.

6. Paul M. Dietterich, *Foretaste: Leadership for the Missional Church* (Eugene, OR: Cascade Books, 2019).

7. Dietterich, *Foretaste*, 6.

8. Dietterich, *Foretaste*, 20–34.

9. Dietterich, *Foretaste*, 23–24, 34.

10. Dietterich, *Foretaste*, 24–25, 34.

11. Dietterich, *Foretaste*, 26–27, 34.

12. Dietterich, *Foretaste*, 27–28, 34.

13. Rensis Likert and Jane Gibson Likert, "The Likert Profile of a Church," Center for Parish Development, www.missionalchurch.org.

14. Dietterich, *Foretaste*, 52

15. Dietterich, *Foretaste*, 62–72.

16. Dietterich, *Foretaste*, 77

17. Dietterich, *Foretaste*, 77–89.

18. Dietterich, *Foretaste*, 88–89.

19. Dietterich, *Foretaste*, 95.

20. Dietterich, *Foretaste*, 102–107

21. Dietterich, *Foretaste*, 120.

22. Dietterich, *Foretaste*, 122–23.

23. Dietterich, *Foretaste*, 132–33.

24. Peter M. Senge, *The Fifth Discipline: The Art and Practice of the Learning Organization* (New York: Doubleday, 1990).

25. Dale Ziemer, "Cultivating a Learning Community," *Transformation* 2/3 (Summer 1995).

26. Lois Y. Barrett, ed., *Treasure in Clay Jars: Patterns of Missional Faithfulness* (Grand Rapids: Eerdmans, 2004).

27. Barrett, *Treasure in Clay Jars*, 159–72.

28. Barrett, *Treasure in Clay Jars*, xii–xiv.

29. Mark E. Tidsworth, *Shift: Three Big Moves for the 21st Century Church* (Pinnacle Leadership Press, 2015).

30. Tidsworth, *Shift*, 7.

31. John Driver, *Images of the Church in Mission* (Scottsdale, PA: Herald Press, 1997).

32. Driver, *Images of the Church in Mission*, 20.

33. Driver, *Images of the Church in Mission*, 175.

34. Christian Smith, *Going to the Root: Nine Proposals for Radical Church Renewal* (Scottdale, PA: Herald Press, 1992).

35. Smith, *Going to the Root*, 14.

36. Smith, *Going to the Root*, 20.

37. Smith, *Going to the Root*, 36–37.

38. Smith, *Going to the Root*, 60.

39. Smith, *Going to the Root*, 75.

40. Smith, *Going to the Root*, 91.

41. Smith, *Going to the Root*, 104.

42. Smith, *Going to the Root*, 127.

43. Smith, *Going to the Root*, 136.

44. Smith, *Going to the Root*, 154.

45. The Presbyterian Church (USA), "Seeking to Be Faithful Together: Guidelines for Presbyterians in Times of Disagreement," August 5, 2020, https://www.presbyterianmission.org/resource/seeking-to-be-faithful-together-guidelines-for-presbyterians-in-times-of-disagreement/.

46. Alfred Wilken, informal comment summarizing a church leadership team meeting, Iowa Conference, United Methodist Church, 1975, quoted in Dietterich, *Foretaste*, 95.

# Benediction

Now,
may you
be the church,
a community of disciples
engaged in God's mission.

May you
love God with all your heart,
with all your soul,
with all your strength,
and with all your mind.
May you know God's love for you, and
may you love your neighbor as you love yourself.

As you walk along the road,
may you look upon your neighbor on the side of the road
with love and compassion.

May you love your neighbor,
your wounded neighbor, your homeless neighbor, your hungry neighbor,
your thirsty neighbor, your immigrant neighbor, your neighbor in prison,
your neighbor with no coat, your neighbor on the side of the road.

May you love your next-door neighbor and your neighbors around the world,
the neighbor who shares your culture and the neighbor whose culture you do not understand,
the neighbor who looks like you and the neighbor who doesn't,

the neighbor of similar religion, the neighbor of different religion,
and the neighbor with no religion at all.

May you love
your rich neighbor, your middle-class neighbor, your poor neighbor,
your LGBTQ+ neighbor, your straight neighbor,
your young neighbor, your old neighbor,
the neighbor you know well, and the neighbor you haven't met.

May you love your Samaritan neighbor.
When you are injured, may your Samaritan neighbor bandage your wounds.
When you are thirsty, may a neighbor offer a cup of cold water.
When you are cold, may a neighbor offer a mug of hot chocolate, a warm quilt, and a seat beside the fire,
When you are lonely, may a neighbor knock on your door.

May your community be loving and close.
May your worship be lifted and grateful.
May your prayers be unceasing and still.
May your teaching be open and living.
May your missions be going and doing.
May your witness be gospel and visible.
May your care be compassionate and healing.
May you follow and may you lead.

May you be at home in Martha's kitchen,
may you sit with Mary at Jesus' feet,
may you go and do likewise,
together.

Amen!

www.ingramcontent.com/pod-product-compliance
Lightning Source LLC
Chambersburg PA
CBHW061935220426
43662CB00012B/1917